THE BOOK OF DAN

THE BOOK OF DAN

Serving Across the 34th Parallel

Dan Hiland

Hiland Publishing
Rexburg, Idaho

Published in the United States by Hiland Publishing
ISBN 13: 9780996873314
ISBN: 0996873317
Library of Congress Control Number: 2017914929
eBook ISBN: 978-0-9968733-0
Printed in the United States of America
First paperback edition
Cover Designs by Tammy Chenault
Manufactured in the United States of America

Disclaimer: This is a work of non-fiction. The people and places mentioned in this memoir are real, but due to privacy concerns, I have substituted fictitious names for real ones.

Website: hilandwriting.com

Dedicated to Chelsea, Carma and Connor

Acknowledgements

The author expresses appreciation to the following individuals, without whom this book would never have made it to the finish line:

Maureen O'Brien, editor, ghostwriter extraordinaire, good neighbor, and the most famous person I know- for preliminary editing, and for telling me repeatedly that my mission was something worth writing about.

Brendan Halpin, published author and mentor- for helping me figure out how to cut the crap, trim the fat, and realize that one can never listen to enough Belle and Sebastian.

Monica Drake, author of Chicken Girl, and the best creative writing teacher ever- for helping me understand that I have something to offer.

Heather Randall, editor- for her encouragement, enthusiasm and example.

Mike Lambert, fellow traveler in Argentina- for being a friend.

Carol- for her critiques of the manuscript, long-standing patience, love and encouragement, when I was down and/or out.

"And I beheld the heavens open again, and I saw angels descending upon the children of men, and they did minister unto them."
1 Nephi 11:30

"When we get out of the glass bottle of our ego and when we escape like the squirrels in the cage of our personality and get into the forest again, we shall shiver with cold and fright. But things will happen to us so that we don't know ourselves. Cool, unlying life will rush in."
D. H. Lawrence

"One day it occurred to me that it had been many years since the world had been afforded the spectacle of a man adventurous enough to undertake a journey through Europe on foot. After much thought I decided that I was a person fitted to furnish to mankind this spectacle. So I determined to do it."
Mark Twain

"Our boat was waiting for us at Kingston just below the bridge, and to it we wended our way, and round it we stored our luggage, and into it we stepped. 'Are you all right, sir?' said the man. 'Right it is,' we answered; and with Harris at the sculls and I at the tiller lines ... out we shot onto the waters which, for a fortnight, were to be our home."
Jerome K. Jerome

Table of Contents

DAY ONE

10 A.M. I PEER THROUGH the bug-splattered windshield at an entry door to the Salt Lake Mission Home. It's now or never. If riding in a roommate's car across eastern Oregon, southern Idaho and northern Utah hasn't killed off any remaining traces of wanderlust, the overnight stay at a cheap motel has. I'm dressed in my brand new, three-piece suit from JC Penney, with matching tie, white shirt, and black wingtip shoes (with inch-thick, patented, Forward-Thrust soles, "guaranteed for lasting comfort").

Out of the car and stretching, I breathe in a biting lungful of December air in a part of the city where it's just another Saturday morning for the locals. Sleeping in late. Off for a full day of Christmas shopping. Starting in on that leaky bathroom sink. But for me there'll be no leaky pipes or shopping on this, the first of 737 days of missionary service for The Church of Jesus Christ of Latter-day Saints. The Mormons.

I grab my light blue suitcase, clothing bag, and gray briefcase and walk through the door to the Intake Room. Maybe that isn't its official name, but that's what it is. Toasty warm inside, the place smells of dated thin

1

carpeting and after-shave, its walls off-white, and not a stick of furniture in sight; a 50' by 50' room solely designed for transition to somewhere else. Some twenty young adults—a few women, but mostly men—are here, more arriving every minute, as small piles of luggage and personal items clutter the shrinking floor space with piles both neat and sloppy. Respective owners are saying goodbye to their parents, sibs, and friends, platonic or romantic. Lots of tears are being shed. It seems like I'm the only elder here with no family to see him off, my own a good 800 miles away in western Oregon. While I assure myself that they'd be present if they could, a small voice inside is instead clamoring for a hastily-assembled pity party: "They'd be here if they really cared. But why should they? They're not Mormons like you. They never did understand, did they? You poor guy, all alone . . ." I shake off toxic thoughts amid the clamor of fare-welling. I know why I'm here. All is well.

I'D SUBMITTED PAPERS three months earlier to serve a mission for the Church. Then the letter arrived, signed by the prophet, Spencer W. Kimball, stating that I'd been called to serve a twenty-four month, proselyting mission in the Palacio, Argentina area.

Many weeks of preparation followed: paperwork, interviews with Church leaders, dental work, shots, clothing to buy, goodbyes to make. With six days to go, I'd stood in front of my fellow Church members during sacrament meeting, feeling quite dapper in a new suit, as I told the congregation how excited and blessed and humbled I felt to be leaving on a mission. None of my family were present, but I chalked it up to their being 300 miles away. With jobs to go to and the expense and all, it just wasn't possible. Yet I wondered if I had somehow made them feel excluded from a church not theirs. Or was it too much trouble for them to see me off? In the end, it was easier to not dwell on the "why." I had to move forward, another Christian soldier marching off to war.

Finished speaking, I walked to the chapel's exit door, where a lot of people shook my hand and wished me well, a few of those hands surreptitiously passing on a personal check or folded currency.

The day before I left for Utah, Stake President Lindsay (a local Church leader) needed to set me apart for missionary service. Before doing so, he interviewed me to make sure I was ready to go. Are you morally clean? Yes. Are your debts paid off? Yes. Have you repented of any past sins that might make you unworthy to serve? Yes. Do you have a testimony of the restored gospel of Jesus Christ? Yes. Satisfied with my answers, President Lindsay placed his hands on my head and said, among other things:

"Brother Daniel Arthur Hiland, I promise you that if you will arise an hour or two earlier than your companion, in the peaceful hours of the morning, you will gain much inspiration and enlightenment while studying the scriptures. If you will put forth more effort than your

companions, you will benefit greatly from the experience. Stay with your companion at all times. Be mindful of and show respect for the customs of other people while in their land, so that you do not offend or anger those you will be teaching. You will discover, during your stay there, how to go about fulfilling your lifelong ambitions. Write home to your loved ones. The words you write will be a testimony and an inspiration to them about the Gospel, and what it means to all people—that the readers might be inspired to search out the truth which the Lord has provided for each and every one of us to partake in, if we only will."

He ended the prayer in the name of Jesus Christ and re-moved his hands from my head.

"Congratulations, Elder Hiland," he said, shaking my hand. "You are now an official missionary for The Church of Jesus Christ."

Though I'd occasionally been referred to as "Elder" before, the title now replaced "Dan" as my first name. I was now authorized to teach the gospel to anyone I came in contact with. With this came the responsibility to live my life in such a way that I would be open to the influ-ence of the Holy Ghost. This meant staying morally clean, avoiding influences or activities that could distract or dis-able me from being able to teach others. There was to be no dating or romantic association with the opposite sex for the next two years. I felt I had crossed a threshold into another state of mind, though *my* mind was still thinking about it. Regardless, I did feel different, a load of responsibility having come down from heaven and now resting on my shoulders.

10:15 A.M.

SEEING NO OPENINGS for conversation-starters, I circle my luggage and look through the condensation-steamed windows. Cars drive by, planes fly overhead, people walk past on their way to somewhere else. But inside the Mission Home, all non-essential personnel are invited to leave. The rest of us are asked to line up our belongings in a narrow hallway, then move to the next room for further instructions.

Now in a larger area, my three-score group of elders and sisters listens to the elderly Man in Charge. We're asked to fill out a questionnaire. Sitting down at a desk, I look the paper over, my attention drawn to the section asking me to describe my driving record and abilities. Of all things, why does the Church need to know about this, one of the darker chapters in my recent past? Having accumulated more than my share of traffic citations during the preceding eighteen months, the state of Oregon saw fit to suspend my driving privileges. I scribble a vague answer and hand back the paperwork, confident that my chances of driving any Argentine vehicle more complex than a bicycle are now dashed.

"Elders and Sisters," says the Man in Charge, I'd like to take this opportunity to welcome you to the Salt Lake

Mission Home. You know, the Lord is pleased with your decision to serve Him here in the mission field. Many of you have made a lot of sacrifices to be here, some having traveled long distances and at great expense."

I think about what I've gone through to now be standing in that crowded room. The bad habits I repented of. The other changes I made to become a better person. The friends and family I left behind. But a quiet assurance comes over me, as it has repeatedly during the last few weeks: that my decision to serve is the right one.

"As representatives of the Lord, you should be clean in thought, deed and appearance."

That latter item being the easiest to remedy, he asks us to stand single-file.

"As I pass by, if you feel a hand on your shoulder, it means you need a haircut."

Though a few missionaries laugh, mainly the sisters (and those elders who've taken no chances by getting a buzz cut prior to arriving), a sizeable line forms. Positive I'm safe, due to a recent trim which I think looks pretty good, the Man in Charge closes in. I feel the Touch of Shame on my shoulder, signifying that I'm one of those present who is not in sync with mission grooming standards.

Off I go, following those more familiar with the territory, across a street or two to the first floor of the tall, business-like Church Office Building. Traveling along one hallway after another I arrive at a barbershop, where multiple chairs are occupied by the Shorn and the Soon-to-be-Shorn. Clumps of blonde, brown, and black hair tumble down the slopes of white cloaks, spilling onto heaps that obscure the checkered linoleum floor. Barbers solemnly shuffle through shifting piles of locks as the rest of us captive customers watch and smirk, trying to appear unconcerned. I ascend a tonsorial throne, lose less hair than I thought I would, then descend, grateful I'm still in possession of something topside. I follow others as we make our way to the cafeteria for a quick lunch.

As I travel on foot across public areas, headed back to the Home, I'm starting to notice a sort of aura, that separation from the common person that comes with "being part of something"—of having joined a cause that sets me apart from the everyday, the commonplace.

1 P.M.

BACK INSIDE THE MISSION HOME, I'm wondering what's next on the schedule when someone hands me a two-by three-inch, salmon-colored card. Apparently, next on the schedule is leaving. I grab my stuff, head outside to the frosty parking lot, hand my ticket to a baggage loader, and climb aboard a chartered bus. Finding a resting place halfway back, I offer a half-hearted greeting to an Elder who plops down in the seat next to me.

Owing to road lag and emotional overload, my friendliness reserves are depleted. I feign sleep, drifting in and out amidst excited talk. Place names like "Provo," "Orem," "Brigham City," "Logan," "Ogden"—ad infinitum Utahn—fill the air. I think about this missionary business. Though I trust those in charge, what's going to happen next? Can I handle what's about to be thrown my way? Will I be able to adjust to all the changes? As if invited onto my mental stage for some script rehearsal, Doubt steps up to the mike.

"Who are you, Daniel Arthur Hiland, to be going forth to preach this gospel?"

"Who are you, period?"

"Why are you here, of all places—the guy who values his solitude above all else?"

And though I've played the Loner for many years, I've never felt as solitary as I do at this moment. Aside from my reflection in the tinted window, the only thing that looks familiar is the Wasatch Front—that mountain range running parallel to the freeway as it always has on my previous trips through the state that Brigham founded. I shut my eyes again and wonder what's to become of me . . .

PROVO: 2 P.M.

OUR BUS LEAVES the interstate and winds its way toward that white "Y" of arranged stones that presides over Brigham Young University from a steep hillside 2,000 feet above. South along University Avenue we roll, rounding the bend past the Carillon Tower. Parking lots to the right, storied white cinder block apartments on the left, where married students and their children eke out an existence while the spouse goes to school every day. At the southwest corner of the campus the bus hangs a right, then *whisshes* to a stop in front of Knight Mangum Hall, the Church's current location for the LTM (Language Training Mission). Consisting of two floors and a basement, KMH is a flat-roofed, squarish, brown-bricked building, three blocks long by one block deep. The nexus of language training and religious instruction for many of us foreign-bound missionaries, this will be my home for the next eight weeks.

Scores of well-dressed sisters and elders line the sidewalks, eager to greet this latest batch of Dazed Ones. Flanking the entrance, and inside looking out through the worn drapery of floor-to-ceiling windows, they watch, their faces a mixture of happiness and a bemused, "You have no idea what you're in for" look. Leaving the warm security of the bus, I descend into brisk winter air and retrieve my bags, then self-consciously walk past folks fascinated at the sight of themselves a few weeks earlier. One thing you can say about missionary work: it's the great equalizer. Whether a lifer in the Church or a recent convert like me, this is all new. No matter how much dedication one possesses, the mountain of work rumored to be just around the corner might as well be Wasatch-sized.

Once in the hall proper, paperwork is handed out and the herding begins. Those destined for one country head This Way, others are sent That Direction. Those going to Southeast Asia are sent to accommodations down the street at a place called St. Francis. Argentina being my destination, I'm assigned to the Santa Fe District, Branch Two. Those standing in my line include two "sisters" and eight "elders." I'm introduced to one Elder Searle, the person who's to be my "companion," Mormon-speak for the person I will study with, eat with, pray with, and generally accompany throughout our days at the LTM, sunup till sundown.

Aside from door-knocking, this is the one aspect of the Work I'm not looking forward to. Being a lone-wolf type and an only son, the prospect of spending inordinate amounts of time with another male, let alone sharing meals, an apartment, a bathroom, teaching activities, and traveling makes me very uncomfortable. Sure, I've had roommates before. But I could always get away by myself, and any time I wanted to. Not so in the mission field. Mission rules state that companions are to remain together at all times, the only exceptions being lavatorial or while sleeping. We share greetings and a few questions, but I'm going slowly. Plenty of time to get acquainted later. Eight weeks, to be exact. *Eight weeks.*

Given directions by one of the handlers, Elder Searle and I are assigned a second-floor room on the eastern end of KMH's north side. I'll never see the western half, where the Sisters are housed. Administrative offices form a central architectural barrier between the ordained male and female members of the species. Dragging my stuff along for the fifth time that day, I walk down a hallway. Up some stairs. Along a narrow crème-colored passageway to an oak door and our room. I dump my belongings on the floor and flop on the lower bunk to test the mattress. But restless, I get up and look out the window.

Our quarters sport a festive view of the back parking lot, its grey concrete steps leading uphill to maintenance sheds and sidewalk access to the BYU campus. A one-hundred-fifty-foot tall, round, brick smokestack blocks my view of the lofty hillside "Y." As with the other boarding rooms at KMH, ours is designed to house four people, interior design on the Spartan side. Light-green walls. White acoustic ceiling tiles. Red-tiled linoleum floor. The fifteen- by twenty-foot space holds matching bunk beds, dressers, and closet. A large desk in the middle separates it all. A light-brown, metal wall heater radiates an odor of cooked, ancient dust, horizontal slots punctuating its front. It hugs the wall below steel-framed single-pane windows, which open via small crank handles. The heater radiates an odor of cooked, ancient dust. Amidst all of this, the other two roommates arrive: Elders Bertram and Short. They're stepping past us, trying to figure out where they and their belongings will possibly fit.

The only thing lacking in our quarters is lavatorial facilities. I walk down the hall to the men's room and it's just as I'd feared: community bathrooms and showers. I hated them in high school and I hate them now. Facing a two-month stint of communal washings, I decide to retain some sort of dignity: I'll beat the rest of the gang to the showers as often as possible. For once the crowds hit, it will be every elder for himself.

After hanging stuff in the closet and populating the dresser drawers with underwear and socks, I read over the mimeographed paperwork I've collected. Class schedules. Study schedules. Meal schedules. Daily schedules. Weekly schedules. But before my eyes can glaze over too much, someone reminds us that it's dinner time. I look at the meal ticket I've been issued: good for three squares at the St. Francis of Assisi school. I don my light-tan, fur-lined coat, Elder Searle the more popular, black trench coat. We join a small group of Elders headed out into dusky, frigid evening air for a southbound, mile-long trek through ankle-deep slush.

As we slosh along, the struggle for communication ensues. Elder Searle and I seem to be on different wavelengths. If I'm FM, he's AM. He's talking sports, and I can only share a few lame slow-pitch softball stories. After a few minutes, my companion moves ahead in the pack to converse with others, as if I lack something of interest. If he's expecting me to follow his gregarious example, he's mistaken. I remain at the back, a role I'm used to filling.

I look at the dark and looming mountains to my left, or missionary backs straight ahead, or the traffic to my right, beyond which are homes and businesses decorated with Christmas lights. The holidays are eleven days distant.

5 P.M.

INSIDE ST. FRANK'S, bright lights, warm air, and the rich aroma of dinner beckon, that meager lunch at the Church Office building a distant memory. Traveling along a short corridor, I see a large room to the right, where row after row of metal-framed beds are arranged, like a hospital ward. The Asian-bound missionaries live here. It's privacy-challenged and looks like a breeding ground for insomnia, making me grateful for my KMH accommodations.

Once in the gym, I grab a tray and join the line. It's standard college cafeteria fare: meat, potatoes and gravy, rolls, vegetables, bread, and dessert. Elder Searle and I sit down and eat, conversing little. Then he's off, working the crowds. Thin-skinned, I'm already resentful of his behavior, as if I'm some creature occupying a lower spot on the Popularity food chain. He reminds me of the jocks I knew in high school.

Dinner over, I head out into the cold world, body temperature lower due to my stomach using much of the available blood supply to digest whatever has happened to come tumbling down the gastric chute. Through the slushy, street-lit night we walk. I try to look and act gregarious while my Forward Thrust shoes skid and slide and twist around in the uneven, rutted, half-frozen slush.

7 P.M.

FROM 7:00 PM TO 9:30 PM I attend orientation meetings, again perusing paperwork I've been collecting all afternoon. The 6:00 a.m. to 9:30 p.m. schedule reads like a Preview of Coming Attractions:

Preparation Day (P-Day). That one day of the week when I can go to the temple, wash clothes, write letters, sleep, go bowling, etc. It ends at 5:00 p.m.

The Live Your Language program. The goal is to have me speaking nothing but Spanish. Before the end of the first week.

Spanish language study. Grammar, vocabulary memorization, pronunciation, and conversation. Six days a week.

Scripture study. One hundred thirty-nine scriptural passages to memorize, and which I'll be tested on every week. The bigger exams will be held during Weeks 4 and 8.

Book of Mormon study. Ten pages per day.

9:30 P.M.

WE'RE RELEASED TO RETURN to our rooms. Lights are to be out by 10:30. Prying off tight shoes, peeling away the black socks, tugging loose my tie, I stretch out on an unfamiliar mattress and close my eyes, feeling my body relax but my mind refusing to unspool. Thoughts are everywhere and NOWHERE, like a compass needle surrounded by magnets. Afraid I'll be laughed at for falling asleep fully clothed, I strip down to my temple garments and slip between the sheets. Too soon, but not soon enough, one of the other three elders switches off the lights. Idle chatter waxes and wanes, then all is quiet. The heater clicks and ticks amid the sound of heavy breathing. I say a silent prayer—not wanting Elders Searle, Bertram or Short to hear me—and assume that God will understand. After the "Amen," I close my eyes and relax. But sleep doesn't come. Despite the fact that Saturday morning seems to have occurred a couple days ago, I'm excited, worried, lonely. I wonder what I've gotten myself into. Then thoughts melt away, out of control, and I drift off . . .

DAY TWO

AT 5:55 A.M. MY EYES OPENED to a view of coiled mattress springs. Then, remembering where I was, I grabbed a towel, garments, pants, shampoo and soap, and ran down the narrow hallway. The bathroom was deserted, a miracle well-deserved. I jumped in the shower and enjoyed hot water coursing over me as I tried to mentally prepare for the known and unknown. Since it was Sunday, I knew there'd be a full three hours of church meetings. Where they'd be held was anyone's guess. Then there were the three hikes to St. Frank's. My hope was that the Sabbath in the LTM would be observed as a day of rest, that quiet ride in the plane before the parachute jump.

Back from the showers, I dressed, studied scriptures, and said my prayers, consulting the Schedule to make sure I was in sync. At 7 a.m. we hiked to breakfast, then hurried back for the 8:00 to 9:00 priesthood meeting. Similar to the civilian version, the elders met together, while the sisters convened elsewhere for a Relief Society meeting.

Our meeting began with a hymn, a prayer, words of welcome, and announcements about upcoming events. A lesson followed. After the closing prayer, we had fifteen minutes to get to Sunday School, where the men and women met together again. It was another opportunity for instruction, most likely from the scriptures.

From 10:45 to 11:30 a.m. was Free Time, followed by an hour and a half of lunch. As a reminder to the troops about the importance of civilized dining, a handout was circulated:

- Follow the schedule or you'll not be served after posted hours.
- Don't crowd in line or save places.
- Keep the line moving quickly by having your meal ticket out.
- Make selections quickly: one main course, one salad, bread (two max), one dessert, one beverage.
- Extra items must be paid for.

Then came Personal Time from 1 p.m. to 3 p.m. What to do with my newly allotted leisure? Sleep? I was too keyed up. Play? There were no sporting or gaming facilities available, nor a basketball court nearby—not that I played the game. Call someone on the phone? There were no pay phones in the building, and mission rules forbade calls home or anywhere else, Christmas Day the lone exception. Watch TV? See the aforementioned mission rules. This left hanging out in our rooms, or going to the campus. Though we were not to fraternize with the general public—for a variety of reasons—the Bookstore and Cougar Eat cafeteria were not off-limits.

THIS PARTICULAR SUNDAY being the kickoff for everything but the rigorous class schedule, I reviewed it to make sure I was ready:

Live Your Language. The goal was to speak Spanish every hour of every day I was in the LTM. Called "immersion," the experience was similar to inching into a pool full of frigid water, lots of ice blocks bobbing around. Monday: two hours. Tuesday: four hours. Wednesday: eight hours. Thursday and onward: 24/7.

Room Care. "Rooms will be inspected on a bi-weekly basis for cleanliness, proper furnishings present in each room, and damage."

Care of Clothing. "Washers and dryers are on a first-come, first-serve basis. You have to furnish your own soap."

Exercises. Participate daily in the Missionary Physical Fitness program. This meant finding some open space in the hallway where one could perform jumping jacks, pushups, and sit-ups.

Scripture Study. One hour a day: thirty minutes devoted to memorization of verses in the Bible and Book of Mormon; the other half hour for reading ten pages from the latter.

Missionary Handbook. Also known as the "White Bible," it was a thin, three- by four-inch booklet that contained all the rules, policies, and guidelines necessary to keep us on the straight and narrow path that missionaries needed to walk. The heart of the booklet was the threefold purpose of the Language Training Mission:

- Become disciples of the Lord Jesus Christ.
- Learn to preach the gospel in a new language.
- Learn to love the people in the mission field.

Underlying these goals was an emphasis on obedience to all the rules set forth by the mission. Without obedience, the whole structure could crash down around us.

From 3:00 to 4:30 p.m. was sacrament meeting. The bread and water (representing the body and blood of the Savior, prior to His death) was administered by priesthood holders to the Elders and Sisters. Talks were given on different gospel subjects, followed by a closing song and prayer. Dinner was followed by a "fireside" or "family home evening," from 7:00 to 10:00 p.m. These three-hour meetings they represented a time when missionaries met as districts to share lessons or discuss their concerns. If someone was struggling with something, that issue could be shared with others in the group, in order to find a solution. It was a spiritual support group, and one that I drew strength from. That meeting over, I returned to my room, weary eyes blinking from the strain of the overhead fluorescents. Lights-out couldn't come soon enough.

DAY THREE

MONDAY. FOLLOWING THE RACE for the showers and the long slog to breakfast, I sat through a 7:45 a.m. – 10:30 a.m. string of lectures (in Chapel Three) by the mission presidency. Subject matter included our calling as missionaries, the goals of the LTM, what was expected of us for the next eight weeks, and more about the mission rules. In Social Hall Room 121, I paid $285 (from a rapidly dwindling supply of currency hidden in my money belt) for housing and a meal ticket.

Unlike some denominations, members of the LDS Church are not paid for their service, whether they be Sunday School teachers, bishops, or stake presidents. They accept the call to serve and then arrange their lives accordingly, continuing with full-time jobs to support themselves and their families. On top of that, they voluntarily pay tithing and fast offerings. It's like a virtual plate being passed around every Sunday, except that the donations are submitted in sealed envelopes to the bishop or one of his two counselors. Missionary service is treated the same way—pay as you go.

But due to my family being unable to foot the bill, and me being short of funds, my bishop in La Grande had determined that I was a worthy candidate for financial assistance. Saying that he'd prefer me serving in the mission field rather than being out on the street, he found folks in the local ward who were willing to help pay my room and board costs. For the Argentine mission, that amounted to $60 per month. The $1500 plane ticket expense was anonymously covered by local Church members in La Grande, as well. I was asked to take care of the bills for pre-mission medical and dental work, my scriptures, shoes, clothing, passport, transportation to Provo, and LTM room and board.

Prior to lunch I took my maiden voyage to the college bookstore to pick up supplies, all the while striving for as little interaction with the campus denizens as possible. Not that we were better than any of them. But complications could ensue when running into family, friends, or suitors (past and present)—especially prolonged conversations with the latter.

Not so my romance with the bookstore. The first time I walked its aisles, I basked in the aura of the tomes. It didn't matter if they were textbooks, reference works, or novels. They were all books. I loved the look, the feel, the weight in my hands. The smell of the pages. The covers. Steeling myself to the task at hand, I bought the inch-thick manual required for Spanish grammar and pronunciation class, along with "201 Spanish Verbs" and a Spanish grammar review book, circa 1945. Trying to avoid looking at the resident goddesses that roamed the store proved to be a challenge, but one I was up for—as long as there were books to look at.

Lunchtime. The rapport I hoped to develop with Elder Searle was not happening. Once he began socializing, there was no stopping him. He bounced Tigger-like from one group of humans to the next. Having played the loner for so long, I was starting to think that the problem might lie with me. All I really knew for sure was that it was uncomfortable as hell. I wondered how long we could go on like this.

BACK AT KMH IT WAS TIME for the first class, conveniently situated next door to my room. Inside was a circle of chairs, bare walls interrupted only by a dusty, green chalkboard. For those whose minds tended to wander, windows afforded a stirring view of the parking lot and physical plant smokestack. Elder Calderón greeted us as we entered the classroom. A native of South America, he was shorter than average, had dark brown, straight hair, was soft-spoken, and of kindly manner. His job was to help us learn how to pronounce Spanish words, as well as what to say. He pushed us into the pool, so to speak, by having us go to Lesson One and start learning words and their meanings. The book was filled with line drawings of the parts of the face, hands, legs, as well as lists: days of the week, months, colors, and numbers.

"Here," the instructor said, pointing at his mouth and lips. "Let's pronounce the word "turista." "Too" (with lips protruded), "dee" (with a wide faux-grin and teeth bared, grimace-like), "stahh" (mouth wide open and tongue pulled back out of the way). "Too-DEE-stah," with the accent on the middle syllable. To say it correctly meant having to make three distinct sounds, while orchestrating the movements of the jaw, lips, teeth, and tongue. In

English, I'd taken it for granted that if I said something close to the desired word, it would be understood. But in Spanish, such sloppiness could mean the difference between a smile and a slap in the face, or worse. It was calisthenics for the mouth. The instructor had us repeat a difficult word over and over and over until any trace of a non-Spanish accent was gone. The exercises were tough to accomplish, but I was promised (by virtue of being set apart), that I'd soon see a drastic improvement in my ability to pronounce words correctly, even if I didn't always know what I was saying.

LATE AFTERNOON WAS TAKEN UP with Gospel Study. Finally, a peace-filled break. Just me and my scriptures. Or so I thought. From the get-go, I found that this was a time set aside for the memorization of scriptures from the Bible and the Book of Mormon: twenty, to be exact. And by the end of the first week. *Oy.* In secular schools, a compressed learning environment relies on rote memorization—that repetitive ingestion of a stream of facts. LDS Church leadership recognized that a missionary had to be more involved in the process—that before sharing the Word one had to first "obtain" it. But what does it mean to "obtain" something, by the Lord's definition? It's one thing to understand something intellectually. Having taken in a set of facts, one can then present that same information to others. And if the instructor is lucky, the student will retain a portion of the presented information. But teachers worth their salt will help the student learn not only the *what,* but the *why.* This helps internalize the concepts being taught. If the internalization doesn't occur, the student may pass a subsequent test, but will forget a majority of the info within a matter of days.

As for language study, there were hundreds, even thousands, of words to memorize. But they had to be framed in a contextual setting to sink in. Facial features, body parts, and food groups would be discussed, then used in a sentence. Spelling, grammar, punctuation—it was all part of the Herculean task of becoming conversational in a foreign language.

DINNER TIME—and more of the same for Elder Searle and me. Then again, lack of conversation was on everyone's minds by late afternoon. We had just experienced two straight hours of LYL, that inverted form of the monk's Vow of Silence, where we spoke nothing but Spanish for 120 minutes—long periods of silence amidst the noisy chatter. I clung to the easy-to-remember phrases like linguistic life preservers: "Que hora es?" (What time is it?) "Cuando vamos a comer?" (When do we eat?"), and the ever-popular "Me voy al baño" (I'm going to the bathroom). But it was frustrating to communicate, with only a handful of words to draw from. For someone like me, who could talk the leg off a piano, that two hours was tough to endure.

RETENTION. From 8 to 9 p.m. I retired to a table to practice what had been covered in class. A welcome relief from the instructor-led sessions, these one-hour periods nevertheless had their own challenge— the goal of capturing as much as one could on the mental hard drive, before the short-term memories evaporated. I could tell I'd need to take measures: index cards full of notes; grammar book pages underlined and highlighted; words scribbled across formerly pristine textbook pages; extra books purchased. And all in the hope that one of these study aids would somehow push me over the line from ignorance to understanding; anything to help my frazzled brain make the connection between theory, practice, and reality.

As if that weren't enough for one day, I mulled over the discovery of a most vexing stumbling block, one sitting in the middle of my path to linguistic enlightenment: verbs. I liked structure, organization, and consistency. But verbs had their own ideas about what the Rules of the Game should be. Sure, there were the well-known tenses of Past, Present, and Future. It was the difference between them that drove me loco. Take ser and estar. Both verbs signify states of being, one literal and the other figurative. To be or not to be. In English, if I'm physically or mentally ill, people can say that I'm "sick." But in Spanish, "Estoy enfermo" means I'm physically ill, while "Soy enfermo" indicates that I'm off my rocker. The challenge lay in remembering which was which, an action I had to exercise before I dared open my trap. "Frio" could mean one is cold, or sexually frigid. "Rico" could signify that one is either rich, or tastes good. Soy or Estoy—which word could it be? A linguistic minefield, to be sure.

9:45 P.M. Nothing meaningful going on in my worn-out brain, I headed for my room. After some exercising and small talk, I collapsed on the mattress, saying prayers to myself but drifting off before an Amen could be uttered.

DAY FOUR

TUESDAY, 16 DECEMBER. Up at dawn. Into the shower. On my knees for prayer. Off to breakfast. Back to class at 7:30. Our seated circle of students was displaying the Various States of Consciousness: present in body; barely awake; aware of surroundings; conversant; inexplicably attentive; chipper.

Residing in the middle of this bell curve, I tried to pick up where I'd left off the day before, poring over familiar textbook content. But the previous session was a blurred mix of grammar, spelling, punctuation, and pronunciation, a few fascinating facts about Argentine culture tossed in, and all in the hope that something might stick. I was backtracking so much that this game of mental catch-up was causing me to fall behind. And falling behind was my greatest fear. Having developed a lifelong habit of comparing self to others, the resultant anxiety sapped me of my strength, like a sprinter looking over his shoulder. To see missionaries pulling ahead fed a panic that spawned frustration.

I was praying, asking God to help me not be The Last. But this was one of those times when I'd need to learn how He worked—not doing difficult things for me, but with me. And only if I let Him.

One of His gifts to me was a departure from the regular morning schedule to attend the on-campus Tuesday devotional. Held in the stately, gray, 1920s-era Joseph Smith Auditorium, west of KMH, our 200-plus number assembled in theater seats to hear motivational talks. Though the discourses were in English, each district was encouraged to sing in its own language. Stumbling through the Spanish version of "Onward, Christian Soldiers," I would pause every so often, thrilling to the mix these different languages produced. And it wasn't just a love for music that gave me chills. I was starting to feel that aura again, sensing I was part of a group effort both holy and transcendent—one that spanned countries, cultures, and centuries.

The rest of the day went according to schedule. Before I knew it, Lights Out was upon us. And though the body was firmly planted in bed, my weary brain—unleashed from the linguistic cares of the day—liked to stagger all over the place. I thought about what it would be like to walk streets and knock doors in Argentina. I thought about family and friends. And I thought about girls, said topic a source of concern—for once I touched that mental third-rail, guilt flourished like a fast-growing, noxious weed. Maybe it would have been easier, had I left a girlfriend behind. Maybe worse. Regardless, I was gaining an understanding of what one must give up when embarking on a mission for God.

It wasn't the notion that sex was evil. Far from it, judging by the average size of LDS families I knew. On the one hand, sex is sacred—God's way of sharing with humans the power of procreation. It's where babies come from. On the other, it's a source of profound pleasure, the mortar holding the bricks of marriage in place—or something along those lines. But nighttime alone in a bed in the LTM was not the place for sexual thoughts. And though the sudden appearance of the sexual on my mental stage was natural, dwelling on it produced obvious effects on my body that would be impossible to control, let alone halt.

The see-saw battle between the Natural and the Saintly had begun, and the punching bag it made of my confidence was not a pretty sight.

DAY FIVE

WEDNESDAY, 17 DECEMBER. On the seventh day God rested. And in that spirit the Church instituted Preparation Day. Not the whole day, mind you. Just from those first waking moments until 5 p.m. Called P-Day, it was a chance to unwind the spring and engage in the mundane, the playful, the laundry. But said rest period was fraught with obstacles. Our modes of transportation were limited to either walking or taking the taxi—the former time-consuming and the latter expensive.

Since we were expected to attend the Temple every Wednesday morning, during prime Laundry Room time, planning was of the essence. If I got everything washed beforehand, there was plenty of free time available upon my return. If not, I'd suffer the time sink of laundry gridlock, forced to spend lunchtime and early afternoon in a humid, noisy room full of washers, dryers, and the pungent aroma of detergent.

As for the Temple, we attended a two-hour "endowment" session there. Doing so was a spiritual uplift for me. I could feel the calm and peace that comes from being in a place where the Lord's Spirit could be felt. Aside from one's home, the temple is considered the most holy of places. It was a ten-minute taxi ride to the Provo Temple. I entered the front doors and presented my temple recommend—a signed card that vouched for my worthiness to enter the sacred edifice. In a locker room, I changed from my suit into all-white clothing, down to the shoes and socks. The sisters wore white dresses with a veil, pulled back. The clothing symbolizes purity, reverence and holiness, and the fact that in God's church, no one is of a higher status than anyone else. The atmosphere is one of peace, beauty, quiet, and reverence. And for the next two hours I sat with others in a white-walled, furnished room, listening to instruction about the nature of the covenants I'd made with God. I left the temple calm and refreshed.

Back at KMH, a mimeographed note had been left behind by anonymous visitors:

NOTICE OF ROOM INSPECTION
"The Lord said, let all things be
done in cleanliness before me"
(D & C 42:41).

These somber words were followed by a list of items, red check marks next to the ones my roomies and I had neglected to take care of:

- Put dirty clothing away
- Make beds
- Clean dresser top
- Clean desk top
- Sweep floor
- Sweep under bed
- Put pillow under bedspread
- Empty trash can

The overall grade? "Very bad!"

After all the work I'd been doing to toe the line, this heavy-handed missive had me saying, "Shove it!" under my breath. I decided not to take the inspection seriously. After all, what could they do? Send me home?

Casting a further pall over what had started out as a nice, calming trip to the temple was the realization that this was the fourth day of LYL. Eight continuous hours of Spanish speaking. Since I'd put off my own effort all morning, I began at 2:30 p.m., uttering a final few sentences in English. Things were quiet that afternoon and evening, a very limited bank of words and phrases keeping me from expressing myself as I wished to. By bedtime I was exhausted. I had just enjoyed the last day during which I could speak English with a clear conscience. Language immersion was complete—at least on paper.

DAY SIX

THURSDAY, 18 DECEMBER. Facing the new day with further concerns about 24/7 Spanish-speaking, I was
on the lookout for those islands of exception when
English could still be spoken: during interviews with
leaders; while asking grammar questions in class;
conversing with non-Spanish speakers; during doctor
appointments and Sunday meetings. And there was always a chance to invoke the much-abused "Que quiere
decir...?" question. Yet when I did know what words
to use, I had to be mindful of verbs. Having assumed,
upon purchase, that my "201 Spanish Verbs" book
would clear up all questions, I was unaware of one
small fact: English uses six verb tenses, while Spanish
has fourteen. *Fourteen.* I would have to limit myself to
three or four common tenses and ignore the rest.

It was on this day that I resumed writing in my journal, a habit I'd developed nine months earlier. It reads
as follows:

"*I have now been in the-*"

DAY SEVEN

FRIDAY, 19 DECEMBER started out like any other. Early rising, showers, prayers and the breakfast hike. But after we returned, Elder Searle told me he had an appointment with Max Pinegar, our mission president. Realizing I'd be getting a break from class, I looked forward to the down time. We walked the long hallway together. Though I couldn't read my comp's mind, that expressionless look was one he didn't normally wear. Something was wrong.

Arriving at the building's central point, my comp announced himself to the President's secretary. We were invited to sit in the foyer and wait. Then the door opened and President Pinegar motioned Elder Searle into his office. As the door closed, I settled into my chair, expecting my companion's reappearance within a few minutes. If it took longer, so be it. I could handle the time away from class. For now, I would just enjoy the unplanned rest. Ten, fifteen, twenty minutes passed. I grew fidgety. My thoughts dwelt on what might be happening with Elder Searle. The only thing I was sure of was that the interview wasn't about me.

"Elder," said someone in charge, "go back to your class."

So off I went, eastward. I entered the classroom and was heading for a seat when-

"Elder Hiland."

"Yes?"

"Where is your companion?"

"Talking to President Pinegar."

"Well, why aren't you there, with him?"

"I was told to come back to class."

"Well, go back and wait for your companion to finish his interview," he said, as if I was supposed to have known this. "Then you can return to class."

So off I went, westward. I'd no sooner settled into a comfortable chair when—

"Elder Hiland, where's you companion?"

Eastward I went. The vicious cycle ended when someone decided I should hang with Elders Bertram and Short, until the mystery was solved. But no one seemed to know anything. And if they did, they weren't telling.

Early-afternoon class ended, the three of us returned to our room. On the floor in the middle of the room sat Elder Searle's bags, but no Elder Searle. Instead, I found a note on the dresser:

> *Elders Hiland, Bertram, and Short:*
> *I'm going home because of a personal matter. Hope you all do well, and may the Lord bless you.*
> *PS: Here are some things that might be a help to you. Find someone who can wear these shoes. Please give the hair dryer to Elder O'Donnell. Here's my address if you'd like to write.*

If swearing had been tolerated in the presence of others, I'd have uttered an oath or two, the shock was that intense. I looked out the window at the campus, and wondered where John might be. Though ours had not been the ideal relationship, I was tempted to go for a walk on the off-chance I might stumble across him. Then I thought better of the idea. I tried to imagine how Elder Searle felt as he walked from Pinegars's office to our room and packed his bags, heartsick and filled with that dread known only by those who return home dishonored.

Years of preparation followed by searching interviews with his bishop and stake president, during which he assures them that he's worthy to serve as a missionary for the church bearing the Savior's name. The final few days arrive. He gives his farewell talk in front of a packed chapel. Family and friends are there, parents and siblings weeping at the thought of their son being gone for two whole years, though for the best of causes. The tearful goodbyes at the airport. The promise of a twenty-four-month adventure in God's service. All that spiritual growth he'll enjoy, evidenced by the changed man—the better, more spiritual person he'll be when he steps off the plane at mission's end. Instead, Elder Searle would be phoning home. After returning and facing everyone, over the course of a few grief-ridden days, there would be one last trial to endure: a disciplinary council conducted by his stake president, during which Elder Searle would most likely be excommunicated.

To the secular world, the word "excommunication" has several meanings, all of them negative. But the process and aftermath vary, depending on the denomination.

In some churches, excommunication signifies a lifetime ban from church activity and membership. In others, it results in shunning—an avoidance of the sinner that denies that man or woman the privileges of fellowship. In the LDS Church, excommunication is sometimes part of a person's repentance process.

Suppose Mr. Smith has committed adultery. After a time, his conscience torments him to the point where he breaks down and confesses the act to his bishop. The bishop convenes a meeting between himself, the two councilors he works with, Mr. Smith, and a clerk present to record the proceedings. After conversation, during which Mr. Smith repeats to the group what he has done, sans the gory details, the bishop excuses Smith from the room. The remaining people discuss the situation, come to a decision, then kneel and pray about it. After the prayer, if they all feel they've received a confirmation from the Lord, they invite Mr. Smith back and the bishop informs him of the decision. The bishop asks Mr. Smith to meet with him on a regular basis. The purpose of these meetings will be to help Mr. Smith find his way back to full Church membership and activity.

But regardless of the outcome, Mr. Smith receives assurances from the bishop that the Church members still love him. For the time being, he may not be able to partake of the Sacrament, or teach a class or hold a position, but the goal is to help him finish repenting and move forward. There is no shunning, no lifetime ban. No punitive measures are taken. In its own way, excommunication is the first step of an arduous repentance process Mr. Smith needs to experience to make things right with his Heavenly Father.

I REMAINED WITH ELDERS Bertram and Short, while the leadership decided who to reassign me to. The trouble with threesomes is the nagging feeling that one is intruding. But in this instance, there was no reason to believe I was a third wheel—especially with Bertram. Mike was energetic and enthused about life. Both of us quick on the verbal draw, we hit it off from the start. Discovering common ground in the pun department, we struck comedic pay dirt upon learning of a shared fondness for the Marx Brothers and The Firesign Theatre. His memory for Abbott and Costello's "Who's on First" routine amazed me.

As I crawled into bed that evening, below Searle's empty bunk, I wondered how worthy I was to serve. Was I any better than my ex-companion? Any smarter? Probably not. More obedient? Probably in at least one area. But what did that matter? I had no idea what Elder Searle had confessed to the mission president. But I knew that in the end there was only one thing separating us: that split-second decision to not cave to temptation. And what a razor-thin boundary it was.

December 22-31

CHRISTMAS WAS APPROACHING. In the interest of morale, the mission president decided that all residents of the LTM should spend the better part of the 25th in the homes of Church members throughout the Provo area. As such, the three of us received a letter from a local family:

"Dear Elders Hiland, Bertram and Short:

We are very happy to be able to invite you to our home on Christmas Day. We hope you enjoy lots food and plenty of company. There are six in our family living at home now, with our oldest son and his wife of two months living one block away. Our home at Christmas is filled to the brim, but no other time of the year is so great. We are happy to be able to have you share your Christmas with us.

Brother and Sister Smith.

ONE OF THE TRAITS of confined humans is the tendency to examine every square inch of their living quarters. It was only a matter of time before each of us, having exhausted

41

all other surfaces, looked heavenward. Someone decided to remove an acoustic ceiling tile. While disappointed that there wasn't a warren of ventilator shafts to explore topside, we did notice writing on the back of the removed square. Excited about this archeological find, we all got into the spirit of things, pulling down one section after another. There were poems, mass signatures, stories and dedications. Illustrations and caricatures—some professional-looking—filled the tiles. Before leaving in mid-February, I would inscribe something on one of those gray spaces, as well.

Soon after my arrival at the LTM, the mission saw fit to bless us with a closer venue for meals, resurrecting the old KMH kitchen, which had been mysteriously idle even before I arrived. At first, the novelty of an on-site kitchen made for long food lines. The queue stretched from the counter past the long tables, then through a narrow doorway at the back of the cafeteria, to the outer halls. The wait was such that one had better bring something to do if they arrived late. But soon enough, the familiarity of a bland cuisine bred contempt, brought on by recurrent bouts of indigestion. The cooks did the best they could with the limited materials at their disposal. But I had little sympathy. Being on the receiving end of their creations was causing me untold grief.

In the beginning were the pancakes. When I was hungry, they looked and smelled great, their seductive aroma a siren call that wafted through hallways, tempting the unwary. But once deposited upon one's plate and butter applied, the trouble began. The cakes were a half-inch thick and uber-absorbent. Poured syrup disappeared into the top layer for the first ten to fifteen seconds, before emerging to undulate down the stack's ribbed sides, carrying away most of the precious butter.

No matter. Let's eat! The first few mouthfuls were great. Then one started to notice the density of said cakes; how they expanded to fill every corner of one's mouth. And the way each bite fell and landed with a rock-like thud at stomach's bottom. These weren't flap jacks. They were *flop* jacks. If able to get more than two of these syrup-saturated pillows down your protesting hatch, you were lucky. Or maybe not so much. Washing the mass southward with a refreshing glass of milk only made matters worse, like tamping down a cannon-load of soggy doormats with lumpy concrete mix.

A few minutes later you've had enough. Alarm bells are ringing in your gut as you push away the partially loaded plate and lumber off to language class, stopping occasionally to lean against a wall and catch your breath. Collapsing in a classroom chair, and with nowhere to run, chronic indigestion sets in.

Then there was the cracked wheat cereal. I filled my porcelain bowl to the brim one morning, then poured on the milk and sugar. Unfamiliar with the properties of the grain in question, I ate the lot in record time, then went to class.

Now, cooked wheat goes through two stages of expansion. The first occurs while it's cooking on the stove; the second takes place after it's been deposited in one's stomach. Apparently, once the wheat is comfortable in its new digs, it relaxes in a recliner, kicks off its shoes (or husks, in this case) and loosens the belt—which is as good an explanation as any. As I sat in class, trying to focus on the lesson, I noticed a feeling of fullness around my midriff. The feeling intensified, soon joined by my old friend Indigestion, as the unprocessed wheat continued to expand. About the time said expansion abated, the pain set in. I was like a pressure cooker ready to explode. I somehow made it to meeting's end before heading to the lavatorium for an explosive end to my suffering.

And lest we forget, there was the Mystery Meat. Anxious to sit down at the cafeteria table and eat what looked to be a cross between steak and hamburger, I dug in. I was struck by its pungent taste. After more puzzled bites I stop masticating long enough to make inquiries.

"Hey," I asked, poking at the entrée. "What kinda meat is this?"

"Turn it over. Look at the other side" was the reply. Flipping it, I noticed that while well-cooked, the meat had a green tinge to it. I looked again, turning this way and that with the fork tines. Maybe the light was hitting it wrong. But yes, it was still green. What meat was the color of grass, anyway?

"It's liver, Elder Hiland," someone said, as if this were something one ate every day—but which, in fact, had never crossed the refrigerator's threshold in the Hiland home. Suppressing a gag, I pushed the plate away, washed the taste out of my mouth as best I could, and left the table, vanquished by the cooks again.

As class ended one morning, I saw groups of missionaries ascending the back steps to the campus. Within a couple days the numbers increased to exodus levels, while the cafeteria became quieter and the lines shorter. My fellow missionaries had found a new place to dine— the Cougar Eat, a huge cafeteria in the Wilkinson Center. Out of a sense of self-preservation I followed suit. Soon I was basking in the glory of well-cooked meals that used up spending money but left me feeling better.

WE'D BEEN COUNSELED to offer vocal prayers every morning and evening. Saying them out loud seemed to generate stronger feelings of closeness with Heavenly Father, and helped me be more articulate about what I was grateful for or needed. Another advantage was that during the evening, I was more likely to make it to "Amen" without falling asleep. But there was something about kneeling and relaxing for the first time that day, elbows sinking into a soft mattress, and Morpheus so close that . . . well, it was better than trying to do so on a tiled floor. The knee discomfort alone was enough to discourage me from making the effort. There were three of us packed into close quarters, making for little privacy and even less elbow room. I tried the closet thing a few times, then decided to take my chances next to the bed.

SUNDAY: SCRIPTURE MEMORIZATION, Round Two, found me considering memory shortcuts. After all, it had worked for high school math classes—in a lame sort of way. I would commit an equation shortcut to memory, then hope a test arrived before the arithmetical images faded from my brain. I was subjecting the latest set of passages to a combination of mnemonics and index cards. But until I actually tried to think about and internalize the content of the verses, they wouldn't hang around any longer than a morning frost in the sun. Upon committing a few verses to memory, though, the sense of accomplishment was rewarding. To have scriptures at my disposal provided a sense of power and confidence.

WEDNESDAY, 24 DECEMBER. Arising at 5:45 was getting easier with every passing morning. What was more difficult was dealing with my emotions. Homesick and a bit depressed, it was good to get out on P-Day for some bowling. During that first game, I could do no wrong, cracking the 180-pin barrier for the first time. But even being out in public couldn't erase the hurt. Playing the Comparison Game, I believed I was the only elder there from a non-LDS family. The outcast. The odd duck. Being the lone wolf had its disadvantages.

FINDING A PAY PHONE on Christmas Eve that wasn't being used by any of the scores of missionaries calling home was a challenge. But despite having Short and Bertram in tow, I discovered a booth two blocks south of KMH at Millet's Market. Calling home, I reached Mom, then Grandma Quigley, who asked when I was leaving for New Zealand. Speaking to Mom again after that, for a good fifteen minutes, I came away feeling much better. It somewhat made up for the fact that I'd be spending Christmas Day with strangers for the first time in my life.

25 DECEMBER

CHRISTMAS MORNING DAWNED bright and early. We did not. There were no trees, no presents, nary a stocking. No half-conscious family members staggering about the house. Just another gray winter morning at the LTM. Some might say it was cruel to deny missionaries Christmas gifts. But if they were allowed, the distractions would have been immense. And how would the mission limit presents: By number? Size? There were plenty of parents out there who could have found a way around any limitations. Only one gift, huh? Well, here's a motorcycle. Merry Christmas! Or maybe they have to be very small. How about a tiny stocking full of twenty-dollar bills? Feliz Navidad!

Suppose one gift was permitted and gift-givers behaved themselves. If it was a game, there'd be no time to play it. If it was music or a book, when could one listen or read? (Not that we were lacking in reading materials at the moment.) And where would it be stored?

No. The only gift to us that morning was from the Lord: no meetings or classes. P-Day on steroids. Showering and dressing in time to get breakfast, I wondered how to make the most of the holiday. Yes, there were meals to consider, and more phone calls home. But as I ate breakfast I marveled at the taste of freedom. Though I'd only been in the LTM twelve days, it felt both strange and wonderful to have no place to go, nothing I *had* to do. Fourteen hours of idleness dead ahead. Would I lose the work ethic I'd developed? And it wasn't like I'd bolt, taking the first bus back to Oregon. I knew why I was there. But the no-strings-attached time off was a delicious slice of guilt-free life.

Breakfast out of the way, the three of us went on the prowl for an unoccupied phone stall. Scoring one in an enclosed hallway entrance, Short went first. Elder Bertram and I walked outside, confident that leaving our companion alone for a few minutes would do no harm. Normally crawling with people, the campus was deserted and quiet, the only sound being a thin layer of snow squinking under my shoe soles. I pulled in deep breaths of snow-cooled air, the exhaled steam wisping away as I looked across the grounds at a new construction site of chilled steel and iron, white mountains beyond. But the purposeful Elder Bertram was restless. We needed to be doing something.

I noticed a maintenance man exiting by a side entrance to the many-storied Joseph Smith Memorial Center. Bored and willing to risk detection—what could they do, send us home? —I tried the door. Unlocked! Calling to Bertram, I pulled the door open and in we went. It was trespassing, but the thrill of being somewhere I wasn't supposed to be overrode any worries. It was so quiet. Strolling through one darkened hall after another, external snow-reflected light guided us, vacant study tables and chairs adding to the holiday atmosphere. The building was full of history, an odor of antiquity lingering at every exhibit. Centuries-old archeological artifacts. Oil paintings of past Church presidents. Utah pioneer exhibits.

We entered a high-ceilinged hall where a fully assembled dinosaur skeleton stood, its upper features rising into the gloom. Heading downstairs, we walked a basement hallway lined with in-wall aquariums. What else did this building hold? I never found out, as it was time to return to Elder Short, who we'd abandoned long enough. After he hung up, we strolled around the campus some more, stopping at one building to play around on a baby grand piano before returning to KMH.

AT NOON, A THIRTY-SOMETHING GUY picked up the three of us in front of KMH for our afternoon with the Smith family, a mile from the college. Along the way, I answered what would become a familiar battery of questions over the next twenty-four months.

"So, you're Elder Hilland."

"Well, uh—that's Hyland," a pronunciation correction I'd been making since grade school.

"Oh, sorry. Hy-land. And you're from . . .?"

"Oregon. Portland, actually."

"Ahhh. Ory-gawn." Another pronunciation problem. Mention of the Pacific Northwest elicited mild surprise. The standard answer was some town in Utah, Idaho, or California, Arizona placing a distant fourth.

The ever-popular, "And you've been out how long?" usually followed, after which queries hopefully shifted from the worldly to the spiritual.

We pulled alongside a modest home, where our host discovered he'd locked himself out. After we helped him find an open window, he climbed in and we awaited the rest of the clan. While I would have preferred to be with my own family, the sweet spirit I felt in the family's home helped me forget my troubles. They lived their religion without wearing it on their sleeves. We had dinner, talked a lot and generally relaxed—except when it came time to play Pit, a noisy card game designed to leave players breathless, frustrated, and hoarse. Before leaving, we sang them a hymn, then bid everyone farewell—especially their good-looking daughter.

IT WAS MOVIE NIGHT, the only one scheduled for the year, a present from the mission leaders to all of us. A projector with twelve-inch reels was wheeled to the back of the room to provide us with four hours of cinematic bliss—or so we were told. The film threaded into the machine and the amplified speakers ready to go, off went the lights and on came . . . Scrooge. While it could have been worse, the 1970 film was not compelling enough to keep me glued to my seat for its entire one hundred and eighteen minutes. After recognizing it as the same plot I'd seen years before in Mr. Magoo's Christmas Carol, sans the humor, I wandered off, returning in time for the stirring conclusion. Don't get me wrong. It's a timeless story and a fine film. But I harbored a vague suspicion that given the place we were in—being missionaries and all—a Shirley Temple film was not outside the realm of possibility, riots not far behind.

I waited with anticipation to see what the follow-up would be. And what to my wondering eyes should appear but "Advance to the Rear," a 1964 Civil War comedy in glorious black and white. All was forgiven as I gloried in the slapstick and satire, the inspired silliness. Everyone was laughing. Well, not everyone. At several points, leading man Glenn Ford had the opportunity to engage in some kissing with Stella Stevens, a blonde bombshell if ever there was one. Once the osculation commenced, so did the catcalls and woo-hoos. The noise level rose high enough that sudden blinding overhead lights came on, followed by some "Knock-It-Off" and "Remember Who You Are" speeches— "OR ELSE."

For a few minutes, there was dead silence. No one wanted to be deprived of further scenes of hilarity or the lovely Stella. But with each successive smooch and corresponding shouts of approval, the leaders' resolve weakened, no doubt realizing it would be better for the troops to let off some steam now than deal with morale problems later on. At one point—starting with the appearance of a riverboat madam and her cavorting call girls—I began to wonder if the Powers-That-Be had screened the film. But left to our own devices, we had a great time—though I doubt that "Advance to the Rear" was ever again shown within a thousand miles of a missionary training facility.

ELDER DEVLIN

INTENSITY AND TEMPERAMENT of our teachers varied. Some, like Elders Calderón and Ellsworth, were humble and easy-going. Then there was Elder Devlin. Rigid, uncompromising, and abrasive, Elder D was the drill sergeant of the MTC. And if he caught you not paying attention, there was hell to pay. One day Elder Bertram was fussing over a shoe heel that liked to fall off every so often. Though one of the better students, he was still human, and needed the mental break.

When Devlin caught Elder B messing with his footwear, he demanded the offending heel. Striding to a tip-out window, our instructor yanked it open and hurled the shoe part outside, where it fell to its death in a snowbank two floors below.

Since there was no way to talk back to him without bringing on the Wrath, I restricted my comments about our taskmaster to other locales. One day, while standing in the food line at KMH, I began to speak about Devlin in a most unflattering manner, to the delight of my listeners. That is until I noticed that my audience had stopped smiling, some looking at me as if I were in some sort of danger. Feeling a breathing down the back of my neck, I turned around. Elder D was standing very close, head tipped forward and brown eyes full of hatred as he stared daggers, knives, and bullets at me. I tried to return the gaze with some joking around, but any words leaving my lips tumbled to the floor in embarrassment. After a very long two minutes he turned on his heel and walked away.

Yet there were occasions when he tried to be nice. During class one day, Elder Devlin took time out from instruction to compliment us. We were one of the "humblest" groups he'd ever taught, said comment taken warily. Whether the words were calculated to make us feel better, offered as a veiled apology for his rough manner, I wasn't sure. He said a lot of things, some of which we liked. But it was the way he said and did things which didn't exactly endear him to us.

LEADERSHIP AND A NEW COMPANION

SEVERAL DAYS AFTER Christmas I had personal progress interviews with some of the leadership. During these meetings, we discussed ways I could improve my study habits and spiritual life, topics I didn't feel comfortable discussing with my contemporaries. I carried around misgivings about my level of worthiness, the way a traveler holds onto luggage in an unfamiliar city. Having played the

Comparison Game too much and for too long, I came to believe that I'd never measure up to my peers.

As with all flawed mirrors, the reflection this one gave off convinced me that it was better to remain meek and humble than be the braggart, the egotist. Based on this misunderstanding of what humility really is, my self-esteem hadn't a chance. And since interviews also served to help leaders choose those most suitable for leadership positions, I was eliminated in the first round. At some point, I came to equate this search for leaders with a popularity contest, when nothing could be further from the truth. Interviews helped leaders make inspired decisions about who was best equipped to lead others. The fellow chosen to be our District Leader was Elder Viktor. Other guys in the group may have had better senses of humor or warmer personalities, but Elder V was the well-rounded one, having had previous experience leading others.

That night we held a Family Home Evening. Our district had developed a camaraderie—a shared concern about the situation we found ourselves in. We were all serving a mission for God, but FHEs gave us an opportunity to relax and discuss how we felt we were doing. The gestalt atmosphere allowed us to speak about each other—what we liked best about this sister or that elder. The support and love were palpable, emotions close to the surface. There was a growing sense that we had been put in the Santa Fe District for specific reasons.

HAVING LOST OUR RESPECTIVE companions around the same time, Elder Stanley and I were assigned to work together. Elder S hailed from Georgia, his strong southern drawl flattening the ethnicity out of phrases like "Coemoe Eh-staw." A lanky, easy-going guy with wavy red hair, he was great to work with. "Mi pelo es muy rebellioso," he'd say as he tried to rake spread-apart fingers through a case of bed hair.

The reassignment meant a room change. Losing the company of Bertram and Short, I moved across the hall. The new room looked out across KMHs snowy front lawn, the street, a flat-roofed Student Health Center, and the neighborhood rooftops beyond, above which presided beautiful sunsets and bittersweet reminders of the civilian life I'd left behind.

We began the penultimate day of the year with companionship prayers, something that at first violated my comfort zone. Not having had the benefit of working with just one other elder on a daily basis, sharing prayers was a new experience. Since we were expected to work toward the same goals, praying together was supposed to help accomplish this. We kneeled, closed our eyes with heads bowed, and then one of us offered a vocal prayer, thanking Heavenly Father for the ways He'd blessed us. Specific help was requested for things we were struggling with. The prayer was closed in the name of Jesus Christ, an Amen signifying that the prayer was finished.

I would make scores of such prayerful requests on my own during the week, such were the demands placed on me. What took a while to learn was that Heavenly Father answered requests in His own time and way, not necessarily according to my desires, which were many times ill-advised. If I was struggling with memorization, my request for "MORE BRAIN POWER NOW, PLEASE" might be honored. But more likely the help would come in the form of more sleep, or encouragement from Elder Stanley, or a mnemonics trick offered by my teacher. And sometimes the answer was NO, which itself was an answer.

CLASS WENT BETTER on the 31st, retention time more productive due to my companion's assistance. We each had things the other person needed. I might be better at pronunciation, but he may have the verbs down cold. Maybe he was a scriptorian, but I understood Church history better. Patience his strong suit. Mine, humility.

During the afternoon, it began snowing. I loved seeing the flakes drift down, the more the better. By evening I was glued to the window, watching heavier snow fall through the outdoor lights. Even the looming Wasatch Mountains seemed tamer under the blanketing white. I felt blessed to be there, grateful for winter beauty. So ended the month and the year, with little fanfare as we went about our way to and from classes, meals, prayers, and meetings. By the time New Year's celebrations had commenced in the real world, I was fast asleep, Knight Mangum Hall as quiet as the heavy snow covering the city.

A New Year

A NEW YEAR

THE NEW YEAR was upon us. Departure for Argentina was a mere six weeks away. And given the fact that missionaries teach what's called a "discussion" during the first full day in their assigned area, it was time to start learning what was in that discussion. Discussions are a set of lessons missionaries present to "investigators" (Mormonspeak for people interested in learning more about the Church). If an investigator wants to become a member of the LDS Church, they have to be baptized. And before they can be baptized, they have to receive, understand and believe what they've been taught.

During the first week of the New Year I recorded in my journal what I'd memorized in class:

"Señor García: ¿Es usted sincero en sus deseos de seguir al Salvador? ¿Cree usted que puede seguir verdaderamente a Jesús, sin guardar los mandamientos del Padre? Leamos uno de los mandamientos del Padre."

Memorizing complete sentences and paragraphs in a language upon which I had, at best, a tenuous hold was a strange and fascinating experience. But once portions of the language were mentally captured, the sense of accomplishment was tremendous. I'd made more progress in three weeks than during Mrs. Habib's entire Beginning Spanish high school class. Being in possession of this skill brought with it a sense of power and influence, even a touch of superiority. Soon I'd be able to stand in a public place and listen in while people spoke a language they didn't think I could understand. A sort of audial voyeurism.

In the early 70s, discussions in Argentina—which will be referred to as "charlas" from here on—represented the Church's Uniform System of Instruction. The word "uniform" implied consistency. And since we were to teach people in a consistent way, the content would have to be memorized.

How much memorization, you ask? Well, there were eight charlas, each printed on half-sheets of paper and sporting pastel Monopoly money colors. Referred to as C, D, E, F, G, H, I, and J, each charla covered a different gospel topic. The mission goal was to memorize the first four charlas before heading south, word count being: C = 1,820; D = 1,575; E = 1043; and F = 1,800. Let's say I'm charitable and replace F with G, which clocks in at a measly 560. That comes to 5,000 words. If the idea was to just sit in front of someone and read to them from a book, there'd be no need to memorize at all. Anyone can do that. What the Lord requires is teachers—ones who believe what they are saying and can reinforce truths and concepts with scriptures, just like Christ's apostles did two thousand years ago.

Amidst the initial battery of classes, I looked over the first paragraph of brown Charla C. It started with us introducing ourselves as representatives of The Church of Jesus Christ of Latter-day Saints—and that the Lord had sent us with an important message. He wanted them to know that whenever God has wanted to communicate with his children, He's done so by means of a living prophet. The paragraph ended by asking the listeners why they believed it was important that God would want to guide us. One hundred six words, some of them duplicates. How hard could it be? I had no idea—though I might have gotten a clue had I looked at the other nineteen pages of the charla.

Maybe it was an example of the Lord's mercy that he kept me from seeing the big picture: a document full of scriptural quotes, vignettes, and strategically-placed questions; one week in which to memorize it all; presenting this to total strangers who would derail my train of thought with questions, or veer off the subject, or start arguing with me. And I thought learning verbs was tough.

Some missionaries were learning the discussions quickly. But not Elder Hiland, aka Mr. Good Speller, Mr. Imaginative Writer, Mr. Prolific Reader. And why? I believed I wasn't "spiritual" enough or lacked sufficient faith. This skewed outlook, a carryover from earlier times, was battering my confidence and self-esteem to a pulp, in turn making it harder to focus on learning new things. Though I continued to seek the Lord in prayer, it was taking me a while to realize that as fast as I wanted things to move along, the Work was geared to Heavenly Father's timetable. Patience with Him and myself was what I lacked. We were supposed to be a team, not opponents.

THE SMITTEN MISSIONARY

REPORTS HAD BEEN emanating from Rumor Central of a pretty blonde seen in the company of an elder in our district whom I will call Elder X. But I was skeptical. I'd heard so many supposed facts about people, places, and things that I was trying to ignore them, distraction the last thing I needed. I thought again of Elder Searle. I recalled another missionary who'd been with us, but was now gone. He'd walk around all day, pulling food from his pockets, munching copious amounts of it, and generally demonstrating that he'd rather be anywhere else but at the LTM. Surely the Law of Averages for mission rule-breaking had run its course.

Elder Stanley and I made our way across campus and into the Marriott Center for the weekly devotional, finding seats off to the left of the stage. With twenty minutes to kill before the meeting began, I was gazing about the cavernous building when I saw Elder X. He was speaking in animated fashion to a young lady. A blonde. Thinking it a fluke, I continued to watch. Elder X continued to talk. So much so that during the next fifteen minutes he attracted the attention of scores of people nearby. I was a stew of indignation, embarrassment, and fear, even flashes of envy appearing, then gone.

Church policy requires that missionaries are not to be involved in romantic relationships with members of the opposite sex. This includes any kind of physical contact or dating. Missionaries are supposed to dedicate their time to the Lord. That's why they mentally and physically leave behind jobs, school, cars, and hobbies. And of all the distractions this world has to offer, a romance has to be one of the most time-consuming and involving.

Thus, while missionaries are not asked to break off existing relationships, there is a shift in emphasis from romance to one of support, via letters or emails—not phone calls, motel encounters or clandestine meetings in the park. Letters from girlfriends or boyfriends are encouraged. Correspondence with a loved one can be a great source of comfort and strength and helps stave off loneliness and homesickness. The only risk one runs is possibly receiving the dreaded Dear John letter, which can be temporarily devastating.

Having lost one companion due to runaway hormones, I knew what was heading this elder's way if he didn't put a stop to the relationship. Where was his companion, Elder Canova? Maybe he'd said something to X, and was told to shove off. Maybe Elder C thought it was somehow cool. Or just didn't care. All I knew was how this public tryst looked to me and anyone else within eyeshot. It wasn't that a conversation between Elder X and a girl was inherently wrong. The fact that it went on and on throughout the featured speech was the problem. This wasn't a quick hello and goodbye. It was industrial-strength flirting.

ELDERS GABI AND Viktor burst into our room, the former upset about the fact that it was 10 p.m. and there were two young women in the lobby. The presence of women at that hour or any other carried with it the likelihood that they'd see half-dressed elders running around or exercising. Further investigation revealed that the intruders were none other than the Girlfriend and another young lady, hanging out again with Elder X. Adult leadership soon arrived and asked the ladies to leave.

While standing in the lunch line at the Cougar Eat a day or two later, I saw Elder X dead ahead, tray in hand. Though Valentine's Day was a month off, X looked like quite the jackass, sporting an irreverent pair of red, plastic kissing lips on his dark blue suitcoat lapel. The goofy look on his face suggested that his mind was not on scriptures, charlas, or conjugations of the verbal type. As we worked our way to the register, I wondered how long he would last. Then again, maybe I was assuming the worst, being judgmental. Possibly the mission president knew about the bad behavior, and had the situation sufficiently monitored. We only had a few weeks left anyway. But that made about as much sense as the lips Elder X was displaying.

When it came my turn, I stepped to the register and there she was—the Girlfriend. She took my money, then resumed her conversation with Lover Boy, who was warming up while his food cooled off. I rushed off to sit with Elder Stanley at a table distant from the young lovers.

A man approached us, looking determined and grim.

"Excuse me, Elders," he said. "Is that fellow a missionary?"

"Yes," I said.

"Okay . . ," he said and returned to his seat. He and another adult continued watching Elder X.

SOMETHING WAS DEFINITELY IN THE AIR. Two days after Elder X's poor display of judgment in the Lunch Line of Life came news of another Christian soldier falling by the wayside. Elder Gonzales, an outgoing, charismatic Guatemalan, told a few district members that he needed to postpone his mission. He said he had to finish repenting, and was soon on his way to the airport. Though I never heard the reason why, I had to assume it was girl trouble. That seemed to be the moral Achilles heel most of the fallen had succumbed to, a sobering reminder about the importance of remaining worthy to serve.

IN CLASS I WAS LEARNING and memorizing "G," the baptismal invitation charla. Shortest of all the discussions, its purpose was to invite an investigator to be baptized on a particular date. It could be given at any time, usually when a missionary felt prompted by the Spirit to do so. Once the teacher determined we'd had sufficient time to learn G, we were each scheduled to pass it off in a face-to-face with one of the other instructors. If the charla was recited word-for-word, the effort was signed off on a tracking sheet. Hands were shaken, backs were slapped, and then it was back to class to begin study and memorization of the next charla. Of course, who should I be passing G off to but Elder Devlin. I was so nervous that I forgot four entire lines.

After licking my wounds and regrouping, I repeated the attempt an hour later in front of an easier-going elder and passed. Grateful and relieved that I'd overcome self-doubt and discouragement, I vowed that the next charla would be easier. But the effort left me emotionally drained. Sleep came easily that night.

MEMORIZATION, SELF-ESTEEM

MONDAY, 12 JANUARY. Four solid weeks of charla memorization had begun, starting with "C." Of the eight, "The Restoration" was the discussion we'd be presenting most often. It served as an introduction to the LDS Church, recounting Joseph Smith's struggles to find the true church he'd been praying for. As a result of his heaven-sent petitions, God the Father and Jesus Christ appeared to Joseph in a grove of trees in 1823. God introduced his son Jesus, who told Joseph to join none of the churches on the earth at that time—that they were not of Him. Joseph would be instructed later on how to restore God's true church to the earth.

This being the fundamental reason for the existence of the LDS Church, I'd be teaching it during my first full day in the field. Knowledge of this fact only added to the pressure I felt during the four daily one-and-a-half-hour classes. The goal was to learn sixty-five lines per day. Thus, the post-class retention periods became essential to memorization progress. During those hour sessions, all lines I'd learned had to be added to what was already lodged in my battered brain. Falling behind would only make matters worse. It was all up to me and those brown-colored, half-pages of Charla C.

Dog-eared, folded in thirds (so I could tuck them into shirt and suitcoat and pants pockets), I tried every study technique I knew to lodge the words upstairs. Underlining words. Circling sentences. Bracketing paragraphs in red colored pencil. Writing words in English above or next to their Spanish counterparts—thus violating LYL, at least in spirit. But when the boat's taking on water, you use chewing gum or candle wax or whatever is lying around to plug the leaks. Surrounding me like bunker walls were a Spanish dictionary, the class manual, *201 Verbs*, my 1945 edition of *Practical Spanish Review Grammar*, and *Spanish: 3100 Steps to Master Vocabulary*" (the latter a paperback touting itself as the "Revolutionary Method of Programmed Learning"). *3100 Steps* being more gimmick than practical, I didn't care. I was a desperate man.

Armed with the knowledge that my support staff would be there for me, I went to class and tried to absorb, saying mental prayers. Then it was off to Retention for study and memory workouts. Then I was back in class. Then retention, mental and physical breaks replenishing my sanity and powers of concentration along the way. At some point, I remarked in the journal that "my brain feels like someone mopped the floor with it." But instead of squeezing the mop out before the next pass, I kept filling it with more. And somewhere along the way, I was learning how to retain large portions of Charla C.

MID-JANUARY. Members of the district began talking to me about my negative self-image, to which I nodded and shook my head. I knew I was messed up. I fell behind no matter how much I prayed. The remedy? Self-castigation. If there was a line forming to beat me up, I made sure to take cuts so I could get in the first jabs. Compounding the problem was a self-defense mechanism that disallowed constructive criticism. But there was one person who could get through: Elder Devlin. Maybe it was that overabundance of confidence that gave his words authority. After Stanley and I failed to pass off the first part of C, Elder D commented on my inability to look him in the eye.

"The eye is the communicator of the Spirit," he said. "This is how people can tell if your words and actions are sincere." I was fighting a lump of self-pity that rose in my throat. I knew he was speaking the truth, and it hurt. But somehow, I saw past the pain and listened, because Elder D's advice was bathed in love and concern. He knew it hurt, too. "You," he continued, "should be able to look anyone—from the Prophet, on down to the devil himself—straight in the eyes."

To receive tough but loving counsel was something I'd always had trouble with. It usually felt like a personal attack. Besides, self-criticism was *my* job, no one else's. Gotta leave these things to the experts, you know. But this day was different. I was seeing something from a new angle, and for my own good, despite my worst habits of thought. Devlin had revealed a weakness but showed me how it could be a springboard to success. I had experienced a miracle.

After several days of intense learning, my group had memorized one hundred sixty lines—roughly one-third of the charla. While this didn't seem like much, in relation to the overall goal, any civilian would have looked at the one-thousand-plus batch of foreign words and run away screaming. But many missionaries retained all those words and more, every day of the week. And if I stumbled and sometimes fell behind, I never quit. I would say that was a miracle in itself.

SHOTS, THE 3ᴿᴰ WHEEL, AND FLIGHT PLANS

Tuesday, 3 February. In order to not contract hepatitis in Argentina, all missionaries had to receive a gamma globulin shot every three months. But I'd have a choice in the matter: in the arm or the butt, Señor? To prepare for this schedule, we all reported to the Student Health Center for the first of two 2.5 cc injections. Not a big fan of shots, I was a little apprehensive—but it was skillfully administered, and with minimal pain. That being said, it went into my gluteus maximus like a glob of wet clay, then sat there. We were advised to walk it off, which meant scores of missionaries striding around the hallways like they were rehearsing for the dancing part in a musical.

But it could've been worse. Due to the uncertain nature and quality of medical services down south, all dental work was supposed to be finished prior to one's arrival at KMH. The last thing any of us needed was to die in a dentist's chair on some back street in the shadier section of downtown Palacio. One-day Elder Canova, companion to the recently departed Elder X, turned up missing. Fearing the worst, I asked around. "Yes, he's still here, but resting up." Not having had some necessary dental work done beforehand, all four of his wisdom teeth were pulled in one sitting. When Elder C did surface, he looked like hell, sporting bruises, chipmunk cheeks, and a general bleariness brought on by the procedure and lots of pain medication.

SINCE ELDER STANLEY was leaving a week earlier than the rest of us, bound for a stateside assignment, he was re-assigned to work with Elder DeFranco. So much for Companion #4. Elder S had been a great help to me, almost like a brother. I'd miss him. Now it was on to another threesome I went: Elders Gabi and Viktor. And two more disparate personalities one couldn't find on earth. Gabi hailed from the mid-west. A red-headed gregarious guy with premature balding and the beginnings of a paunch, he looked like he'd stepped off a used car lot. Self-named "Gabby," he was the life of the LTM party, slapping backs, cracking what he called "jokes," and giving life a jab in the ribs every chance he got. Utah-born Elder Viktor was mellow and easy-going, and had probably never spent much time around a fellow like Gabi. But despite the differences, they got along. For my part, I was uncomfortable. Feeling like a pass-around guest at the party, I knew my assignment to these two was made more out of expediency than inspiration.

As A SIGN that the end of the beginning was near, my flight plans arrived. The oft-discussed but seldom seen schedule stated that we'd leave early on February 17th, arriving in Palacio, Argentina, two calendar days later. That kind of news gives one pause. For one thing, it meant twenty-two hours in the air—and I hated to fly. Well, I'd just have to cross that phobia when I got to it. The bigger concern was the approaching reality of missionary work.

Soon, very soon, I'd be out there walking around streets and neighborhoods. Knocking doors. Talking to strangers. About Religion. And not just any religion. I wasn't sure how I felt about it all. Probably a mixture of excitement, anxiety, and grave responsibility. It was almost time to leave the cocoon.

CONTINUING TO HAMMER away at Spanish, I discovered more stumbling blocks the further out into the periphery of the language I ventured. Variations in verb tense included Past Subjunctive, Present Participle, Command Form, Possessive Nouns, Reflexive Nouns, and Personal Pronouns. Cries of "I don't even know this stuff in English" (from one of my classmates) did no good. I believed it was time to cut my linguistic losses and focus on other things. I was tired of beating myself up over an inability to pick up the language quickly. I'd have plenty of time to practice, once I arrived in the land of the Gauchos.

WEDNESDAY, 4 FEBRUARY. News arrived of a 7.5 earthquake hitting Guatemala, Elder Gonzales's homeland. Striking at 3:01 a.m., when everyone was fast asleep, some twenty-three thousand people were killed during the main quake. Subsequent aftershocks injured another seventy-six thousand. Two LTM missionaries scheduled to leave for that part of the country were re-assigned elsewhere in Guatemala. We received a report that only one missionary was harmed, said elder pinned under a fallen beam for six hours before help arrived. In serious condition, he was flown to Panama, where he'd make a full recovery.

During Flight Meeting, I learned that parents weren't allowed to see their missionaries off at the Salt Lake City airport. But since my folks weren't LDS, Branch President Tuttle said the mission leaders would make an exception.

As the departure date grew closer, time was set aside for purchase of teaching equipment unavailable in Argentina. One of these items was a filmstrip projector—the kind teachers were still using at public school. The instructor would thread a thirty-five-millimeter film into the opening, then start a cassette tape. At certain intervals a beep would sound, meaning the film had to be advanced to the next frame. The recommended model for our purposes was a fifty-three-dollar Singer, the same company that made my mom's sewing machine. While excited to see it in action during discussions, I hadn't considered how we'd get it to or from appointments. After all, we were supposed to be on bikes the whole time.

This being our last week in the LTM, only Elder Short and Sister Warnoc had passed off the required four discussions. The rest of us struggled along, heads barely above water. Standing in the food line I read Charla D, sick of looking at the salmon-colored pages but knowing I had to keep studying them. Letters from home and elsewhere helped keep my spirits up when prayer didn't. One way or another, there was usually something that came to my emotional rescue.

FRIDAY, 6 FEBRUARY. The news that Dad was going to see me off at the airport was a huge lift. The last time I'd seen him was at the hospital, where he was convalescing from a life-threatening illness. He'd woken up as I entered his room, then fell asleep during our parting words. As for other farewells, President Pinegar held a special meeting, given in the form of an extended talk. He expressed his love and concern for us and stressed the importance of keeping the commandments. He reminded us that we were about to embark on the adventure of our lives, and that though the Lord would be watching out for us, we'd be subject to temptations of a variety and frequency we'd never before encountered. Being that we were on a mission for God, the adversary would try to tear us down and stop us from being effective missionaries.

Then President Pinegar quoted a scripture from the book of Doctrine and Covenants that I'd never considered before: "Yea, I tell thee that Thou mayest know that there is NONE ELSE SAVE GOD that knowest Thy thoughts and the intents of Thy heart." The Lord was making plain that Satan doesn't know what any of us are thinking. But to get power over us, he watches where we go, what we say, and what we do—and then takes his cues accordingly. When he sees someone about to do something bad, he puts thoughts into his or her mind to encourage them along. President Pinegar assured us that the adversary could have no more power over us than we were willing to give him. This was news to me. I found comfort in knowing that I was more in control of spiritual things than I had imagined. Less of a puppet, more responsible for my choices.

RED TAPE, A TOENAIL, AND FAREWELL

THURSDAY, 12 FEBRUARY. It was a time of lasts. Last P-Day. Last Temple session. Last day spent in the muggy laundry room. And now the last day of charla classes. The relief that came from knowing I'd be spending my last few days studying in the cafeteria was immense. Though I hadn't passed off a single charla (aside from memorizing most of diminutive G), I had hopes of knocking off C before we hit the road.

After returning from the temple at 8 a.m., I packed things to send home and helped clean our room. After lunch was clothes-washing and letter-writing, followed by profuse amounts of picture-taking on the KMH front lawn, the weather sunny for the first time in days. Then I took an hour-long van ride with Elders Gabi, Viktor, Stanley, and De Franco to the SLC airport to see off the latter two, on their way to California. The ride back was quiet. In five days, we'd be the ones leaving.

Somehow the Singer projector showed up. It was housed in a twelve- by eight- by ten-inch, off-white box, a plastic carrying handle hinged to the top. Metal clips at front and rear were snapped open for lid removal. Though not more than eight pounds, the thing was damned bulky. How would I transport it from place to place without looking like some sort of a salesman?

FRIDAY, 13 FEBRUARY. In a last-minute letter from Grandma Net she told me that she and Dad would not be able to see me off, after all. Was it a money problem, or did he just not give a damn? Unwilling to invest time in a potentially painful effort, I had to shrug it off and try to move on.

As for the rest of the day, it turned out to be as off-kilter as I was feeling. Following breakfast and two-and-a-half hours of study in the cafeteria, Elders G and V were summoned to another part of the building for charla tests. Grateful to not be involved, I tagged along, trying to remain inconspicuous. Elder Gabi, on the other hand (or foot), was limping every step of the way due to an infected big toe. As we waited, the pain got bad enough that Gabi could no longer study. One hour and much deliberation later, a nurse told him that he'd need to see a specialist before he could leave the States.

The appointment set for 3:30, Elder Viktor and I dropped Gabi off at the testing center, then walked to the cleaners to retrieve our suits. Upon returning, we found that Elder G was still being tested, so we waited. After Gabi was released, a teacher asked us to find Bertram and Short, so off Gabi and I went with him to the cafeteria, in search. Never one to miss an opportunity, Elder Devlin spotted us and asked why we were walking around so much, then went with us back to the testing area. I longed for another trip to the cleaners, anxious to stop running around for no apparent reason. Calling us outside, Elder D pointed in the direction of the doctor's office, a good twelve blocks distant. I wondered how Gabi would make it there without us having to carry him most of the way.

We ate fast, then walked, limped, and ran to the bookstore for last-minute items, while Elder Devlin visited a bookbinder to have copies of the Book of Mormon and the Doctrine and Covenants bound together. Returning late for grammar class, we discovered that the other district was crammed in with our group. Due to a chair shortage, Elder Short and I shared a seat while Bertram wisely sat on the floor. Perching on a folding metal chair with someone else proved to be very uncomfortable. After class, it was back to the cafeteria for forty-five minutes, then back to the testing center. Finished at 2:30, we stopped by our room to get ready for the doctor appointment. President Ostergaard, who was on his way out the door, gave us a ride, sparing Elder G a hellishly painful hike. After a half-hour wait, Gabi was called in, the operation taking place twenty minutes later.

During the interim, I sat in the waiting room, trying to avoid looking at magazines which seemed much more interesting than waiting room reading material had ever looked before. I was soon distracted by a young couple seated on a sofa. "I don't know'f I can trust you with a pound over the weekend," the guy told his girlfriend/wife/recent acquaintance. Mumbled back-and-forths ensued as they tried to work out their business plan. After they left, Elder Viktor and I went back to see how Gabi was doing. Why, I don't know. Parts of Gabi's bloody toenail rested on some cloth atop a stand. The doctor had had to tear out most of the offending nail. Then he killed some cells so they wouldn't grow out again and cause further infection. About the time I'd seen my fill, the doctor sent Elder G on his way, $97 covering the half-hour's work. It cost him all of ten bucks, thanks to Blue Cross.

Time evaporated during the last few days. My greatest challenge shifted from learning charla content to packing. I had two suits, two pairs of shoes, one heavy overcoat, eight pairs of garments, socks, jeans, tee shirts, a shaver, toothpaste, towels, books, a journal, discussions, a five-pound flip chart binder, scriptures, a camera, a projector, a tape recorder, filmstrips, pens and pencils, stationery, important "official" paperwork, and a few other things. But where to put it all? Some went in the suitcase, other stuff in a bag. If I could have gotten away with wearing both suits at once, I would have done it just to conserve space. As for the overcoat, I filled its two immense outer pockets with books, papers, pens, my journal, and the tape recorder. In the end, I was able to carry it all, but felt like a pack mule. Overloaded pockets swayed back and forth, impeding forward motion while banging against my legs, everything else I was carrying, and that damned projector.

ON THE LAST night a storm blew in, carrying with it blizzards, wind, thunder, and lightning. It was as if Mother Nature were performing a dress rehearsal for Armageddon. I'd run from one window to the next, trying to catch the flashes, but only seeing swirling snow bash against the glass and fly away, wind beating the shrubbery every direction at once. Sleeping was rough. Several hundred thoughts streamed through my mind, when I wasn't ducking thunderclaps.

L.A. and Beyond

L.A. AND BEYOND

EARLY IN THE MORNING the taxis came. Leaving the warm confines of Knight Mangum Hall, I loaded my stuff into a waiting trunk. We rode through deep slush and snow to an off-campus house where the sisters were staying. Watching them come down the steps, I saw myself. This was it, and my feelings were a jumble.

We headed north on I-95. Then we were at the airport under clearing skies, last night's maelstrom only a memory. Carrying what I couldn't load into my pockets, I walked through the terminal, swaying back and forth with the weight, excited at the reality but anxious about how it would all turn out.

It was only when we'd boarded that I remembered how much flying scared me. It was only the second time I'd ever been on a plane and I was nervous as a cat. The airliner taxied across the runway, roared into the sky, and it was white knuckles all the way. I felt every bump, every sideslip, convinced that our plane wasn't much more technologically advanced than the Kittyhawk on its maiden flight.

Coming into airspace over Los Angeles I was in awe of its size, with neighborhoods that went on forever. Then the ground came up to meet us, too fast for my liking. Okay, maybe landing was a good thing. At least we were back on earth.

Disembarking, I noticed warmer air through the boarding area. Past the gate, some of our group waved and rushed forward. It was Elder X, greeting his chums from the sidelines, sans the Girlfriend. I wasn't sure when he'd been given the boot from the LTM, but he looked happy—though I couldn't help believe that somewhere inside he knew he'd missed out on the opportunity of a lifetime. If he didn't care, why show up at the airport? After they got caught up on the latest, we continued on, dragging our luggage behind us.

Outside we went, to wait for the Holiday Tours van. Ten, twenty, thirty minutes went by, but the van was a no-show. Two of our group contacted their parents, and soon we were in a couple station wagons headed for the Sheraton. Our luggage placed there for safe-keeping, we took three cabs to the consulate to take care of visa and passport business. Packed like sardines, we did enjoy a brief moment of humor when the lead cab ran out of gas, causing a third of our group a thirty-minute delay. Waving, we passed them by. Fingerprinting, paperwork, and visas finished, we returned to the hotel.

We secured our rooms, and then it was time to eat. Being without a companion, I accompanied Elder

Canova to a large, crowded restaurant. Feeling conspicuous, I found a table seat fifty feet from Elder C. It felt strange to be solo in a public place. I wondered if others could tell I was a missionary. To all outward appearances I was not. For reasons I would better understand later, Argentina-bound missionaries weren't allowed to wear the black name tag most elders and sisters bore on their clothing. So much for that giveaway. I glanced at Elder Canova every so often, out of duty and habit, and noticed he was watching me too. It was as if we needed to keep tabs on each other, less for protection than to see if some gorgeous woman would try to pick him up. Or in case he bolted. Or if someone was in the mood to persecute Mormons in the middle of a crowded eatery. Later we met at an exit and headed back to the Sheraton, unnerved by the experience.

For the next few hours I milled around, trying to work off nervous energy that was accumulating like storm water in an undersized barrel. I napped, snacked, and read, but my nerves were on edge. Before midnight, I laid down on a fully-made bed and slept, fully clothed.

AROUND 1 AM IT WAS TIME TO HAUL OUT. I forced myself out of bed, donned shoes and heavy overcoat, grabbed my bags and joined the group at the taxis. At LAX we were herded to the baggage check-in. Though bleary of eye and mind, it felt good to be rid of everything but my overcoat. Then we were off to the boarding gate, and the walk to Argentine Airlines Flight 371. I gained a window

🖈

seat, got my coat off, settled back to relax, then leaned forward. The flight crew—were they Argentines? I had no way of telling, so I lay back and tried to relax by looking out the window at a black night punctuated by overhead lights and ground crew activity. Then we were cruising along the runway, the pull of heavy acceleration even less enjoyable than I'd expected, as the plane tipped back, back, back, banking enough to make me cringe.

Then we were level and stable, the lack of a view out the window giving me no reason to believe we had actually left the ground. Grabbing my journal, I tried to write, but couldn't concentrate long enough to form but a couple sentences before closing the book. What was I doing here? How would it all end? A slight bump made me flinch. I looked at the passing clouds and the dark city far below, and the cabin lights no longer seemed bright enough.

The stewardess came along with food: chicken coated with some sort of white sauce. Normally a picky eater, I was hungry and then some. Then came drinks, followed by a dessert. A few of the missionaries passed, but since it looked like chocolate, I took a serving. After a couple bites and a swallow, my tongue felt strange, a bit numb. The cake was loaded with *alcohol.* Unsure whether or not I had sinned, I gulped down the rest, leaned back, and kept my mouth shut.

Having been assigned a seat on the ocean-side of the plane, the nighttime view was limited. But I kept thinking about how high up we were. How the wings flexed too much for my liking. How any little bump up or down sent me into prayer mode.

As the naps came and went I relaxed, but still wished my feet were on solid ground. When over the ocean I wanted to be above land. If the plane went down, at least we wouldn't drown. But when we were over land, I wanted to be over the ocean when the plane failed, for it would be a softer landing. In the end, my only comfort came from believing that nothing would happen because I was serving the Lord. Surely He wouldn't allow the plane to go down with all of His servants aboard. Knowing that He is no respecter of persons, I should have been praying instead for comfort and peace, regardless of what might happen.

WE FLEW OVER MOUNTAINS AND A VOLCANO, then to Mexico City for a quick stop. Then over the Pacific again, giving my nerves another workout that left me drained and sleepy. I drifted in and out of countless naps as we passed over Guatemala, El Salvador, Honduras, Nicaragua, Costa Rica, and Panama, stopping at one of the afore-mentioned for a forty-five-minute break. Wandering about the airport, dazed and seized with thirst, I spied a drinking fountain. I hesitated, then took a tiny sip, ignoring previous warnings about drinking unbottled water. It was lukewarm but wet. I guzzled. Thirst slaked, I returned to the plane blissfully unaware of the possibility that I may have ingested a multitude of bacteria that were ready, willing, and able to enjoy a working vacation, while wreaking havoc on my southern gastrointestinal estate.

Daylight. We passed over the Northwest tip of South America, hugging the coastline. I was transfixed by the sight of an ocean-bordered outline that looked just like maps I'd seen of the continent. Familiar yet surreal. Then over the Venezuela-Colombia-Ecuador triumvirate and Peru we flew . . .

Well into Brazilian airspace, then past the beautiful, mysteriously dusky lights of São Paolo we descended to another airstrip. Bolivia. Paraguay. Uruguay. Then we were above the muddy Río de la Plata and down into Buenos Aires. We'd landed in the New World.

IN COUNTRY, THEN WEST TO PALACIO

AT 11:15 P.M. OUR GROUP DISEMBARKS, a clump of Americans, each taking turns in the middle, then at the outer edge of the mass we constitute. The air is much warmer here in the accordion-like tunnel and past the boarding gate. Into the terminal we walk, getting the feel for terra firma again, stretched out into a line, like a long piece of human clay. Through Customs, where each individual member of the host body has to start interacting, has to start saying more than the "gracias" offered to the flight attendants and pilots upon disembarking.

"How many bags?" they ask.

"Your documents, please."

I hand them over. The rest I pretend to understand. We're moving again, past the Inquisitors. Suited representatives from the mission are nearby, poised to shepherd us as we gather our belongings— those articles that are our only tie to past life and present identity. Then we're outside, looking for taxis amidst the balmy, humid air. It's summer, I tell myself. But I don't believe it just yet.

I'M SITTING IN THE BACK SEAT OF A TAXI that's hurtling through the summer night, two other elders along for our ride to a hotel, somewhere. Gone are the overcoats, our white shirts radiating a bluish glow under the cab's fluorescent black lights. Windows rolled down, short hair blowing every which way as I try to understand the driver through the wind gusts. He's talkative and friendly, but the radio blasts a mix of words and music that tests and then defeats the prowess I'm trying to show with a language not my own. Thundercloud-induced raindrops splatter the windshield infrequently.

I give up listening to the driver and the other elders, lying back in my cushioned seat, the glow our missionary shirts radiate drenching everything with a surreal look and feel. But relaxing isn't what this trip is about. The driver is hauling eighty-mile-per-hour ass on a poorly-lit, populated interstate, the cab barely recovering from every near-miss we have with his co-combatants on the road. It's exhilarating being swept from side to side, but I wonder if we'll reach the hotel alive.

Eventually our conveyance screeches to a halt in front of a fifteen-story building somewhere downtown. We crawl out, say "gracias" to the driver for not killing us on our first day in the country, and haul our stuff into the lobby. Up ten flights or so to some rooms we go, where I try to unwind. By now, I'm having trouble processing much that I see or hear. All I care about is that there's a bed to lie on, and that I'm not alone in this foreign place. And finally, sleep . . .

SOMETIME AROUND 7:30 AM I OPEN MY EYES. It's Thursday. The 19th. Drab stucco ceiling and walls. We're still in Buenos Aires. I take my time getting up, scrabble around in a small bag for toothpaste, soap, underwear. Stagger to the bathroom. My lower regions are gurgling with pressure that comes and goes, murmuring storm warnings. Not sure what this means, but it can't be good.

Looking out of our high window, I snap pictures of the congested streets below. On its face, the scene is no different than that of my hometown. Buses and cars fighting for position. Rooftops stretching off across the city. Giant neon signs and billboards mounted high, advertising food and drinks and cigarettes. But something is different. These lit-up signs are for products and services I've never heard of, the building architecture deliberately unfamiliar. Even the vehicles look foreign: makes and models from the thirties and forties. Panic courses through me. What am I doing here? Who do I think I am, going to another country to preach the gospel? But the thoughts feel inappropriate, as if whispered from some dark place of doubt and unbelief. I dismiss them and focus on the sights.

LUNCHTIME. We're rushed along a freeway to a restaurant perched above the muddy, toffee-swirled Río de la Plata River. I look at the menu, see a familiar-looking culinary phrase or two, and order. I speak little with the other missionaries, due to my limited vocabulary and the fear of embarrassing myself in front of these Argentines. Once the meal comes, I wolf it down. Then the taxis whisk us off to departing Austral Airlines, #412, at 12:30 p.m.

THE CITY OF PALACIO still hundreds of miles distant, our plane climbs away from B.A., the urban giving way to farmland, forests, and barren landscape. And for the first time since touching down in this country, I'm enjoying the trip. Amazing what a full night's sleep and a decent meal can do. My lower regions are still in disarray, but they'll straighten themselves out in a few hours, I tell myself. Sunshine bathes everything in agreeability, not a snowdrift or freezing fog bank in sight.

The plane begins its angled descent. Aerial, map-like views of geographical features give way to grassy fields, houses and huts, rivers and bridges, train tracks and streets, sidewalks and dirt roads. Then the city and the airport, rough crosswinds buffeting us at the last moment, as the plane reluctantly bumps onto the runway at 1:40 p.m.

Through the oval window I see lush greenery pushing through the fenced-in landing strip. Tropical-looking. But descending the portable stairway is when it really hits me. Hot, humid, verdant air from an evaporating rain shower wafts over us, and I feel the thrill of standing in a foreign, exotic place. It's mid-February, yet it's summer. I'm really here. I follow our speechless group of ten across the tarmac.

THE MISSION HOME

OUR TAXI PULLS UP to an ornamental, wrought-iron security gate in a residential neighborhood. We exit while our guide, a missionary like ourselves (who's been assigned to work in the mission home for a few months) pays the driver, then pushes the doorbell button. A click sounds and we're through, walking along the gated driveway of the Palacio Argentina Mission Home. This larger-than-average, stucco-covered, two-story house is the dwelling of mission president Aldo Parón and his wife. The LDS Church-owned building houses the president's office, mail room, dining area, a dormitory (where the mission staff sleep and visiting Church members stay), as well as the amenities needed by President and Sister Parón.

We're escorted inside and formally introduced to the Paróns. In his forties and balding, Aldo is medium height, of pleasant demeanor, bespectacled, and sports a neatly trimmed moustache. Dressed in an ever-present suit—one of the requirements of the calling—he introduces us to his staff, composed of two assistants and a secretary (all young, full-time missionaries). We're shown around the place, which includes a kitchen, a dormitory full of bunk beds, a dining area, showers, and bathrooms, the latter of which I make haste for. Something bad is happening to my guts.

During an orientation meeting replete with slides and pep talks, we learn that the Argentina-Palacio mission comprises the country's upper left-hand corner and western mid-section (the northwestern provinces), representing an area four hundred sixty miles wide by eight hundred seventy long. Images of firemen, the military, wine-making businesses, gauchos, and other scenes are shown. We're told about how vitally important it is to keep our "documents" with us at all times. Bearing legal proof of who I am, and that I'm in Argentina legally, this small set of papers represents my visa and passport records. Without these documents, any policeman, soldier, or other authorized representative can have my butt hauled off to jail, or worse.

We're asked to insert the documents into the same plastic holder that houses the White Bible. Immunization schedule cards are also distributed, gamma globulin medication the main line of defense between myself and hepatitis. I accept mine with some apprehension, the anxiety increasing with the news that I'll need to get an injection every twelve weeks—seven more shots coming over the next twenty-two months.

We enjoy a light meal, then meet with Parón one at a time for personal, getting-acquainted interviews. I enter the small office, shake hands with the president and take a seat across the desk from him.

"Well, Elder Hiland, welcome to Argentina and the mission."

"Thanks."

"I want to personally thank you for your decision to serve the Lord here in my country. It is a beautiful place. It has its problems, as all countries do—but there are many wonderful sons and daughters of God here, just waiting to hear the message you have to share with them."

I strain to understand what he's saying, but most of the words get through, as does that smile of his. He's excited to see me, another stranger at his gates.

"Well, Elder Hiland, you're probably wondering where you're being sent."

"Sí." It's the best I can manage at this stage of the game. The President looks at a sheet, then turns to one side.

"Here is where you will serve first," his index finger pointing to a spot on the wall map.

"It's called *Temprano*. It has a population of about a hundred thousand people."

"Muy bien," I say, nodding my head.

"Do you have any questions for me?"

"No. I'm okay."

"Well then, Elder," Parón says as he steps out from behind his desk, hand extended. "Welcome. And thank you for being here. Hasta luego."

Temprano

TEMPRANO

ELDER BERTRAM AND I climbed aboard a southbound bus. From the way it was decked out, I could tell that Argentines took great pride in their public transportation. Ours was built like a Sherman tank and painted in bright colors, flags flapping from the front corners, the rest of the body covered with acres of chrome and lights. The interior, aside from the dashboard, was more pedestrian—full of brown, Naugahyde-covered seats, advertisements plastering every available bit of reading space.

The feeling I had as we bounced along reminded me of the first day I rode a yellow school bus home from elementary school. Clutching my first-grade lunch box like a talisman, I listened as the driver announced every stop. Even then I made several trips to the front to ask the man if he was familiar with my address. Though assuring me he knew, I moved to a front seat. If he screwed up and overshot the address, I could dive through the folding doors and find my own way home.

Though Bertram was accompanying me, I wasn't much comforted. If we got lost, we'd be together, but alone in a city full of strangers. Regardless, I wasn't about to stand behind the driver, badgering him about where to get off, especially when there was a good chance he wouldn't understand. And that was all I needed now—to make the driver laugh so hard at my crappy Spanish that he crashed the bus, killing us all.

Elder B and I conversed a little but spent most of the ride just taking it all in. It was the first time I'd been in a public place here with only one elder between me and Them. The safety-in-numbers throng that had served as a force field between me and those I'd be serving was evaporating.

THE TAXI STOPPED IN FRONT of a metal door set in a stuccoed-wall, the address being some numerals paint-ed on the cement. Unloading everything, we paid the driver, then pushed open the door and drug our stuff along a wall-enclosed alleyway. I could hear voices as we arrived at a sunlit patio. Several elders were seated at a table, laughing and eating in the early afternoon summer sun.

"Hey, hey, elders!" they greeted us. "Welcome."

"Hi, guys," I said, Elder Bertram smiling as we shook hands with our new companions.

"I'm Elder Hartman," the blonde-haired fellow said. "Carl," his first name, would have been too informal, a distraction from the Work.

"Elder Hiland," he said, "you'll be working with me."

"Elder Bertram, is it?" Elder H continued. "Elder Hamilton will be your companion. Have a seat, brethren. We're just finishing lunch."

I left my baggage in a pile and took a chair at the end of the table. I was beat. The constant barrage of new time zones, sights, words, smells, and sounds had taken their toll. The weather was sixty degrees warmer. And now I was sitting in another unfamiliar place, talking to total strangers, a bunch of unrecognizable food and liter bottles of pop—drinks called Pritty Limon and Mirinda Manzana—scattered across the table. And all the while my lower digestive tract grumbled, in disarray. But I tried to focus on the conversation. I wanted to make a good first impression. Soon I was laughing along with my new friends. It felt good to let loose a little, like a rescued sailor enjoying the newfound security of a lifeboat. I was among my countrymen.

And it was while laughing that I let my guard down. Something erupted in the vicinity of my back lot, and I knew what that something was. Cringing, I maintained composure and the brave face. But I couldn't sit a minute longer. Getting to my feet, I asked where the bathroom was, then performed a nonchalantly clinched walk through the door, followed by a much quicker stroll across a darkened bedroom. Undressing in haste and disgust, I tossed defiled garments and pants under what I assumed was to be my bed, then dashed to the bathroom. No porcelain throne was ever more needed and appreciated. After a heavenly five minutes in the shower, I donned fresh clothing and returned to the patio, no longer a marked man, the others none the wiser.

Unbeknownst to me, I had just joined the ranks of the Brown Spot Club. To say it was an elite group would be incorrect. The number of members was quite large, taking into account how many state-side missionaries resided in Argentina, as well as the frequent incidence of gastric distress suffered.

And though no awards were ever bestowed, being a Brown Spot Club member was considered an honor. Just as the Saints had suffered dysentery-like afflictions, crossing the plains more than a century earlier, so did modern-day missionaries fertilize their unders. And all for a good cause. Recognition came in the form of a few snickers, a knowing smile, a shake of the head, or simple acknowledgments like "You poor sucker. That's the worst case I've ever heard of." Most of the elders I knew were members. I'm sure a lot of the sisters were, too, though the topic wasn't one I'd be likely to discuss freely with the fairer sex. And though there was comfort to be had from realizing this was a shared experience, I was the only missionary I knew who'd signed up first day in the field.

After Elders Hamilton and Bertram took off for their apartment, Hartman gave me the short tour: a back-yard consisting of an L-shaped patio enclosed by high walls, the latter festooned with cemented-in-place shards of bottle glass—effective, though lacking in charm. A shared room with two twin beds, a desk, and a bathroom with shower.

Tour over, I unpacked. Books went in a pile on the floor. Garments and socks in a dresser drawer. Dress shoes and tennis shoes by my bed. Suits and ties and the now-irrelevant overcoat in the armoire. The Singer projector box and cassette player on a table. My thirty-five-millimeter camera somewhere safe, out of sight. Toothbrush, toothpaste, shaver, and deodorant in the bathroom. Everything else was left for the morrow. The elation I felt upon realizing I could stop lugging my stuff around was indescribable. But so too was the sense that my gut was being rearranged by some foreign invader. War had been declared, and a diarrhea attack might come without warning. The only problem for this Christian soldier was that there was no place to hide.

There being not much left of the day, Hartman and I talked about ourselves, family, and where we came from. And at some point, Elder H filled me in on the Schedule:

- Up at 5:30 a.m.
- Exercises and a shower
- Breakfast
- Scripture study
- Personal and companionship prayer
- Planning Card review
- Fire out by 9 a.m.
- Lunch at noon
- Siesta until 3:30 or 4:00 p.m.
- Back to work

- Something called the Merienda
- Back to work
- In at 10 p.m.

"As for the charlas, Elder Hiland, you need to pass them off as soon as possible."

"Yes. The charlas …"

"Well, you'll be teaching them a lot, so it's important to know them inside and out."

"I understand."

"Good. Now, here's the deal. I expect you to study the charlas and study them hard."

I nodded.

"Until you pass them off, don't read scriptures too much—except for the ones you're to memorize and pass off."

I nodded.

"And no Church magazines."

I nodded.

"No Church books."

I nodded.

"No journal writing, either."

Huh? Journal writing was one of the few good habits I was in possession of. A source of consolation, it was the friend I could turn to when there was no one else around. One way or another, journal-keeping was going to stay on my daily schedule.

"Now," Elder Hartman said, "once you've passed off all those charlas, you'll get to serve as a senior companion. Then you can trade off with your other comp when it comes to leading. You'll also get to train greenies (new missionaries). But for now, I'll be finalizing all the daily planning."

Saying evening prayers with Elder H, then silently by myself, I crawled into my bed and fell asleep, the suspense of the unknown forgotten for a few hours.

THE PLANNING CARD

UP AT 5:30. That was my first real test. The second was seeing whether or not I was still sick with the runs. And yes, I was. As if a giant something was squirming around in my guts, trying to escape.

Shower.

Exercises. Sit-ups and jumping jacks—but not when I was sick.

Breakfast. Check.

Scripture study. Check.

Personal and companionship prayer. Check and check.

Planning Card. What?

"Okay, Elder Hiland," my comp said, holding some light-blue, accordioned-into-four sections card stock.

"Aside from the White Bible and your documents, this is the most important piece of paper you'll carry with you."

A different day of the week was printed at the top of each three-inch-wide section, clock hours down the left edge in half-hour increments. A line ran the full width of the card for each thirty-minute period. The last portion was titled "Notes."

"Every morning we'll plan what we're doing, and we'll write it on this card—nowhere else. This is your brain, your memory bank. Our teaching appointments, people's names and their addresses and their phone numbers all go on here. Keep this card on you all the time."

Reaching into a box full of Planning Cards, Elder H handed me an empty one. We proceeded to fill it out. The last task was to fold it in half so it could be tucked into that shirt pocket that held the Documents.

Fire out at 9:00. We grabbed a couple worn out bikes from the porch, wheeled them along an enclosed alley to the street, then stopped for a second time so Elder H could double-check the Card. Then we were off, riding fast along the city streets, taking care at intersections, the majority of which were sans traffic lights. Past the nice homes we rode. Past the business district. Past even the pavement, our destination the homes along pothole-filled roads. There were shacks and nicer homes, cane-roofed two roomers and adobe-walled residences. The further out we rode, the more fields there were, homes sparser and further apart.

On one of those first days we were visiting a family two miles from the *pensión* (apartment). Despite being the novice, I'd helped give a charla concept and borne my testimony. But as we were finishing up, the rumblings began down below. We kneeled and I offered the prayer, but did so under duress. The pressure was building and dropping in my guts like Braxton Hicks contractions.

"And I say these things in the name of Jesus Christ. Amen," I intoned. Then—

"Elder Hartman, we need to get home *fast*," I said, pointing a finger at my stomach. Saying a hurried "adiós" to our investigator, we were on our way, me pedaling like a mad man in hopes of arriving at the pension before my semi-digested food crossed the gastrointestinal finish line. The irony of the situation was not lost on me, the guy who'd suffered chronic constipation for the first fifteen years of his life on Planet Earth. The same guy who would, if possible, have had a monument to Metamucil erected—one bearing a plaque engraved with a dedicatory prayer about the wonders of my favorite fruit-flavored, effervescent laxative.

Lunch at noon.

Siesta until 3:30 or 4:00. Being assigned to serve in Argentina afforded me the unique privilege of working in a land where work was not a top priority. Spending time with family and friends was. Drinking wine with every meal was. Playing soccer was. Partying at the drop of a hat was. And so was the National Afternoon Nap.

"So, Elder," I said, "What are we supposed to do for the next three hours?"

"Study your charlas," my comp said as he curled up with a Church book.

Back to work at 4 p.m.

Merienda at 5 p.m. In line with the siesta observance was a thirty-minute break. We sat down on a curb somewhere and drank pop, munched a few cookies, and waited until 5:30. Then it was back on the bikes for more visits.

Dinner. Shoehorned in somewhere during the early evening.

In at 10 p.m. I looked at the Planning Card. It held a lot more information than it had that morning.

Companionship prayer and personal prayer—the latter of which I don't remember finishing. At some point, I awoke in the dark, still kneeling over my mattress. It was a quick crawl under the covers to oblivion.

THE RUNS

So BUSY WAS I, trying to keep up with Elder H and the increasing demands of my lower GI tract that, despite my resolve to scribble the day's events, journal writing went by the wayside. And though the new schedule was tough to adjust to, I had an incentive for rising early. When my eyes first popped open, all was well in Zion—until I sat up. Or moved even one muscle. Any skeleto-muscular activity set in motion an evil process in my guts. All the rest of the day I'd be on guard, whether on foot, bike, or bus, hoping against hope that the monster within had accepted my morning lavatorial sacrifice. But I could never be sure.

Maybe I'd have suffered less had I received that green-colored, four-page pamphlet, *Preventing Diarrhea, and What to Do If It Occurs,* during my first days in the country—instead of five months later, after the damage was done.

Published by the Church, the front page bore an illustration of two missionaries in suit and tie, sitting at the dinner table, enjoying a quiet meal. The placid looks on their faces bore witness to the fact that they had not yet been afflicted with the Hershey Squirts. Then again, a more realistic drawing—that of an elder or sister lying on their side on the bathroom floor, grimacing, doubled over in pain as they tried to not defile their underwear for the fourth time that day—well, that would probably be too much information for new missionaries.

Page Two talked about The Causes of Diarrhea. The suspects included microorganisms, virus germs, bacteria, parasites, and food allergies. Drawings to the right portrayed an artist's rendering of viruses, which looked like a cross-sectional view of sliced kiwi fruit. Bacteria were represented by a string of furry beans. And the lowly parasite resembled a swimming T-bone steak, if said creatures had tails. While I appreciated the effort, knowing what they looked like would do me no good in the long run (no pun intended). Even if I could see them coming, how would I defend myself? With all the tools at its disposal, my body had mucked up the job pretty well. What chance had I?

The next section was about Prevention. "Wash hands after using the toilet, and before eating. Water may be boiled with an inexpensive electric coil dipped into a glass of water." Considering the frequency with which we ingested food from questionable origins, there was no time or means with which to easily boil water, and dumping an electric coil into a glass of water seemed a risky proposition, at best. Following this were reminders to boil fruits and veggies five minutes before eating them and to politely avoid unsafe food and water when they were offered. Then came the clincher: "You do not have, and will not develop, the immunity that the local people have." I could understand why the Church decided it was safer to inoculate us every three months.

But during the first few days in country, I had no idea what was going on inside of me. The sudden exposure to full-blown summer heat, humidity, foreign food, mosquitos, and skin-burning sun was taking its toll. My body decided that nothing I ate would make it to the Southern Regions without first being liquefied. Maybe it was the Coriolis Effect, or the likelihood that my lower GI didn't recognize or trust what I was sending down the hatch. Regardless, it refused to treat food with due process, or the courtesy it had afforded American food. And to make sure that the food I was now eating didn't stay in my body very long, it made damned sure that my internal psi was cranked up a few notches during waking hours. Even if I did want to hold something in until within striking distance of the nearest bathroom, it would ensure there was a steady supply of feceous gases ready to expel any and all foodstuffs from my body with extreme prejudice.

KNOCKING DOORS, KIOSKOS AND RAIN

MY FIRST DOOR-KNOCKING EXPERIENCE was a leap of faith into icy waters, despite the fact that it was hotter than hell. The late summer sun beat on us as we walked from door to door. I watched Elder Hartman rap on a few. Then he told me it was my turn. Gulp. Approaching one, I knocked, then stood there in the hot sun, half-hoping that the responder would either be nice or not at home. No one answered. Another door. Another knock. Several approaches later a latch rattled, and the door swung open. The person looked us over and said "Sí?" upon which I, with heart in throat, said "Hi. We're representatives of The Church of Jesus Christ of Latter-day Saints. We have a message for you."

To my surprise I got it right—after which I fell silent, a strong signal to my companion that I'd exhausted my inventory of usable Spanish words and he needed to take over. After a few more doors I was past the jitters, able to focus instead on the person's demeanor, then on what I felt the Spirit was guiding me to say—that is, when I wasn't drawing a blank in the spirituality department. Sometimes I knew I was being guided by heavenly forces, while at others it seemed God was leaving me to my own devices.

Sometimes the person would listen, followed by:

"Sorry, but I have my own religion, so …"

"No, thank you." Followed by the closing door.

"What did he just say?" the person would ask Elder Hartman, pointing at me.

No response and a slamming door.

No response and a closing door.

A head shake and a closing door.

In a few cases the person would invite us in, which led to the next stage of proselyting: the charla, which is where all that memorization in the LTM came into play. Once the person allowed us to start teaching, the discussion could last twenty minutes to an hour.

Knocking doors is hard work. Just ask your local Jehovah's Witness. Besides the heat of the sun sapping my energy, hunger came into play. And since we did most of our door-knocking far from home, in the poorer sections of Río Four, any appetite was magnified by the absence of supermarkets or other stores.

But all was not lost. We'd been out doing the Work. I was hot, sweaty and tired, my clothes turning brown from the dust of the dirt roads we struggled along. The houses seemed to be growing further and further apart, grassy soccer fields and wilderness just beyond us—when I spotted a possible sign of civilization: a small, whitewashed, flat-topped edifice not much larger than a bus shelter.

"Elder Hartman. What's that?"

"That building? It's just a kiosko."

"Huh?"

"A little store. You can buy soda and cookies and . . "

"Elder," I said as I mounted my bike and started pedaling, "Let's go check it out."

Just a kiosko? It was a palm tree-filled oasis in the middle of the Sahara. Dropping my bike, I walked up to the small window.

"Yes?" the man said, stepping away from the soccer broadcast on his portable radio.

In no time, I was sitting on a curb, devouring shortbread cookies and Pritty Limon, the latter being the Argentine equivalent of Seven Up. Bottled pop never tasted as good as it did on that hot, dusty day. Some fifteen minutes later I stood and brushed the cookie crumbs off my clothes, revitalized. From then on, church buildings weren't the only havens on the map.

WE RODE TO AN INVESTIGATOR'S HOUSE and parked our bikes out front. Not entering the gate—for that was a breach of courtesy to some—my companion clapped his hands several times. The homeowner came out to greet us.

"Me llamo Elder Hiland," I said, then fell silent as my comp took over. I was in watch-and-learn mode. We were invited inside and shown to the living room. After an opening prayer, Elder H started the charla. Resting a thick black binder on one knee, he described the origins of the LDS Church, occasionally opening the binder to show a picture or printed words that reinforced what he was teaching.

I stared fixedly at my companion, a technique that directed the listeners to also look at him. I could follow what he was saying, but would then lose the verbal thread, like trying to stay tuned to an elusive radio signal in the mountains. It was during those lost moments that I feared Elder Hartman would ask me to comment. But he didn't. Instead he asked me to bear my testimony about what I believed. Though sharing memorized sections of the charlas gave me the willies, testimony-bearing was something I'd practiced a lot in the LTM. It was a simpler set of words to pronounce, and needed be no longer than a few sentences. So I let fly:

"Señor Moreno, I know that Heavenly Father and Jesus Christ live. I know that the Book of Mormon and the Holy Bible are the word of God to us, in these latter days. And I say these things in the name of our Savior, Jesus Christ. Amen."

It felt good to contribute. As we were riding away, Elder Hartman told me I'd done a good job. After watching him talk for forty-five minutes while I played the mute, I felt more than a bit humble. But it was a start, and one of my first spiritual experiences in the country. And that's the way it went all day, my companion doing the heavy lifting while I watched and listened and learned. By evening I was so tired I wanted to crawl into bed fully clothed. It was good to know I'd earned my exhaustion.

THE DAYS STILL WARM, I enjoyed the cleansing freshness that rainstorms brought to the air. But being near the city—one without below-the-street drainage systems—flooding was a regular occurrence. One day during that first week, it rained hard for several hours straight, then subsided. Elder Hartman called me to the street to take a look. The curbs serving as river banks, foot-deep rainwater flowed past us toward the central avenue, getting deeper the farther it traveled.

"We've gotta ride through this."

"Why?" I asked, looking at the current and thinking about my shoes and pants and whether they'd survive a swim.

"To get across town for an appointment."

"You're kidding."

"Nope."

So we walked our bikes down the sidewalk on our side of the street. Within the first hundred feet the waters were washing over the curb, and as we splashed along, shoes filling up, residents looked out their windows at the flood and at us. The further we descended, the higher the cresting waters rose, within inches of residents' thresholds and open doors. The looks those people gave us said to not bother asking if we could render assistance, an attitude borne of their mistrust of foreigners. Or maybe because there was little anyone could do by that point, short of closing their doors in the hope that little water would leak through before the flood receded.

Several blocks ahead was an intersection where water was noisily converging from several tributary-streets, having developed into whitewater rapids of undetermined depth and ferocity. Smaller vehicles bobbed around like giant, colored corks. A city bus tried to fight its way to higher ground. I looked at Hartman and he shook his head. We turned around and pushed upstream a short distance, lifted book-laden bikes above our heads and crossed to the other submerged sidewalk, the lukewarm rainwater having reached my hips. We must have been a sight: well-dressed men with bicycles, wading to who-the-hell-knew-where. I followed my companion to shallower depths and our eventual appointment.

THE BRANCH, P-DAY AND BICYCLES

By the time my first Sunday in the country had arrived, I was ready for the peaceful hours that Sabbath church attendance could provide. The Temprano Branch met at a nicely maintained building near the city center. White spire marking the location, the edifice was of cinder block construction, a short, white, wrought iron fence surrounding the narrow strip of lawn out front. The building included a chapel, a gym, a stage, a kitchen, an administrative office, numerous classrooms, and a baptismal font. Out back was a basketball court that, given its present state of disrepair, was more suited to a game of volleyball or soccer.

Temprano membership had grown to the point where the Church was justified in constructing a nice-sized building. There were about fifty people attending every Sunday. With a branch president as its leader, the members were fortunate to have such a fine place to worship. Church-goers in other branches were meeting in homes, school buildings, maybe even the stray bar or tavern, affordable housing a problem throughout the land. Once the Río Four Branch membership increased enough in size, they'd be designated as a "ward." Instead of a branch president, they'd have a bishop as their ecclesiastical leader.

It felt good to sit and listen to someone else teaching, for a change. I needed the rest, and partaking of the sacrament was a welcome respite from all the unaccustomed running around I was doing. The members spoke a different language from mine, hugged and kissed each other a lot more than their American counterparts, but the spirit of love and fellowship was the same. It felt more like home than anywhere else I'd been in the country, my apartment included. But as to the Sabbath being a full day of rest? Maybe for the rank-and-file, but not us. No sooner had meetings adjourned than we were out riding the streets again. The only other time we would visit the church building would be for baptisms, district meetings, or some special event like a branch-sponsored dance or dinner.

"OKAY, ELDER, IT'S P-DAY. We've got until 5 p.m. to do whatever we want."

"Cool," I said, looking forward to a lot of goofing around and sightseeing.

"But first we need to write letters home and to the mission president. We'll take turns sending that weekly report letter to Parón."

Elder H handed me a Weekly Report form. On it I had to enter the number of hours we'd spent teaching charlas, knocking doors, or otherwise finding people to teach. The names of our investigators as well as the number of baptisms had to be included. Expenses had to be noted, as well. And all of that information was gleaned from the Planning Card.

The bottom half of the report was reserved for a letter to President Parón. Because the president was responsible for over two hundred missionaries, he relied on feedback from two elders called APs (assistants to the president), several sets of ZLs (zone leaders), many DLs (district leaders), and our weekly missives. My first letter to Parón was a wobbly affair, but I had to start somewhere. An hour later I signed the report form and handed it to Elder Hartman, who'd mail it that same day. Then we were ready to go out into the world to buy toothpaste, writing paper, pens, postage stamps, food, and medicine. Deliver clothes to the washer woman. Visit the post office. Fun things like that.

ONE DAY OUR EIGHT-PERSON DISTRICT rode bikes out to a park, away from the city. It was a beautiful place, featuring a large running track, gazebos, a small lake and bridge, rose gardens crisscrossed with gravel paths, benches scattered along the way. I rode my bike on almost every path, breathing in the cool, fall air as I scurried around the track a couple times, then sat on a bench in the warm sun and wrote letters, when not squeezing in the occasional journal entry. There were chances to converse with other district members, but most of the time, we were all just relaxing, thinking either about the trees and the lake and the nice weather or about nothing at all, especially if sleep overtook one while resting.

Since some companions could get on each other's nerves, district outings gave us some social breathing room. And if there were sister missionaries around, so much the better. To hear a friendly female voice and be in their presence had a calming effect on me. I admired them to no end.

BICYCLES PRESENTED SPECIAL PROBLEMS for missionaries. Due to their many moving parts and the amount of abuse they suffered, they were prone to breakdowns on a regular basis. The bike's reputation for causing cancellation of important charlas and meetings gained it a reputation as the "Tool of the Adversary."

Tires were the worst offenders. Lying in wait along all roads were enormous, gaping potholes, washouts, wash boarding, cobblestone (that tires loved to wedge themselves in-between), brown and green bits of broken wine or beer bottle glass scattered everywhere. And lastly, the efforts of boys young and old whose goal in life was to puncture tubes whenever and wherever we parked (needles being the tool of choice). But regardless of cause, flats were a clear and present danger. It wasn't uncommon to see elders doubled up on one bike, a practice I found humiliating on the few occasions I had to endure such an ordeal. People stared at us enough as it was.

By March 3rd, I had tired of riding a borrowed, worn-out bicycle. It was time to buy one of my own. There's something special about owning something you depend so much upon, and the missionary bicycle was no exception. Sure, there'd always be flat tires to deal with, but if I was using my own bike, at least I'd be familiar with its idiosyncrasies. I'd be able to see trouble coming. On this particular day, Elder Hartman and I searched all over town for the right model, but every candidate was either too expensive or the wrong color or not stout enough. Much of the decision-making was my comp's, since he knew better what would survive the daily rigors of missionary travel.

Then we entered the bicycle shop of one Joachim Albuixech, and I saw it: a shiny, brand-new, jet-black Mundo one-speed. Sporting motorcycle-sized metal fenders, a wide spring-loaded seat, a heavy frame, two-inch wide tires, and thick spokes, it was perfect for the worst road or trail Temprano had to offer. No wonder most missionaries preferred to call this kind of convey-ance a "tanque" (tank).

Above the rear fender was a spring-loaded carrying rack. Since the only backpack available back then was the type one would take camping or on military maneuvers, I'd load my full-to-bursting black leather attaché bag on the back of the bike and hope the spring held. Those valises could get pretty heavy when stuffed with scriptures (ours and new copies), pamphlets, a five-pound flip chart binder, cassette tapes, filmstrips, a tire pump, and a patch kit. If I didn't keep a close watch on the cargo, it would fly loose without my knowing it. I was always looking over my shoulder. But unsightly as the Mundo may have been to the average cyclist, it was the bike for me. Sturdy and ugly, it could handle the roughest terrain and still be parked outside after we finished a discussion.

During this period, I attended the first of many zone conferences. All the missionaries from our group of districts convened for instruction by the ZLs and President Parón. The talks were instructive, even if I was straining to understand the Spanish they were speaking. One of the fringe benefits of these get-togethers was the chance to see old friends. Though we'd only been apart a few weeks, strong bonds of friendship had been forged.

REGULARITY AND CONFIDENCE

IT HAPPENED DURING THE NIGHT of March 7th, my body saying "Enough is enough!" I assumed it was so busy fighting some loathsome form of bacteria in my food-processing facilities that it couldn't devote the proper attention to incoming shipments. All I knew was that when I awoke that morning, there was no internal grumbling, gurgling or inflation. I sat up in bed and waited. Nothing. I stood and casually looked in the direction of the bathroom. My bowels shrugged their shoulders and said "So what?" My seventeen-day war with diarrhea was over. So overjoyed was I that I devoted a special entry in my journal to the occasion.

According to the missionaries I talked to, getting sick in Argentina was an adventure best avoided. During medical exams, serious health issues might be glossed over or just plain missed. Conversely, a routine exam could yield bizarre recommendations for a treatment that had nothing to do with the real problem—if one actually existed. While childbirth was handled well, the rate of post-operative infection for a simple appendectomy was fifty percent. That led me to better understand why the Church administered hepatitis shots the way they did.

ONE DAY WHILE Elder Hartman was teaching, I shared my testimony. My comp then felt impressed to challenge the guy to be baptized—and he accepted. As the investigator was getting up off his knees after offering the closing prayer, there were tears in his eyes. The experience was beautiful, and I was grateful to be part of it—yet I believed it was too small a part. My companion seemed to be doing all the work. From there I made the illogical jump to believing that I was unable to help much because I was not "spiritual" enough. It was the same dispiriting train of thought I had boarded and rode during the LTM days.

We all have a "thorn in the flesh," as Paul described it. An Achilles heel. A chink in the spiritual armor. Mine was the belief that, aside from my prowess at Scrabble, I didn't ever stand quite as tall or mature as others my age. The damning habit of comparing self with others was becoming a larger millstone around my neck with every passing year. The sad part of it was that other missionaries viewed me as a person with many talents. They saw a young man who had chosen to serve a mission under less than favorable circumstances, lacking the type of support they had grown up with and taken for granted. Some of them said that they didn't know if they could have traveled the road I had.

But one of the blessings of serving a mission is that it's the great equalizer. You can be an expert in human behavior, fluent in many languages, even a gifted orator. But when it comes to sharing the gospel of Jesus Christ, any person guided by the Spirit of God can teach a lesson that will pierce the heart of even the staunchest unbeliever.

With God's help, I was experiencing little victories over self almost daily. Speaking and understanding a foreign language. Talking to total strangers with little or no fear. Developing a heightened appreciation and love for nature, the weather, animals, music, little children, and babies. I was even getting up at 5:30 a.m. on a consistent basis. That alone was worthy of some level of wonderment. But for every victory there was another arrow of self-doubt flying my direction. Maybe it was God's way of keeping me humble. Maybe the adversary saw another chance to tear me down. And maybe it was just me, self-programmed by past experiences and resultant misconceptions to start a scripted tape running—one that set me up as Punching Bag #1. Regardless of the reason, the battle for my self-esteem was on.

ELDER H AND I WERE WALKING around town. Seeing a person of interest, my comp approached.

"Hello, Sir. We're representatives of the Church of Jesus Christ of Latter-day Saints, and we have a message we'd like to share with you."

The man being amenable to further discussion, Hartman continued, engaging the fellow in a question-and-answer exchange. Once at a point where the topic turned to the origins of Christ's primitive church, my comp turned to me.

"Now my companion Elder Hiland would like to tell you the story of Joseph Smith."

With a whopping ten seconds to prepare, I accepted the flip chart binder (that book full of visuals) from Elder H, and started talking—like I knew what I was doing.

"As Jesus Christ began His ministry on the earth, he knew he would need the help of others in order to spread the gospel."

I was doing it. That is, until the third or fourth sentence, when a case of nerves clouded my memory. I stammered, then stopped talking, feigning concentration though knee-deep in panic. After a few eternally painful seconds of silence, Elder Hartman nonchalantly took back the binder and continued. Acting as if that was the way the teaching was supposed to go, I nevertheless felt my cheeks flame on. But it was the kind of shame I was willing to endure. I'd been put into the game for a few minutes; exposure to a total stranger on that city street had strengthened and emboldened me.

On the home front, though, I chafed at the grueling regimen of charla study Hartman subjected me to. Scribbling away at my journal one day, I was trying to catch up on recent happenings and current affairs—all those things I'd forgotten to include in letters and postcards home, those events my Petri thirty-five-millimeter camera could never record. Sure, there was P-Day, but with the many things that happened in any twenty-four-hour period, I hated to not get them down on paper. If they weren't recorded quickly, they became etched in my memory inaccurately, or worse, evaporated into the ether.

Returning from the morning shower, Elder H stopped and looked at me.

"Elder Hiland."

"Yeah?"

"Why are you writing in your diary?"

"I like to catch up on what's been going on and this is the only time I have for it."

"How do you ever expect to pass off your charlas at the rate you're going?"

"Well—"

"Well, nothing. Get cracking on those charlas. You gotta get them passed off."

Understanding the import of what he was telling me, I nevertheless renewed dedication to my journal. In the future, I'd need to be more careful and record things only when not in Elder H's presence.

POSTAL SERVICE AND A NEW COMP

IN A MARCH 12TH LETTER TO DAD, I noted that the Peso had again been devalued, sending the local populace into a frenzy. Though I was in about the same financial condition as them, I'd paid off my room, meals, and the laundry service. Knowing that trouble could erupt at any moment, President Parón reminded us via letters and leaders that we weren't to write anything about the government. And given the shaky state of postal security, there was no guarantee that our mail wasn't being monitored or read on a daily basis, jail being the last place anyone wanted to land, innocent or guilty.

The quality of the postal system was a matter of conjecture. I could go for weeks with every letter arriving unscathed. Then the mail would stop coming, period. Or envelopes and packages would be opened sometime after entering the country, then sealed again. One day I received a letter from Mom. Enclosed was a photo clipped from the local stateside newspaper. Why my mother thought that a picture of scantily clad women would not be distracting is beyond me. But upon closer examination I noticed that someone had drawn anatomically-correct features on the ladies. I never looked at the local mailman quite the same after that.

THE FOLLOWING MONDAY, Elder H revealed that he'd be leaving on transfer to the north within a few days. My being privy to such information ahead of time was unusual, since only the president, the APs and ZLs usually knew about transfers that early. To have advanced notice could cause any number of problems, the main ones being distraction and disruption of the missionary work.

But this pending change wasn't of much concern to me. I'd already served with seven other elders. If it'd been a case of my comp's mission coming to an end, his departure date would have been common knowledge (as flight plan details didn't stay unknown for long). Then his challenge would be to avoid becoming "trunky"—a condition where the missionary starts dwelling so much on their return to civilian life that he or she loses all desires to do the Work.

Elder Hartman's departure meant the zone would have to find another DL, which meant us having to find a new place to live. The new leader would need our spacious apartment's proximity to downtown, from which to conduct district business. And though we didn't have that many belongings, our move took the better part of two days. It's tough hauling clothing, books, food, and supplies across town via bicycle.

The new pensión was in a neighborhood more worn around the edges than our present one. The house, situated at the end of a back street, was fronted by a five-foot wall, in the center of which was a masonry arch surrounding a locked gate. Past a short walk to the front door was a living room and a door leading to the kitchen. To the left were the bathroom and our bedroom. The landlady in the new place was a woman in her early forties, eager to please and always smiling. And given the state of the economy, having paying tenants must have been a blessing.

For the moment, life was good. Eight thousand pesos ($60 American) bought a lot, including laundry service, rooms cleaned, beds made, plenty of hot water for showers, and three squares a day. Breakfast was Café Malta (a Postum-like beverage) mixed with milk and sliced bread covered with marmalade or dulce de leche. Lunch was the main event. Along with water or soda there were soups (vegetables, rice, fideos, or cheese), bread and pasta (fideos, raviolis, or gnocchis), meat (chicken, meatballs, asado, or roast beef), potatoes, carrots, sliced tomatoes marinated in onions, or milanesa neapolitana. For dessert there was cake, mandarin or regular oranges. Dinner was more of an afterthought: soup, bread to dip in it, vegetables, and arroz con leche or mandarin oranges.

At 4:30 Friday morning, we saw Elder Hartman off at the bus terminal. I was sick with my first Argentine cold, but looking forward to working with my new companion, Elder Noland. As he'd be going home in two months, I was curious to see how he'd handle the short time remaining to him. After he arrived, I discovered that he arose no earlier than 6:30 a.m. Life had just gotten a little easier.

A COUP AND PERSECUTION

WEDNESDAY, MARCH 24TH. We were out in the campo (countryside) for an evening teaching appointment. After we closed with a prayer, the man of the house had a question.

"So, elders, have you heard about the curfew?"

Elder Noland said that we had not.

"Well, Isabel Perón (Argentina's president) was just removed from power. It's a military takeover."

I didn't understand what this fellow was telling us, but from the look on Noland's face, it was a bad thing.

"So, elders," our host continued, "How are you getting home?"

"On our bikes. Why?"

"Well," he said, "you better be careful. There's a 9 p.m. curfew and—" he looked at his watch. "Oh! It's after 9 o'clock now. Oh-oh."

Oh-oh, indeed. My companion motioned me toward the door.

"Elders, anyone seen on the streets between now and daylight tomorrow morning will be arrested and taken to jail."

Saying goodbye to our friend, Elder N filled me in on what was happening as we loaded our bikes with books and teaching materials.

"Elder Hiland. We need to get home, *now.*"

Oh, crap.

"Get on your bike and ride as fast as you can to the house. We can't be seen by the cops."

Slapping my shirt pocket to ensure that the documents were still there, I tore off after Noland. Being in the campo worked in our favor, since we were on dimly-lit dirt roads little traveled by cars or trucks, even in the daytime. But it was tricky, trying to haul butt when I couldn't see much in front of me. If I hit one of those crater-sized pits, I'd be sailing headfirst over the handlebars before I knew what was happening. It was a matter of pedaling hard but staying loose so I could bail if I did hit a big one.

Slow at first, then accelerating through large sections of darkness, then sudden overhead lights, I looked to the right (toward town) at every intersection, the paranoia building before each upcoming cross street.

Standing on the pedals, I pumped my legs, pushing the Mundo faster than ever. More glances right, then left, even straight ahead. If a cop came upon us, we'd need to either stop and surrender, or ride like hell into the shadows. But at each intersection I saw nothing near or far. We were riding though a ghost town—no cars, buses, bikes, or people in evidence. Then we were on our own street, pedaling like mad as we coasted into the driveway at twenty miles per hours, then skidded to a stop—not an easy task on those hulky bikes, unless one is scared to death.

Safely inside, we joined the señora and her mother as they listened to the radio. All over town and across the country, TV stations had ceased programming anything but the static profile of a soldier's helmeted head, military march music droning in the background.

The media blackout continued over the next few days, doing nothing to calm the fears of a nation that had been through too many government coups and meltdowns. In letters home, I had to reassure everyone that I was okay, and not hanging from a telephone pole in the town square. The mail took about seventeen days to get to the States, so the sooner I dispelled whatever drivel the network news was peddling, the better. As for the mission, President Parón had a contingency plan in place in the event of civil unrest. The ZLs would get a call from Parón telling them to "send the books," a signal for all missionaries to head to the mission home ASAP. Once there, stateside missionaries would be hustled off to the nearest airport.

During the third day of curfew we stopped by a contact's house. His front door was open. We knocked. We knocked again. But no one answered. A helpful soul walking by told us to go to the back door and call him. But no one answered. From where we stood I could see the back yard. And a man running into the dense brush. Our contact. Dashing out front, we mounted our bikes, raced down the street and around the corner. There he was, trotting over to rejoin the helpful soul who'd told us to keep knocking. Ticked off about having been played, I rode over and glared him straight in the face—since swearing was out of the question—then rode off. That night we dropped him from the teaching pool.

Not everyone tried to avoid us, though. The Jehovah's Witnesses sought us out at every opportunity. For having so much knowledge about the scriptures, they seemed to only want to argue with us about narrow points of doctrine. Called "Bible-bashing," this unsavory event occurs whenever those of different faiths try to defend their respective interpretations of the Word. Rules of civil discourse fall by the wayside as each party demonstrates their prowess at using verses to back up their claims, while pointing out how badly their opponent is misinterpreting said passages. Long before the discussion has degraded into a no-holds-barred verbal fistfight, the Spirit of the Lord has vacated the premises. The best thing we could do in those situations was to bear testimony and leave.

Then there were the children. They flew kites and played soccer, but since we were primarily teaching adults, kids weren't on our radar. But the longer we worked in a neighborhood, the more familiar a sight we became. And once the little ones realized we weren't cops or spies, a type of mob mentality took over. We were the strangers in their midst, and everyone knows how kids treat strangers, especially ones they aren't scared of or have no reason to trust.

One day we rode past a group of youth using sling-shots on some hapless birds. As we gained distance from them I started hearing things whiz by my head, various objects hitting the ground all around us. Now under di-rect fire, we ducked our heads and pushed pedal.

Yelling only emboldened the punks. Chasing them down would look bad and get their parents, relatives, friends, or the police after us. The only thing that worked was to lock eyes with them as I approached, then main-tain stink-eye contact until we were out of range. If they were slingshot-challenged they might resort to asking for the time, so they could laugh at our accents. As this seemed to happen at least twenty times a day, I started telling them that I didn't have a watch, which usually shut them up. Other kids would yell things like "Hey, faggot," which didn't require an answer, just more incentive to pedal away as fast as possible.

POLICÍA, A TALENT SHOW, AND GUILT

LATE MARCH. During the 150-kilometer bus ride to a mission conference in Villa Maria, our bus comes to a sudden stop. It's a roadblock. The policemen manning this barricade look more like soldiers than cops. My hand goes to that shirt pocket where the ever-present documents reside, while formerly noisy passengers are reduced to whispering. I look out windows on both sides, trying to reassure myself about a situation of which I know nothing. Then an official-looking fellow boards.

"Please step off the bus," he says in flat tones. "Have your documents in hand, ready for inspection."

It frightens me to see first-hand how much power this government has over its people. It's been going on so long that they're used to it—but it seems a huge price to pay to keep order in one's own land. Not excited about taking a walk outside where all those military types are, I rise from my comfortable seat and follow everyone, anyway. Out into the bright sunlight we file.

"Your papers, please," a uniformed official says, hand held out as a sign to stop walking and comply. He looks over my documents, then motions me over to a line of people facing the bus, side by side. So this is how it feels to be treated like a criminal, and by the people who are supposed to be serving us.

"Step forward and place your hands flat against the bus," comes a no-nonsense voice from behind. We all step forward. I can hear some of the men in charge laughing and joking, making small talk. Placing my palms on the cool metal sides of our vehicle isn't as easy as I thought, for once they are in place I want to readjust them so I'll look even less threatening. But once fixed in position, I don't move. I just want to get this over with, for the longer it goes on, the more frightened I become.

I study the side of this bus more intently than any scripture in recent memory, and since the surface doesn't reflect much, I'm taken by surprise as a man runs his patting hands quickly, superficially, up and down my body. Then he moves on. I get the impression this is being done more for show than out of any concern about a possible terrorist presence on our bus. Words are murmured to the driver, followed by silence.

"Okay," an official says. "You may now board the bus."

Later I note in my journal that "it was an interesting experience," and that "there was nothing to fear," basing my comments on the lackadaisical manner of the soldier-cops. A lot I knew. In the larger cities—Palacio, Santa Fe, and Buenos Aires— police activities were no laughing matter. Since missionaries were forbidden to talk about politics, I had no idea what was going on outside my bubble. But occasionally I'd hear stories. Even with proper documentation, any citizen could be whisked away for questioning. Either you'd be returned home later, probably roughed up a little but still intact—or never seen again. If you were tortured but allowed to live, you'd then be blindfolded, shoved into the trunk of a

Ford Falcon—referred to by those in the know as "death cars"—taken to a cemetery somewhere and dumped. You had to find your own way home. But at least you got to return home.

In weekly letters to my parents, I described the businesses I saw during my travels through town and country—noting an inordinate amount of bicycle shops. Having come from a car-saturated nation, it wasn't hard to see that a dysfunctional economy forced the majority to own bikes. Cars were too expensive to maintain, and only the well-to-do owned vehicles that weren't falling apart. I wrote too about warehouses large and small, all full of vino, as well as the soda-bottling businesses crammed into garages next to homes. Fruit and vegetables and firewood were sold from truck beds. People were doing whatever they could to survive the economic hell.

I told them that my daily schedule had improved a bit, Elder Noland and I arising at 6:30 a.m., thus allowing me an extra hour's sleep every morning. Since President Parón had announced during the Villa Maria conference that we could no longer knock doors after sunset, we had to plan ahead to avoid having nothing to do late in the day. With the exception of Sunday meetings and P-Day, it was all work.

One evening we put on a talent show for the ward. Some fifty people showed up, a nice mix of Church members and their non-member friends. Normally one to avoid the spotlight, this event brought out the ham in me. I did a magic act where all the tricks went wrong. Humming a little tune as I performed, the audience laughed harder, the more tricks I messed up. It was a thrill to get the timing just right and make people laugh. In the end, we succeeded in showing the ward members a good time, an event they were able to share with each other as well. We helped visitors see that Mormons were just like them.

WITH APRIL SPEEDING BY came the realization that I needed to start passing off charlas. I spent part of a day studying C, but forgot thirty lines while trying to pass it off. The resultant frustration of the LTM days returned home to roost like a flock of diseased poultry. But I knew I had to keep at it until I got it right. By the 14th I passed off Charla C to Elder N. My triumph over that set of battered, brown half-pages put me in a pro-active mood. Believing I could now conquer anything, I decided to stop biting my nails, a deeply entrenched, fifteen-year habit. Before I knew it, seven days had passed with nary a mangled fingernail or torn cuticle in sight. I believed that if I could keep it up for thirty days, the new habit would stick.

FROM TIME TO TIME I'd get a case of the Guilts. As usual, the culprit was my thoughts about women. Adding to the mix was my low self-esteem, fed by the belief that no one else struggled as much as poor Dan in his attempt to not think about girls. One might as well tell the sun not to rise as to keep a young man or woman (who was forbidden to date, kiss, or even hold hands with the opposite sex for two years) from noticing or thinking about them. It didn't help that many of the girls had an exotic demeanor and look about them. Deep brown eyes. And that accent. Though I preached repentance to other people every day of the week, self-application of said process was sometimes difficult.

CHILDREN, A NEW COMP, AND BARTOK

BY THE END OF APRIL, the weather seemed to be going in reverse—mid-fall and getting colder by the day. On the positive side, Elder Noland and I had taught eighteen charlas in one week; more than anyone else in our district. But with the good comes the bad. One day we became disoriented somewhere in our area.

"Elder—Elder," I said, slowing as we rode past a large group of school kids.

"Stop for a minute. Let's figure out where we're at."

Coasting to a halt some fifty feet from the children, it was time to look at a map. While my comp scoured the paper, trying to get his bearings, I took in the scenery. It was a beautiful day, if a little cold. I was in a good mood.

"Elder."

"Yeah," he said without looking up from the map.

"Don't those kids look nice in their white uniforms?"

"Mmph . . ."

They did look respectful and dignified, and I wondered why more school districts in the States didn't adopt similar policies. Some of the kids had stopped talking and jostling. They were staring at us. I waved and continued musing, glancing at my companion. Did he care? Not one bit. But surely he could see that the wearing of a uniform might inculcate a sense of civility in the Youth of America that was so sorely lacking, these days.

Hearing a THUMP, I noticed a rock rolling past my shoes. Another landed nearby. Wondering where the stones were coming from, I looked in the direction of the children. The little cherubs were aiming for us. And though their initial accuracy was wanting, it would quickly improve, judging by the supply of potential projectiles lying nearby. I wondered if I should return fire or confront the little juvies, when my comp said, "Elder, let's get outta here!"—he already on his way down the street, and in the opposite direction.

There was something about bike-riding young men in formal attire that brought out the worst in the younger set. One day we decided to cut across a large field, instead of going all the way around the huge block. But the rutted path bisecting the area was a gathering place for a dozen youth of all ages. And we were headed straight for them. Deciding to show no fear and barrel on through, I picked up speed. The crowd was ready by the time we arrived, lined along both sides of the trail.

One kid sent a kick at my butt, but I stood up and his foot missed by a cheek. "Ha-ha," I exulted, unprepared for the next kid in line, who doused me with wine of some hellish vintage. Though I was tempted to retaliate, we were outnumbered—that and the fact that starting a brawl would not contribute to the missionary effort. And the timing couldn't have been worse. We were on our way to someone's home for a charla about the Word of Wisdom—the one about the evils of drink. I walked into their home smelling like a ditch dweller.

By the start of May, Elder Noland had gone home, replaced by Elder George, from Utah. After noting in my journal that almost all missionaries seemed to be from Utah or California, I would hold off making any comments about this new companion until I knew him better. While not a misanthrope, I was no longer willing to heap praises on the elders I worked with. I had discovered that they were human like myself, and prone to the occasional error.

FOR NEARLY FIVE MONTHS I'd been denying myself a lot of things to be out in the mission field, one of them being music. Mission life restricted all manner of input, from books to music to movies to TV; anything that did get through was filtered, based on content, noise level, and reputation. On P-Days I'd started listening to music on my low-rent, General Electric cassette player.

According to the mission rules and the White Bible, we were only to listen to "uplifting" music. Since that term was open to interpretation, the only type of music specifically recommended was either classical or religious. As to the latter there was the Mormon Tabernacle Choir, of which nary a cassette could be found in the stores I frequented. But as for classical, I soon discovered a world of beauty. Fidelity being a non-issue, I would base my enjoyment on an artist's musicianship and song-writing ability.

Once I determined I was in sufficient control of my finances, I ventured forth into the music stores. First there was Bach's Greatest Hits, the Deutsche Grammophone release opening my ears to a formerly closed musical door. Though I'd been exposed to "early" classical music a couple years earlier in college, I maintained a bias toward compositions from the 1850s forward. All older works were considered too stuffy and archaic. How ignorant can a person be? Though the Bach tape was only a sampler, it was a revelation to me.

During another store visit I stumbled across a colorfully illustrated cassette tape case bearing the name of an old friend: Bela Bartok. This Hungarian composer had become my hero back in my college days. Anyone willing to carry an old Victrola into the mountains to record gypsy music was someone worth paying attention to. The tape contained a recording of the *Concerto for Orchestra*, a work of Bartok's I was unfamiliar with. But taking a musical leap of faith, I bought the cassette. From the opening notes I was taken prisoner, released from melodic bondage only after the final movement's echoing tones, the music was so impressive.

As for the "Not Recommended" genres, there was a gradual erosion of my resistance to temptation. A Cat

Stevens tape here, a Beatles release there, a copied James Taylor cassette elsewhere. Soon I had the makings of a nice collection to draw from when I needed background music while writing letters. I rationalized my musical choices away in the belief that man does not live by Tab Choir and hymns alone. In the end, I made a truce with the World, an effort similar to that of the little Dutch boy trying to hold back the sea with a well-placed finger. In my case, though, it wasn't a matter of self-sacrifice as much as self-indulgence. I would allow a judicious amount of secular music through the earthen wall at the risk of distractions that would occasionally dilute my missionary efforts but also "enrich" my life. Or so I thought.

FILMSTRIPS, A FUNERAL, AND ENGLISH CLASS

WHEN I WAS RECEIVING THE DISCUSSIONS in 1972, the mission-aries used flannel-covered boards and paper figures—operating on the same principle as Velcro—to help explain gospel concepts. Some four years later, the Church had replaced the board with a binder full of eight-and-a-half-by eleven-inch visual aids called "flip charts." There were times, though, when something more absorbing was required. This was where the Singer projector and cassette player came in. A music-accompanied filmstrip could hold a person's attention longer—especially if that person was illiterate. For twenty minutes, the investigator could enjoy a gospel message in perfect Spanish, replete with music and images. The one drawback to this setup was that every time the dialogue advanced to the point where the frame needed to be advanced, the tape recording emitted a loud "BEEP."

One evening we hauled the Singer and tape player out to a country house. After we discovered that the home had no electricity, the homeowner ran from one neighbor to the next, in search of an extension cord long enough reach us. By show time there were fifteen people packed into a small living room to watch the flick.

The filmstrip cued, Elder George turned on the tape recorder, but no sound issued from it—just the whirring of motor and spinning capstans. Swinging open the cover, Elder G pulled out the cassette, several feet of brown tape trailing after it like a bad magic trick. The crowd started laughing. Spinning a pen in one of the case's holes, my comp wound the tape back inside, then snapped the cassette into the machine and pressed the PLAY button. Again the GE began eating the tape. It took ten minutes of fiddling around to notice that the motor was running backward. This was followed by the discovery that the batteries had been installed the wrong way.

In the end the group enjoyed the presentation. The subject matter touched upon Life's Three Questions: Where did we come from before birth? Why are we here? What happens after we die?

We attended a funeral the following day for one of the ward elders, who'd died of a heart attack. Our district was asked to sing "O My Father." It was an open-casket affair, only the second I'd seen, the first being for my Grandad Quigley a few years earlier. Unlike that earlier occasion, when I'd refused to join the line for a last gape at Grandpa's mug, we were now assembled a scant four feet from the deceased. In his elevated, topless coffin I thought he looked quite natural, but I was still wary. This was a former living human, now laid out in suit and tie and not breathing. Forcing my roving eyes to look anywhere but at the still figure, I did my best to maintain an appearance of solemnity and reverence.

Opening prayer was offered. Then we sang the assigned hymn, but it was hard not to glance at the dead man. The song was about the afterlife, and he'd beat us all there. I wondered what he'd been up to since passing.

Branch President Del Río gave the eulogy, recounting the man's life. His mention of the fact that the elder was better off now, in the Lord's presence, touched me, taking the morbid edge off the proceedings.

Sometime during the service, though, thoughts of a less serious nature were running through someone else's mind. After standing at reverence-induced attention, Elder Bertram leaned over and broke into a muttered "Sing, a-round, the cas-ket. Join, the Camp-fire Girls." While I found Elder B's sense of humor hilarious, the same couldn't be said for those times when nothing seemed to go right.

ONE DAY EARLY IN MAY, Elder George and I spent the afternoon putting up English class posters—seventeen of them—in stores across town. Then we headed out to teach some charlas before 9 p.m. rolled around. On the way to the first house, my comp suffered a flat tire. Walking fifteen blocks home, we got the other bike—the one with the loose chain that liked to fall off every few blocks just to piss off its rider.

We arrived for appointment Number One. "Sorry, elders," said the man of the house, "but I'm leaving on a trip out of town. We'll have to reschedule."

Within a block of appointment Number Two, a kid emerged from the shrubbery and grabbed the back of Elder Gs bike, the juvie's feet plowing furrows in the dirt road, dragging the bicycle to a dusty stop. I leaped from my tanque, ready for action as another kid appeared.

The two youngsters screamed and yelled at us, then ran off into the darkness from whence they'd come.

House Number Two: "They're not here," said a stranger who'd answered the door. "The family went to Palacio. I don't know when they'll be back."

Officially out of places to visit, we stood on a well-lit street corner to regroup, the evening schedule shot to hell. On cue, our little friends reappeared, this time from behind a wall.

"Where is your church?"

"Why do you want to know?" said my pissed off comp. "So you can make fun of us again?"

"No!" the kid said. To prove it, the two youngsters screamed and yelled at us, then ran off into the darkness from whence they'd come. Taking that as a sign that our work there was finished, we pedaled home, getting attacked by three dogs along the way.

CURSING, CHASTISEMENT, AND PARADE

BY MID-MONTH, several days of relentless rain had turned every dirt road into a slimy mud hole that made bike riding and traction a challenge. And though these rainy periods were always followed by weeks of cloudless, clear-blue skies, fall was turning colder, occasionally frigid. If momentum was lost in the midst of a muddy stretch, I'd have to stand on the bike pedals and push as hard as I could. When a slippery shoe sole slipped off the pedal, I almost crashed, letting loose with a well-deserved "*S**t,*" one of those words held in reserve for special occasions. I felt instant shame for having cursed, and hoped my comp hadn't heard, but unleashed another expletive when my foot slipped again. It seemed the only appropriate thing to say.

On the bright side, Elder George and I were teaching twelve families, the logistics involved being a welcome challenge. But trying to schedule enough appointments that we could devote equal attention to each family was tricky. Finding them at home every three days was even trickier. Some forgot. Others lost enthusiasm. And a few just skipped out on us. But the abundance of opportunity was wonderful. For the moment, we were fulfilling the measure of our creation. We were teaching.

MID-MAY. English class was in full swing. Those in attendance included ward members, ten new people, and one drunk. Starting with a diagnostic test, we separated the students into several groups, my class getting four people. Nervous at the start, I relaxed once I saw how excited these folks were to learn. It didn't hurt to realize that it was my chance to teach a foreign language to someone else, for a change.

Around this time, we gained a new investigator- Señor Córdoba—with whom we were very impressed. He asked questions throughout the first two discussions but wasn't antagonistic. A longtime Catholic, he was questioning his church's doctrine, asking us at one point, "Which church is right?" We taught him how to pray so he could ask the

Lord if what he was studying and being taught was true. We gave him a copy of the Book of Mormon, along with reading assignments in the Bible.

After a six-day absence we returned for a visit with Señor Córdoba. He came to the door, scowling, and handed back the Book of Mormon. "I am no longer interested. I don't believe that this book came from the Lord." Shocked, we bore our testimonies to him. Then he said, "Adios," and closed the door. We didn't understand. He'd been progressing better than any of the other investigators. I was very upset as we rode away from his house, and the further we pedaled, the worse it got. We agreed it was time to return to the apartment.

As soon as Elder George was through the front door he headed for the bathroom to pray, I to the bedroom. The more I prayed the worse I felt. I prayed some more. Then came the obvious realization: we had neglected Señor Córdoba. To initiate charlas with an interested person, then not return for visits every two to three days was a cardinal sin. In the case of Córdoba, we had taken for granted that he'd be okay in our absence. Remorse, guilt, and depression washed over me in stinging waves as I continued trying to converse with Heavenly Father, feeling like the world's biggest jerk. After a while the tears and the pain subsided. I felt cleaned out and forgiven. But the memory of having been chastised by God was one I wouldn't soon forget. I vowed to never neglect an investigator again.

Monday night the ward put on another talent show, followed by a dance and refreshments. Not on the ticket this time, my district and I mingled and got to know people better. Between the show and the dance, we grabbed some dinner, while the Church members and one investigator did most of the missionary work. We ended the evening with twenty-one referrals.

THE DAY OF THE MAY 25TH REVOLUTION was upon us, a celebration of the First National Government's inauguration. Scuttling plans to bless homes, we instead went downtown to view the festivities. The Plaza was packed by 10:30 a.m., so we took up a position on a bank for a better view of the promised parade. Soldiers were standing at attention, uniformed schoolchildren arranged in lines. A reviewing stand in front of the Catholic Church slowly filled with local religious leaders, followed by military and political representatives. Patriotic music was played, then the national anthem, courtesy of a tape recording. The monsignor offered an opening prayer, then the soldiers marched by, followed by row after row of schoolchildren, ordered by grade level and dressed in white.

The sense of well-being the government was trying to instill—fortified by a displayed love of nation, security, order, youth, and tradition—was impressive. But the people knew that all was not well. The unease was palpable. While I was photographing the lock-stepped marching soldiers/police, a uniformed, sun-glassed official in a thick, dark overcoat approached.

"What are you doing?"

I held forth the thirty-five-millimeter Petri. The uniformed man was not impressed.

"What is that?"

"I'm just taking pictures of the parade," I said, exuding pleasance. For a moment he hesitated, looking at the camera as if considering confiscation. Then he gave me a hard look and walked back to parade edge.

An hour later the gauchos arrived on horseback. Easily the most interesting group in the parade, they waved and turned their animals around to give us all a better look at a lifestyle in decline. Old men in sombrero-type hats; necks scarf-wrapped; baggy pants tucked into accordioned, spurred boots; eight-inch wide belts full of shiny coins; gold- and silver-plated daggers tucked in back.

BEING IN POSSESSION of a rather overactive imagination has its perks, one being a very entertaining dream life. While I talked in my sleep a lot, the rigors of missionary work made my companions so tired that they rarely heard my displays of verbal somnambulism. Sometimes the dreams were in black and white, other times in color. One dream would have a music background, the next silence— which could feel a little creepy. And while nightmares were rare, there was never a lack of dialogue. On more than one occasion I'd find myself sitting up in bed, giving some non-existent investigator a discussion in Spanish, and probably doing a better job than when awake. Some dreams were silly, others so funny that I'd wake up laughing.

Then there were those occasions when the dream made sense. In one I was present when the Savior returned to the earth. Initially, I felt unworthy to be in His presence. After a time, though, I learned that all my sins had been forgiven. The experience was so beautiful and penetrating that I woke in the morning refreshed.

DISCOURAGEMENT, INFLUENZA, AND MORALS

DURING THE FIRST WEEK OF JUNE, our DL (Elder Gordon) called a work session. While his comp and mine were at work in another part of town, Elder G helped me plow my way through Charla D. We stayed in the pensión all morning, studying.

"I can't get this concept down," I said, frustrated beyond words. "It just won't sink in."

"Let's go for a walk."

Crossing the dead-end street out front, we stepped onto a well-worn path that ran between and behind and around homes of the rich and the poor, the route Elder George and I used every day to get to the more rural parts of our area.

"I don't know why, but these charlas are killing me."

Elder G nodded.

"I pride myself on knowing the English language pretty well. Better than a lot of other people do. So why is it so hard to learn these discussions? Everyone else in my LTM group's passed them off. I feel like an idiot."

Elder Gordon listened as I vented. We kept on walking. Soon we were a couple miles from the apartment. My diatribe at an end, it was his turn.

"We all have choices to make. It's one of God's great gifts to us, the freedom to choose. But in your case, you seem to have developed a bad habit."

What? I was expecting consoling words. Some magic verbal potion to cure my memory ills.

"When you're faced with a choice between feeling good or bad about something, you usually choose the latter."

I was starting to get upset. His words were supposed to make me feel better. By this time we'd reversed direction and were heading back to the apartment.

"And when you get into this toxic place, it hinders your ability to learn."

"Yeah," I said fighting back tears of frustration and self-pity. "You're right."

I felt like such a loser. But Elder Gordon went on and on, his voice gentle, carrying understanding and compassion as I validated his explanations. And as the walking and talking brought us closer to home, my bitter, caustic feelings melted away—replaced by a sense of well-being and gratitude. And then I passed off Charla D.

P-Days came and went. While I usually looked forward to them, a dreadful combination of cold winter days and influenza had sapped my enthusiasm for the weekly day off. Accordingly, Elder G and I spent a lot of time at Elder Bertram's pensión. Though their room was cold, unpainted, and bare, we didn't care. We were too busy with "Estanciero," the Argentine version of Monopoly. The opportunity to play a board game was such a novelty that things like the laundry, letter writing, and firing out on time went by the wayside. We were having too much fun.

Thursday, I passed off the diminutive Charla G (the Baptismal challenge), shortest of all the discussions. But when I gave it to Señor Maldonado that evening, I choked, the situation made more embarrassing by having failed in front of Elders Bertram and George. Our investigator was also challenged to get married before his proposed baptism date some eight days distant. If he couldn't get hitched by then, the baptism wouldn't be happening.

While Señor Maldonado had no quarrel with what we were teaching, other people did. One morning, Elders Bertram, Gordon and I met with Randy, leader of a group called Alpha-Omega. As we discussed our beliefs with him, he began asking questions based on his interpretation of Bible passages, focusing on salvation by grace, not works. We didn't agree, but weren't there to argue. We did some teaching, then bore testimony to him. When the first four principles and ordinances of the gospel (faith, repentance, baptism, and the gift of the Holy Ghost) were referred to, Randy stopped the conversation.

Handing his scriptures to Elder Gordon, the man said, "Show me where the four principles you speak of are mentioned in the Bible. And where does it say that baptism is essential for salvation?"

Elder G took the Bible in his hands and looked thoughtful for a moment.

"I can't find specific reference to them in the Bible, but I can explain them."

Disliking this answer, Randy drew us into a contentious discussion that dwindled to a theological draw. Deciding to cut our spiritual losses, we offered him copies of the Articles of Faith, the Book of Mormon, and Jesus the Christ.

"I appreciate the gesture," he said, "but I have a responsibility to my sheep."

"We understand," Elder Gordon said. But Randy wasn't quite done.

"I don't want you coming around here again until I know you are speaking the truth."

Though we agreed to disagree, I found the minister's treatment of us unsettling, and felt drained the rest of the day. I equated the inability to answer Randy's questions with a lack of knowledge we should have possessed—that this lack of preparation cast doubts on our teaching methods. This train of thought was bound to run off the tracks eventually, given the unsound rail bed it was traveling on.

When it comes to things of the Spirit, it's not the better scriptorian or the more skilled linguist or even stunning charisma that triumphs. It's simple truth spoken by the guidance of the Holy Ghost that touches the soul. We'd have been better off just bearing our testimonies and saying "adios" to Randy than try and match wits with him. Our strength lay in what we knew to be true: knowledge revealed through personal revelation.

By June 8th we were in the middle of a full-blown flu epidemic, many members of the branch affected. One fellow asked us to give him a health blessing. Not only did he feel terrible, but his job was at risk. My companion produced a small plastic bottle from his pocket. Opening the screw-on cap, he let a drop of olive oil fall onto the crown of the man's head. Then he placed his hands on the fellow's head and gave a short prayer, stating that by the authority of the Melchizedek priesthood, he was anointing this man for the healing of the sick. Then Elder George and I placed our hands on the recipient's head and I spoke, sealing the anointing previously performed. I blessed him that he'd get better. The next day we stopped by his house and found that he'd almost fully recovered.

Two days later we spent P-Day playing Estanciero at Bertram's pension again, not tearing ourselves away until 5:30 p.m.—a half hour after we were supposed to be out working. Elder G and I whipped through the streets, as if a show of speed might mitigate our latest act of slothfulness. But guilt followed me around the rest of the evening like a vile cloud. I expected some sort of karmic payback. Then we learned that the baptisms we and the sisters had planned weren't going to happen. And while I couldn't see the Lord making others suffer due to our unwillingness to abide by mission rules, we did seem to be making life hard for ourselves.

THE IDEA BEHIND the ZLs new "purification" program was as follows: if the "inner vessel" is clean, the outer surface will be, as well. In my case this cleansing involved blocking off thoughts about girls. It was the natural result of me looking at them and then dwelling on what I'd seen. And the more I thought about women, the greater a sinner I became. Worst of all, I started believing that having thoughts about women was, in itself, a bad thing. I didn't yet understand that there's a difference between having a thought and developing it into something more, or being tempted and acting on that temptation. If I'd understood the scriptures better, I'd have realized that even Christ was tempted. Being tempted is not a sin; it's part of the human condition. The difference is that He never gave in, while the rest us have a much poorer batting average.

The tendency to dwell and obsess about things that caught my eye, ear, or taste buds was evident. I was consuming Choc-Choc candy bars on a daily basis. Melodies from a growing collection of classical music tapes followed me around, in sync with my steady pedaling as we rode from one house to the next. And last but definitely not least was the physical reaction of my body to repeated thoughts about females real or imagined. The resultant guilt was a load I continued to struggle with.

People I talked to before my mission said that it was unreasonable to expect young men to sacrifice their libido while in the Lord's service. Such repression would lead to a warped sense of what is sexually normal, making prudes or deviants out of anyone who had to endure twenty-four months of sexual abstinence. But what price does one put on learning self-control? Is there value in mastering something as powerful as sexual desire? Having been through the experience, I answered "Yes" to both questions. Without the self-discipline I had adopted, a promised reverence for the sacredness and beauty of sex would never develop. And without a reverence for the power of procreation, humans would eventually behave no differently than animals.

OFF TO PALACIO, THEN BAPTISMS

IT's 6:30 AM, and it being document renewal time, Elder Bertram and I drag ourselves through cold, dark, winter streets to the bus station for a two-and-a-half-hour ride to downtown Palacio. And though it's an inconvenience, I'm grateful for a break in the routine—even if it's only a quick jaunt there and back.

9:00 a.m. Once at the Palacio bus terminal, we hike downtown, then over to the building where our paperwork will be updated. The red tape takes twenty minutes to process. Then we race back to the terminal with enough time left over to miss the bus home by five minutes.

9:05 a.m. Skulking off to the ticket booth, we book passage for the 1:30 p.m. coach, then go upstairs and sit.

9:10 a.m. While comparing receipts to figure out who-owes-who-what for breakfast and bus tickets, we spot Elder Bertram's former companion and another elder coming down the stairs, and we call them over. After exchanging hugs and greetings, we talk for a bit and then they're on their way.

9:30 a.m. Two hours at our disposal and with nothing to do, we leave the building, our destination being the electronic games at a local arcade.

9:50 a.m. Back at the terminal after some fruitless searching for the arcade, we consult an indecipherable map. Inquiring at the Information Desk, we receive the address and are on our way, again. We return to the terminal with time to spare.

1:25 p.m. Elder Bertram approaches the driver of what appears to be our bus.

"Is this bus going to Temprano?"

"One-Thirty" says the driver. We understand this to mean that this is *not* our bus. Our bus is number 130. Apparently, it hasn't yet arrived.

1:30 p.m. We take up residence on an outside bench, where we have a commanding view of all vehicles coming and going. No mistakes this time.

1:31 p.m. Several buses depart, including the one driven by chatty "Mr. 130." Ours is probably just a little late. Happens all the time.

1:40 p.m. Suspecting something has gone horribly wrong, we discover that our bus left for Temprano without us. The one driven by the chatty Mr. 130.

1:45 p.m. Skulking off to the ticket booth, we book passage for the 2:30 p.m. coach, then go upstairs and sit, embarrassed but not angry—for how can you be mad at someone else when you're up to your neck in it, as well?

2:20 p.m. "Is this the bus going to Temprano at 2:30?"

"Yes," the driver says.

2:25 p.m. "Is this the bus that . . ."

"Yes," the driver says.

2:30 p.m. Finally in the correct vehicle, Elder Bertram and I are headed home.

Sometime Later: The bus stops. The driver spends forty-five minutes repairing a tire.

7:30 p.m. We arrive in Temprano. We try to come up with a plausible story that doesn't make us look like morons. We fail miserably.

BY THE MIDDLE OF JUNE, the flu epidemic had affected 200,000 people. I could feel sickness creeping into my body throughout P-Day. As I wrote letters. Copied music from the GE to George's recorder. Played Estanciero in Bertram's pension. It was going to be bad, and I especially dreaded the arrival of the Sore Throat, that harbinger of all things flu-like.

The following morning the flu was worse, so Elder George and I slept in—until 8:30, when I heard yelling out front. It was Bertram and Watkins. My comp resurrected himself and opened the windows in time to see Elder B vaulting the wall, Olympic style. He told us to get on our grubbies. It was our turn to clean the chapel. I told him we'd be there if I got to feeling better. But due to a case of terminal boredom, I was willing to suffer at the church rather than lie in bed, staring at the wall and hating life. Groaning, I arose, head pounding, ears plugged, throat sore. After breakfast we headed out. Once at church, Elder George cleaned the front windows while I dusted and wiped chapel pews for an hour and a half. By the time we finished I was exhausted and in a daze.

Just before noon we found out there was a baptism scheduled for 4 p.m.—and that it was at risk, due to a faulty water heater. Some would ask, "Where's your pioneer spirit? Didn't you Mormons used to baptize people in freezing water in the middle of winter?" Maybe they did. But this wasn't the 1850s. We no longer crapped in the woods. And we sure weren't pioneers. And if we didn't get some water heated up for the impending baptism, those investigators wouldn't be the only ones refusing to step down into an icy pool at the appointed moment. The only solution was to start fires in the church's back lot to heat the needed water.

Working in three teams of two each, we divided up the work. One group started looking for wood. Another started the hunt for three kettles. The third would get fires started with any scrap wood lying around the lot.

Once the fires were lit, screens were placed over the flames. For the rest of the morning and afternoon we all took turns chopping wood and tending fires. And somewhere along the way I forgot about my troubles.

Every so often when the water felt hot enough, several of us would haul a 300-pound container full of it across the lot, in through the back doors, over several yards of slippery linoleum, then dump the water into the font, where it cooled off faster than we could heat it. After several hours of this the water was luke-warm, at best, and the font still not full. We stopped heating water and placed a propane tank in the bottom of the font for displacement. The baptism went on as scheduled. To ensure that the fires didn't go to waste, we had a barbecue later on.

BETWEEN MY RECOVERING FROM THE FLU and our growing lack of desire to work, Elder George and I arose at 11:30 a.m., one day—just in time for lunch. Afterward, I tried to study the charlas, but my mind kept wandering, distracted in part by my companion, who was copying music from one tape recorder to the other. About the time we overcame inertia long enough to tire out, in walked Bertram and Watkins. Their electric-powered shower had blown up, so they needed to use ours. This led to a talkfest that didn't end until 7 p.m., when Elder G and I escaped the apartment long enough to visit Maldonado.

We wanted to see how he was preparing for his Saturday baptism.

Two days later we accompanied Señor M and his girlfriend to a city office for the morning nuptials, having brought some flowers for the bride. With fifteen of us crammed into that small room, the couple stood in front of a desk where a man and woman took turns reading official documents. Then Maldonado and his fiancé took turns signing the documents. The couple then took their vows and the officiators pronounced them Man and Under-Aged Wife. Then we shook hands and congratulated them. For better or for worse, the business took all of ten minutes.

Saturday, we spent most of the day preparing for the Maldonado baptism by tending fires in the chapel's back lot. Shortly before the service, Elder Gordon rode with the mission director to pick up the newlyweds. Señor Maldonado was sick with a hip infection, the swelling causing him great pain every time he took a step. But we said we'd wait. Elder G and I stood around outside, making small talk and watching gliders miles high, doing lazy loops and mile-wide swoops. Eventually we got the young couple to the church, only to find out that the white baptismal clothing was locked safe and sound in a cabinet, the key's owner nowhere to be found. While the mission director went in search, another member started picking the lock with a stiff piece of wire. Sensing a break in the action, my fellow missionaries and I traded off going to the store to buy kilos of mandarin oranges, while the rest of us tended fires and took turns worrying.

Once word went out that the cabinet door had been jimmied open, Señor and Señora Maldonado were ushered off to respective restrooms and fitted for baptismal clothing. Then the service began. Meanwhile, we lugged in one last tub of hot water, dumped it, and tested the temperature. Calling it luke-warm would be generous, evidenced by the little gasps that Señora Maldonado subsequently made with each descending step into the font. I wondered why we'd gone to all the trouble. But baptism is a sacred ordinance, the entryway into the Lord's Church. Anything we could do to make the experience more pleasant was worth the effort. Afterward we invited the couple to the church for a small wedding celebration party. Theirs was the first baptism the branch had seen in three and a half months.

CHARLA E, THEN MALAISE

June 29TH. Having told everyone within earshot that I was going to pass off Charla E by the following day, I decided to stay up late Tuesday evening, studying. And fervent study it would take, since I didn't know the last three concepts, the first four more than a little fuzzy. I blamed the tardiness on my "slothful nature," as I called it in the journal. Study consisted of the usual pattern: read a paragraph, then try to recite it from memory, then on to the next paragraph and more reciting, and on and on, flip charts incorporated into the flow, when necessary. After accumulating enough strung-together paragraphs in short-term memory, I'd go for longer and longer groups of words, connecting the associated pieces of this mental quilt. I only lasted until midnight, when reasoning and cognitive functions—unwilling to further support my impulsive plan—said the hell with it.

The next morning, we remained in the pension as I continued studying and cramming. After lunch I started in again, then attempted to pass off said charla an hour later. Due to my unfamiliarity with Concepts 1 through 4, I failed miserably. Beaten by the written word, I gave up and we went to work, ending up at Señora Miranda's house for a charla with her and her daughter. The family was progressing well, and attending Church activities. We believed we could baptize all three family members. From there it was on to Señor Gallardo's, where he dropped a bombshell: he was not married to his "wife." He'd been living with the family for eleven years. But since his wife couldn't get a divorce from her current husband, they were in a common-law marriage. Their road to baptism was blocked.

INDEPENDENCE DAY FOR THE U.S. was two days away and here we were, entering the coldest part of the year. The reversal of seasons was still hard to comprehend. It had been a crisp thirty degrees the last few mornings, wind blowing the entire time. The apartment felt like forty, our only defense being a small gas stove. We could easily use up a whole tank of propane in a week and a half, but it was worth every peso. Despite the frigid air inside and out, my cold was gone, except for the cough and an occasional sore throat.

As the early days of July came and went, my image of what constituted a normal, productive work day began to blur. There were too many variables at play. Regardless, I was still willing to chastise myself and whoever I was working with (within the confines of my journal, of course) when we got little or nothing done with the precious time allotted us.

On 3 July, I noted that at 2 a.m. my companion and I awoke. It took me two hours to get back to sleep, Elder George four. Up at 8:30, we wolfed down some chow, then went to a contact's house. The wife told us her husband wasn't there, so we dropped off our weekly reports at the church, wasting time there for one and a half hours. Then Elder Bertram and I went to the post office to mail off his letters. We stopped by a candy store on the corner of the plaza before returning to the church. Elder George and I studied in the pensión until lunch. After the siesta, we taught the Gallardo family, and there was a good spirit in the home. Though the rest of the time isn't described, it seemed a little harsh to be calling the day a waste of time.

That said, we were entering a period of "slackness," with understandable results. During district meeting we spent most of the morning discussing the Work, and the way that some of the members felt about us. Due to the immature and disrespectful behavior of a few missionaries over the last couple years, the members didn't appear to trust us much. We talked about how to repair the damage done, and identified members who did trust us. We reminded each other of the Prophet's promise—that the Argentina-Palacio Mission was ready for the "harvest." But in order to baptize more people, we'd need to work with the members. Accordingly, we spent the rest of the morning either looking for members who weren't at home or knocking doors, the latter a task we performed without any enthusiasm or desire—or any degree of success.

Returning home at 5:30 p.m., we went to the chapel to prepare a lesson for English class. Racking our brains for a half hour, we came up with nothing, said event coinciding with the arrival of the other elders. We then shot the breeze until 9:00 p.m., the useful part of the day now officially at an end.

At 2:30 a.m. Elder G's incessant snoring penetrated my defenses. Awake and pissed off at my companion, who continued to rest in the arms of Morpheus, I stewed for a while before being able to go back to sleep. At 6 a.m. I again awoke, residual righteous indignation stirring within. Remembering our recent laxity with the mission rules, I did some exercising for the first time in a month. But due to sleep deficit, my emotions were on a roller coaster the rest of the day. Along the way Elder G kept playing jokes on me, saying to turn down one street while he went the other way. After the third time, I was so angry I slammed the front end of my bike down hard, bending the forks at a dangerous angle— which meant a trip to the bicycle shop.

ONE MORNING AT 4 AM, Elder George left for a trip with Elder Gordon to a DL/ZL conference. Since the other elders were at the mercy of a less than punctual bus system, we had no idea when, or if, they would return. In their absence, I was to work with Elder Bertram. Though there's no record of us having done anything of substance that day, I did end up in his pensión for quite a while that evening, writing letters and staving off hypothermia. The room had no access to a heating system. Being ten by ten feet and with a high ceiling, it was the equivalent of a concrete-lined refrigerator.

In a letter to Mom I asked about the Bicentennial celebration, then told her that ours was a bust, it being Sunday, us without firecrackers or a place to celebrate—unless we wanted every cop in the vicinity on our backs after the first Black Cat exploded. I mentioned the approach of July 9th, Argentina's version of Independence Day—that it would be a repeat of May 25th with a short and not very exciting parade. I thought it sad that few people would be attending the festivities because they were afraid of someone shooting them or tossing a bomb into a crowd. But they had reason to fear, based on current news reports: a bank bombed; five Catholic priests shot to death in Buenos Aires; people being hauled away for "questioning" and never seen or heard from again. But at the time, this was not part of our experience. We were there to help people find God, regardless of what was going on in the world.

It was 1:30 a.m. With no sign of the other elders, letter writing continued. Bertram's room grew colder by the hour, our only respite being a can full of flaming alcohol. The upside to this substance was that it wouldn't explode when lit, though the warmth it provided was more psychological than substantial. At 1:45 a.m. I said goodbye to Mom, then began another letter as Elder B and I drifted into the quiet, early morning oblivion . . .

ON JULY 14TH I passed off Charla E. The load was feeling a little lighter, though I had to ignore the shame I'd experience if I dwelt on my tardy progress. There were four of the buggers left to go.

MALAISE REDUX, THEN HUMILIATION

THURSDAY, 15 JULY. We boarded the 6:30 a.m. bus for a zone conference in Villa Maria. I hadn't seen Elders Wales and Rodriguez get on at the station, but soon spotted them ahead, through the windshield. They were waiting at a bus stop near the city park, on the edge of town. As the bus sped past, they realized it would've been a good idea to signal the driver. It was hard not to laugh. Sometime after we arrived in VM, they showed up, having to buy a new set of tickets before they could catch another bus.

The conference was good, the emphasis this time on the importance of baptisms, not mission rules. Afterward there was the usual lineup for Hepatitis shots. I got light-headed just watching. This was followed by a queasy lunch of milk and hot dogs. We then went to a restaurant for real food, my intake limited to a banana liquado. Running to the terminal, we missed our bus by five minutes, which meant another round of ticket buying and letter writing.

I sent a missive off to Mom, recounting the reports we'd received about two missionaries up north in the Uruguay/Paraguay area. They'd been kidnapped by extremists who wanted $500,000 ransom. The President of the Church refused to pay. One thing led to another and eventually the police tracked them down, but not before one of the elders took some friendly fire during the rescue effort. Nine days shy of going home, the missionary recovered from his wounds. I was told by someone familiar with South American justice that the authorities tossed the crooks into a pool full of piranhas.

WEDNESDAY THE 21ST MARKED FIVE MONTHS in Río 4. My comp sick in bed, I went to the other elders' pensión to work. As I walked into the room, they pulled a large package out from behind a bed—from Grandma Net. We ripped the box open, tossed aside the tee shirts and socks, and went to work on the enclosed candy. The only thing the post office stole was a few pieces of chocolate and two rolls of Certs.

After five days in bed, Elder George was stir-crazy. He wanted to get out and do something. Anything. So we engaged in some less than enthusiastic door-knocking, then visited members. Adding to our down mood, the evening appointments fell through. Back to the pensión we went before 7 p.m. Later I wrote in the journal about how much Elder Bertram and I were discussing transfers. I seemed to be thinking about it "too much," waiting with bated breath every Thursday night—that time of the week when transfers seemed to happen. But like the Biblical thief in the night, so were transfers for me.

IT WAS LATE JULY and Elder George was getting on my nerves, my anger flaring about "stupid little things" he was doing. I blamed the adversary for the situation, reasoning that it was just one more way for the powers of darkness to hinder the Work. It didn't make sense, otherwise. We were doing fine with our personal and companionship goals; getting up on time, exercising, having regular study class. In the end, I decided to swallow my pride and roll with it.

The month almost over, we spent another day engaged in fruitless door knocking, but tried not to let it get to us. That evening we visited with Señora Gallardo, since her hubby hadn't shown up for the appointment. We somehow got into a lengthy discussion with her and her daughter about birth control and why Mormon families were so large. Having run out of things to do, we returned home an hour early and were unwinding when Elders B and his comp appeared. We got carried away with transfer talk, but change was in the air and we could feel it.

After all the weeks of goofing off we'd been engaged in, I believed I'd have to work my tail off in order to regain the spiritual balance in my life, not to mention restoring the Lord's trust in me as a fit purveyor of His word. Maybe He wanted to see how hard I was willing to work to find and baptize sincere truth-seekers. All I knew was that regardless of how crappy the day seemed to go, it felt good to go to sleep at night having done a full day's work. Amidst it all I occasionally dwelt on the old days when I was away from church. It bothered me that there seemed to be a dark corner in my mind that missed the party life. I didn't want to return to that lifestyle, but the temptation to revel in past follies would sometimes surface, then disappear below the waves.

FRIDAY AT 5 AM we traveled to the Palacio area conference, grabbing some bus sleep before arriving three and a half hours later for a dash across town to the church. There were eighty missionaries in attendance. The theme of the meeting was baptisms: how to get them, why we needed them and why we hadn't been getting them the way the Lord wanted us to. President Parón then brought up a sore subject.

"Before you can receive the Spirit's help, you must *obtain* His word. By a show of hands, how many of you have not finished passing off your charlas?"

Embarrassed, I raised mine, one of only fifteen. Despite the public humiliation, though, I enjoyed the meeting, revitalized by the messages we received.

One of the byproducts of conferences was transfers. After the area meeting we found out that Gabi, Clark, and Nakona had been transferred south to Santa Fe. The notification did little to allay Elder Bertram's conviction that before the first week of August ended, he'd be on a bus. He even had the destination figured out. As for my destiny, I hadn't a clue. I had enough problems with my thoughts, without the transfer speculation game complicating matters.

Before heading back, we stopped by the mission home, as the President wanted to talk to my companion. I wanted to talk to Parón, my struggles with the charlas along for the confessional ride. Nervous about the President's reaction to what I'd tell him, I was starting to think I should just keep my mouth shut. But he did nothing more than listen, and gave me loving counsel. The sorrow I'd been experiencing was now gone, a great weight lifted from my soul.

AUGUST 2. Suffering a stroke of common sense, Elder George decided to sacrifice his numbered-in-sequence peso note collection. He handed over the $2,000 he owed me, yanking one loose for himself. Making a morning trip through cold, depressing rainfall, we dropped our bikes off at a bike shop in the Centro, then rode a bus the long way to Nievas' house in the country. It would have been faster walking. We played with their kids, and I drank maté (mixed with milk) for the first time. The chilly weather made the scalding brew all the better. Ninety minutes later we caught a bus back to the pensión.

During the afternoon, we hiked twenty blocks to the bike shop. The embarrassed mechanic had done nothing with our conveyances, but told us to come back in an hour. At 5 p.m. we retrieved the bikes and made our freezing, wet way to Gallardo's house—but he was gone on a three-day truck driving job. So off we went to Hermano Torres's place, making small and not so small talk while imbibing maté straight, sans milk. Bitter like dandelion leaves, I hated it. After having a bite to eat we played with their dog and cat for a while, then went home two hours early. But being inside was better than riding around, exposed to the elements, killing time.

The House of Usher mood continued the following day, my comp falling ill that morning. After a few member visits, we spent the better part of the afternoon riding around in the wind and rain before returning home to change our soaked socks and shoes. Unwilling to turn in early, we rode around in the dark, then decided to visit members. But one had company, another was too busy to let us in, and the third family wasn't home. We rode back to the pensión frustrated and dismayed. Three days of door-knocking and we had nothing to show for the effort. Four days of rain and chilling, relentless wind was not helping.

TRANSFER SW

SOMETIMES THERE'S NO ANNOUNCEMENT. You come back to your apartment after a long morning or afternoon and there sits a missionary you haven't seen before. At least you don't remember him being there when you left the place earlier. He smiles and puts out his hand, telling you he's Elder So-and-So, and he's here to replace you. And by the way, you're going Somewhere Else. As a bonus, he may even know who your new comp is. But if he didn't come from where you're going, you'll be in the dark. What you do know is that you're history, and that you'd best get packing.

You drag out the suitcases and bags that you long ago shoved under the bed or into the armoire—no one has a closet in this country—and start looking for everything that's yours. You give back those ties and socks and books and the Frisbee your companion loaned you way back when, and hopefully he gives back all the stuff he borrowed from you. When you're done packing it doesn't all fit. You start tossing things out. Maybe your comp or the New Guy wants the stuff. If not, you chuck it in the armoire or under the bed or into the trash.

Then the wait begins. It could be a few hours. Or half a day. Or twenty-four hours later. You sit around, trying to find something to do. Maybe the three of you go out for a meal. One thing you notice is how crowded the room has become. You are the one taking up valuable apartment real estate. You've been here the longest. You're the old

167

hand. You should be the one staying, but you're not. Conversation becomes awkward. If you and your comp got along great, the New Guy struggles for things to say. If your comp and you have had enough of each other, the New Guy is being asked all sorts of questions, and not by you—which makes the New Guy uncomfortable, while you shake your head and say, "Yeah. Just like him. Can't wait to get rid of me . . ."

And so it came to pass that at 9 a.m. on August 5th, Elders B and W stopped by to inform me that I'd be accompanying Bertram to the bus station that afternoon. We were on transfer to Santa Fe. It had finally happened, and I didn't know how to react. I was glad for the change of faces and scenery, but scared about leaving what had become a familiar port in an otherwise unfamiliar sea. All the friends I'd made, the streets I'd traveled, the well-worn dirt paths, an apartment that felt like home, and most of all a companion who I'd gotten to know like a brother.

I started packing, but gave up after three and a half hours. Then we took my bike to the depot and sent it off by train. After going downtown one last time, we returned home and I finished packing. The end result was a briefcase, portfolio, two suitcases, a camera case, and that damned Singer projector—a tough load to carry all at once. Saying goodbye to what had been my home for over five months, I rode with Elder George via taxi to the terminal. We met with Bertram, and at

4 p.m. he and I boarded a bus for the eight-hour trip west to Santa Fe.

You enter the bus in a daze, feeling every particle of the transition. As the bus pulls away, you try to settle in and relax. The task is easier if there's another missionary there. If not, you're left alone with your thoughts for what could be hours and hours. Once the bus arrives, you disembark, a new companion and DL waiting nearby. You shake hands and are off to your new adventure.

IT WAS AFTER MIDNIGHT when we arrived in the big city, exhausted from a 400-kilometer trip across the provinces of Palacio, San Luis, and the better part of Santa Fe—a blur of unfamiliar towns, cities, and countryside that all looked the same before or after sunset. Half-stumbling off the bus, I unloaded my stuff onto a rolling cart and joined Bertram in search of a taxi.

Our driver was a friendly sort who rambled on about the sad state of the world and why people needed more faith in God. Then we were on our way to Bertram's new digs. The location of my new place—Jugo—hadn't been a concern. Probably the next neighborhood over from Elder B's. We arrived at the right address and unloaded everything. I asked how much the fare was: 400 pesos. Thinking that a little overpriced, I paid him anyway, but being short of change, I handed him a 1,000-peso note. He shoved some one-hundred-peso notes back at me. I looked at him and he looked back in a strange way. As the engine revved up and I counted the notes, he pulled away. "One hundred pesos short," I mumbled as the taxi raced off at high speed. Evidently, the driver needed more faith in God.

Entering the house, we discovered several things: 1) The other elders didn't know Bertram was coming; 2) There was no place for me to sleep; and 3) Jugo was a twenty-minute bus ride south. Odd elder out, I lugged my worldly belongings—now referred to as "my crap"— to a bus stop and sat down. Too tired to be pissed, I tried to stay warm, wondering if city buses ran at 2 a.m., when one lumbered in my direction.

The last few bleary miles were along a two-lane road, our headlights illuminating a canopy of overarching trees that looked like the inside surface of a green tunnel. A beautiful ride, had I been awake enough to appreciate it. I wondered if the driver would know where to stop. Street lights ahead, the bus turned to the right. We ascended for a half mile to an intersection, where the bus stopped and the driver motioned to me. Then I was down the steps, the vehicle roaring off as I crossed the street, crumpled address in hand: Jose Correa 181. Thankfully, the place was only a couple blocks distant—a Spanish colonial with tiled roof and a palm tree out front. It was 2:30 a.m. I knocked on the door and a small, sixty-ish woman peered out. I introduced myself, then she invited me in, pleasant and meek, even at this hour. She pointed me through a doorway past the kitchen to another door on the left. I opened it and fumbled with my left hand for a light switch. A sleepy figure turned over in his bed and looked up at me.

"Oh—you're the new elder!"

We talked for a bit. Then I collapsed on my bed.

JUGO

I OPENED MY EYES TO THE TRINITY. They were standing on a long, reddish-brown tapestry that hung on the far wall, above an armoire and a small table. Past the empty night stand, a clock showed 10:45 a.m. Past Elder Stephens's bed was a view out the window of a brick wall and blue sky. As I sat up, the effects of a leaden head cold made me wince.

I staggered out the door and across a tiled studio floor, the scent of lacquer heavy in the air. Tables and easels held brushes, paint tubes, and rags, surrounded by canvases empty and full. Leaning against two walls were seascapes, landscapes, and religious images in various stages of completion, unoccupied wooden frames resting here and there.

The bathroom being my immediate goal, I approached a semi-opaque, stained-glass door that gave the narrow room a churchy, reverential feel, despite the crude facilities within. Accordingly, I was expecting more than the concrete bench, a tapered foot-wide hole in its center, with nary a handhold in view. Following the business portion of the program, I reached heavenward for

173

an oval-shaped handle dangling at the end of a chain. One pull and the water from a gravity-fed tank washed all troubles away. Exiting the baño, I saw a glass-paned door to the right. Beyond this lay the patio, a frost-burned garden, small trees, and a grape arbor. A tall, brown-brick wall surrounded the back yard.

Seated on his bed, Elder Stephens was biding his time until I could recover enough to rejoin the living. Tall and lanky, with brown hair parted down the middle, he hailed from Utah, and had been in the LTM the same time as I, but a month ahead. Since he'd passed off his charlas long ago, he'd be the senior companion, by default. He introduced me to the landlord-painter, the painter's wife, and their jet black, Heinz 57 dog, Negro (pronounced NAY-guh-doh, meaning "black-colored"). We ate a quick lunch and wrote letters like mad until 5 p.m. With a little more than an hour of winter daylight left, Elder Stephens introduced me to the area.

WE TAKE A TWENTY-MINUTE BUS RIDE along a beautiful tree-lined highway—the same one I traveled the previous night—to a zone conference at the stake center in downtown Santa Fe. There are inspiring talks aimed at lifting our spirits, reminding us of our duties, and giving us ideas about new ways to teach. Afterward, Elder Stephens and I choose to walk back to the city center with Elder Southern (our Zone Leader), his comp, and Hermanas Maldonado and Gruen.

Elder S has been joking about going to the movies. Since movie attendance is against mission rules, I assume the ZL is playing a joke on me, the new guy. And it stands to reason. Southern has a reputation for rule-breaking. Having gotten into a contest with another ZL, the two of them tried to see who could break the most mission rules. While interesting, I consider Elder Southern a dumbass for behaving in such a way. After all, what's the point? Is he some sort of evil genius, or merely a gifted practical joker? Has the Lord given him some sort of pass that exempts him from punishment? Since that doesn't make sense, I stick with the dumbass scenario.

Stopping in front of a theater, our illustrious leader approaches the ticket box.

"Elder Stephens," I ask. "What's he doing?"

"Buying tickets, from the looks of it."

"But that's—"

"I know, Elder . . ."

Southern finalizes his transaction and hands tickets to the sisters, then heads our direction.

"Well, Elder," my comp says. "We can't just let them go in there by themselves. Two-on-two, you know."

And with that bit of rationalization we accept our forbidden fruit from Elder Southern and enter the theater doors. Briefcase in hand, I feel horribly out of place. What am I doing here? What will be the aftermath of this heinous disregard for the Rules? Even at this stage of the mission, rule-keeping is still on my mind. I want to do the right thing. But life doesn't always present us with cut-and-dried situations, custom-made for a binary thumb up or down. Compromises must be made.

I cross the lobby and give my ticket to the doorman. Then I'm through a curtain and down an inclined walkway, feeling about as conspicuous as a flashing light on a cop car. What is the crowd thinking of our group of well-dressed people? At the very least, we're overdressed for a night at the cinema.

"Crime on the Moon" is the first feature, and it stinks. Even with sub-titles, it's hard to sit through something so poorly acted and written. After what seems like four hours, the second film begins. It's *Doc Savage*, but unlike its predecessor, this movie is thoroughly entertaining, a tongue-in-cheek affair after the manner of all good comic books. And for the first time in a while I'm able to relax and laugh at some mindless entertainment.

At 11:45 p.m. we part ways with the other rule-breakers as Stephens and I go off in search of a bus stop. Sometime later we find one on a dim street corner. As we discuss the day's events, a well-dressed, middle-aged fellow approaches, and he's more than tipsy.

"Please stop talking in English," he says.

Chalking up the offense to his inebriation, we apologize. Then he moves closer.

"You know," he says, as if confessing, "I come from France, but I've been to your country a few times. God bless America!"

We nod. He sways.

"I speak French, Italian, English, and Spanish."

From there he launches into his life story, vignette-by-vignette, a few more "God bless Americas" tossed in for good measure, before the bus mercifully arrives. I hate drunk-talk, and his borders on the belligerent. Hoping we're done with him, we climb the steps, but he raises his hand at the top.

"Please. I will pay for your tickets. Please."

Thanking him, we find a seat halfway back and settle in for short naps, already two hours past our appointed bedtimes. Our benefactor makes his shaky way through the bus, plopping down in the seat ahead of us, where he continues his lively repartee for the next forty-five minutes. Then he says, "Adios," descends, and shambles off into the dark.

Once at our stop, we trudge home, falling into our beds, exhausted. So ends my second full day in Jugo. A few days later I relate my cinematic adventure in a letter to Elder George, swearing him to secrecy.

CHURCH, ISABEL, AND CODEINE

THAT FIRST SUNDAY was an adjustment. Downsizing from a church building to a house, sacrament meeting was held in what would have been the living room. Subsequent classes took place in former bedrooms or the kitchen. But being in a sacrament meeting where only twenty-five people were in attendance made me realize how much work we had ahead of us. Before the meeting ended, I was introduced to President Gonzales, a soft-spoken, humble man who served on the local police force.

Within the next few days I learned the routine for meals: on our own for breakfast, next door for lunch, and in the evening a small meal awaiting us, prepared by the Señora. The bicycles were stored in the alley outside our window. As for the Work, I had met many of the branch members, as well as our small group of investigators.

At mid-week, we were scheduled to teach Charlas F and H to Isabel, a pretty woman in her early thirties. She had accepted the baptismal challenge, and had to receive two more discussions before her interview with the ZLs, two days hence. We stayed in the pension all morning, studying. I didn't know either discussion very well, and by fire-out time in the afternoon I was still a bundle of nerves. Maybe it was due to lack of preparation. Possibly the fact that a lot was riding on the double lesson.

Dressing in a hurry, I searched for a shoehorn, knocking my red alarm clock off the desk. The glass face smashed to bits, jarring my nerves as I shook out the glass shards and put it back. Swearing, I pulled too hard on a shoelace and it snapped, as had my composure. I felt as if someone or something was trying to drive me over the edge. Finally escaping the clutches of the apartment, we raced our bikes to Isabel's home. She wasn't there.

The following day we met with Isabel, but I was still nervous. Despite the extra preparation time we'd gained,

I forgot most of my assigned concepts, and reluctantly handed the teaching reins back to Elder Stephens. By the time the discussion ended, Isabel was having second thoughts about baptism. We knew she'd felt the Spirit's influence and had a testimony; the trouble was her family and boyfriend. Both parties were staunch Catholics and were giving her a hard time about investigating a church so different from their own. Accordingly, Isabel skipped out on her subsequent bap interview with the ZLs and was absent from church the following Sunday, as well.

On the upside, I was able to give a decent ten-minute talk in sacrament meeting on missionary work, despite my deficiencies with the language. It was my first experience doing so. Having succeeded, the fear of failure evaporated for the time being. It was so satisfying to organize and deliver something substantive that I could share with others.

On the downside, the head cold I'd brought with me from Temprano persisted. Brief coughing spells turned into 3 a.m. hacking sessions that made my stomach, chest, and head ache from the exertion. The cold had also developed into a sore throat, a stuffed-up head, and a plugged right ear. Pressure would build, resulting in an ear ache for which there seemed no relief. I tried to work through it during the day, but it was becoming an increasing distraction. During church I asked one of the women about possible cures. She suggested rolling a newspaper into a cone, then placing the tip of it in my ear, the other end held over an open flame, thus pulling the trapped air out. Not trusting the local doctors, I was willing to try anything.

MONDAY FOUND US STILL LOOKING for Isabel and failing. But we began teaching C to Jaime, a young fellow who told us from the very beginning that he wanted to be baptized. While heartening, we told him he'd need to learn the basics; then he could make up his mind about joining the Church. That evening we met the Coronel family, and taught them all of Charla C. The Spirit's presence was strong in their humble, two-room, adobe home. Señor C told us he was searching for the true church and believed we were showing him where to find it.

Later, while teaching D to Jaime and his father, all was well until Concept Three, when I fell victim to a coughing attack. By the time the hacking subsided, I'd forgotten where I was at in the lesson, as had our students. While I caught my breath, Elder Stephens took over. But having never taught D before, it was his turn to struggle. Regardless, we made it to the end, father and son enjoying the lesson.

TIRED OF FEELING LIKE HELL, I made a trip to the pharmacy and bought some cough medicine. It wasn't until returning to the house that I read the label, the main ingredients being alcohol and codeine (essence of chloroform tossed into the mix, just for fun). I was concerned about the Word of Wisdom. Would I be breaking it by drinking this elixir? There's the letter of the law. But there's also that component related to intent: the spirit of the law. If I were buying the cough syrup to merely get a buzz, I was violating the spirit of the law *and* the letter. But that was not my intent. Besides, if I didn't find relief soon, I'd end up in the ER with a separated rib, detached retina, or worse.

I cracked open the bottle, measured out the pre-scribed dose, and downed the cherry-flavored syrup. As it blazed a warm, druggy trail down my throat and esophagus I was reminded of the way schnapps and other liquors had felt, in my party days, a mere eighteen months before. What in the world was I doing? *No, Dan,* I reminded myself. *This is different.* After ten minutes or so I had to admit that the medicine made me feel pretty good. The buzz was back. But the throat-ripping cough was gone.

As for Isabel, she decided she didn't want to be bap-tized, so she hid from us, afraid we'd give her a hard time. Early in the week we stopped by a member's home at 10 p.m., and there sat Isabel and her boyfriend. They'd had a long talk, coming to an agreement about her further involvement with the Mormons. The decision had not been in her favor.

Despite this setback, though, Elder Stephens and I were progressing with other investigators. With this suc-cess came a closeness to the Lord that I'd never experi-enced before. His support was palpable, and I was deeply grateful. I was teaching discussions with confidence. My testimony was growing. I was learning more by the Spirit about the nature of Heavenly Father and Jesus Christ. But I was also learning that with great blessings come more temptations and trials. It reminded me of a warrior in the midst of battle, slaying the enemy, at the same time taking the occasional arrow for his efforts. And all the while his thoughts are darting here and there—focused one moment on victory, then distracted the very next by fear, doubt, or the desire to flee.

In the case of the cough syrup, what had begun as a blessing soon became an ethical challenge: was I taking the stuff due to the sickness, or for the buzz? Yes, I was finally getting a good night's sleep. And yes, the early morning cough attacks were subsiding. And yes, I could breathe normally again. But I was waking up in the middle of the night to take a justified swig. I had also taken to carrying the bottle in my overcoat while we were out visiting people. The air was cold, and to make sure I didn't cough again, I'd stop every so often and take a pull at the bottle. But the cough was nearly gone. What the hell was I doing to myself? After a week of this behavior, I tossed my former-friend-turned-hell-brew into the trash.

As for the cold itself, I was still waking up every morning with a plugged right ear. And the condition was worsening every day. Desperate for relief, I took the church lady's advice. I rolled a newspaper into a cone, started the heater and assumed the position. Due to the fact that the end of the cone kept catching on fire, the enterprise was a failure. But I *was* able to do a passable imitation of Nipper, the RCA Victor record label dog, its ear cocked toward an old Victrola for time and all eternity.

EVENTUALLY THE ILLNESS PASSED. My senses returned. I was finally able to appreciate the beauty of the town I was in. Jugo was situated in a valley at the base of the Cordillera mountain range, some fifteen miles distant. It was as verdant a place as I'd seen since leaving Oregon. Though the immediate neighborhood was one bare-dirt yard after another, a half-mile away began mile after mile of olive groves and vineyards, grapes being the principal product. One had only to look three blocks from our house, to the famous bodega Giol. Surrounded by fences and walls, the processing plant worked night and day producing wine that was shipped across the country and around the world. Along the property's edge—attached to the power line poles—ran eight-inch diameter aluminum pipes through which sloshed grape juice or wine. What spilled out ran in purple streams through the ditches below.

POVERTY AND A PISSED-OFF ZL

THE FOUR-MONTH OLD GOVERNMENT was struggling to govern, the resultant strife nowhere more apparent than in the economy. Inflation outstripped pay raises, and prices at the local markets rose every day, the Argentines feeling a familiar pinch in their pocketbooks. Though mild by comparison, I was struggling too.

Due to a bank error, I and my fellow missionaries were broke. There were no ATMs. No checking accounts. None of us was allowed to carry credit cards or American currency with us. We had to fend for ourselves until the mission home could get money sent to us. With only a few pesos to my name I spent my 22nd birthday/P-Day in the pension, writing letters and listening to Beatles music. In such a fiscal state of mind, I wrote to my mother, explaining the best way to send money so the postal authorities wouldn't find and steal it:

> *"Take a large, thick magazine, and place the currency in between the pages somewhere near the center of the magazine. Then glue the two pages together—the ones on either side of the bill. Then you fold the magazine— double it over, that is. Then make sure the crease is good when you fold it. When the people in Customs open the package, they are going to start leafing through the magazine. But they won't be able to straighten the magazine (because of the crease), and who has time to look through every page?"*

After describing the vineyards, I talked about the grape vines that would soon be budding with leaves. Spring was still eight weeks away, and I looked forward to the season I'd been robbed of upon leaving the States and going straight into summer. I wondered if there was such a thing as "season lag."

During the evening, we stopped by the home of Hermana Perez/Celoni, a good friend of ours from the branch. A single mother with three kids to feed, she'd prepared a birthday cake and party for me. Not a rich woman, her sacrifice was beyond touching, one of the many reasons I loved the people in this country. Following the party and a hike to the church building to see how a dance was going, we arrived back home at 2:30 a.m., exhausted.

The following evening, we were returning from an archeology presentation at the Guaymallen chapel when several soldiers or policemen—it was hard to tell which—strolled out in front of the bus, arms raised high. I felt for the document pouch in my shirt pocket. The driver stopped. Uniformed men boarded. Small, sinister-looking machine guns swung from their shoulder straps as the officers moved slowly along the aisle.

"Documents, please."

I handed mine over, having separated them from the White Bible they were bundled with. As usual, the paperwork was a comfort to be carrying. I shuddered to think what would have happened had I left them at the apartment.

Within a couple days the ZLs called, saying they had money for us. We dropped everything and caught a bus to Santa Fe, only to find out there was only 400 mil available.

"Sorry Elders, but the checks still haven't been cashed," Elder Southern said as he approached me.

"Elder Hiland, we just received a letter from Elder George in Temprano."

"Really?" I gulped.

"He asked if it was true that our district went to the movies. He says that you sent him a letter with *all the details.*"

My ZL sounded pissed.

"So—is this true?"

"Yes. I sent him a letter. But I told him not to say any—"

"Elder Hiland. News of our trip to the cine has spread all over the mission."

As I tried to return his glare, I wondered why Elder G hadn't kept his trap shut. I thought we were friends.

"Well, Elder—you have a big mouth. From now on you are never to be trusted with confidential information again."

Shocked at his outburst, I didn't know what to say. I was embarrassed, yet angry at his twisted set of ethics. In his mind, it was okay to break mission rules, yet not kosher to speak of it afterwards. It reminded me of what the Book of Mormon refers to as "secret combinations," those corrupt, Mafia-like organizations that eventually bring down any society they're allowed to flourish in. And though I despised any good old boy network, I was complicit as well. Hadn't I sworn my former companion to secrecy?

"You shouldn't have taken his guff," Elder Stephens said as we headed for the bus stop.

"What?"

"You should have yelled at him. He didn't have any right to talk to you that way." Stephens sounded disappointed in me, as if I'd been cowed by authority.

"Yeah, but—"

The truth was that I didn't yet know how to respond to this kind of crap. I hated looking like a wimp and vowed it wouldn't happen again. It didn't dawn on me until later that by letting the gato out of the bag, I may have caused our illustrious ZL some serious grief with President Parón. Well, at least I could hope so.

Later, I struggled while presenting Charla I to Jaime and his dad. I believed it was due to the business with Southern, and I felt terrible afterwards, convinced I'd lost the ability to teach.

As teaching went, though, things were looking up. We had a new investigator, a woman named Regules. After seeing several flicks, she told us she felt good about what she was reading in the scriptures and believed she'd be ready for baptism in the near future. The fun part of the morning over, we went from store to store passing out flyers for English classes at church—an activity I loathed. I'd been through this in Río 4 and didn't see it yielding much of value. In the afternoon, we responded to another call from the ZLs about funds. Traveling to their place, I received 10,000 sorely needed pesos, sans demeaning lectures from ZL Southern. Furthering my good mood, we were able to teach Charla E to the Coronel family that evening.

INVESTIGATORS, A FUNERAL

As THE DAYS PASSED, so did teaching appointments with Regules, the Coronel family and their relatives. A package from home arrived, which I ripped open like a drowning man grabbing at a life preserver. Its bounty included letters from family and friends, the sacred Beach Boys tape I'd requested, a batch of homesickness-inducing slides from the Portland area, two packages of Kool-Aid, a blank tape, postage stamps, and a slip for another package soon to come. If there was one thing my mother specialized in, it was letters and packages.

The Guidarellis, relatives of Coronel, joined our growing pool of investigators. While pleasant people, their home was sometimes a crap shoot when it came to teaching appointments. But they enjoyed our visits, the wife understanding a lot more than her hubby. The Coronel's were progressing, but in order to be baptized they had to start attending church meetings.

The first morning that we helped them get off the launch pad, they brought along sister-in-law Elsa Riveros. We were late for the first meeting, but in time for the investigator's class. Next came fast and testimony meeting. Though there were only eighteen of us in attendance, the Spirit's influence was strong, intensifying when my comp stood and bore his testimony. As I shared mine, I looked at Señora Riveros. Tears were rolling down her cheeks. After I offered the closing prayer, Señor Coronel and Señora Riveros told us how touched they were by the feelings they'd experienced. Something different, something special they'd never felt before.

By MID-OCTOBER, life caught up to Brother Arce. An unmarried elder in our branch, he'd been a heavy drinker and smoker, until cancer started eating away at his esophagus. Unable to eat the normal way, he was fed via a tube in his stomach. We'd been visiting him to lift his spirits and offer comfort. But his malady was a death sentence that soon took him away. On the day of his burial, a wake was planned, so Elder S and I and a few branch members stopped by to pay our respects. The casket was set up in a main room, a fluorescent crucifix at its head, ornate flower arrangements nearby. The family having decided against an open casket, the coffin was tipped at a thirty-degree angle so folks could catch a glimpse of Arce's face through a glass window. Not a fan of open-casket services, one glimpse was all I could stand. He did look natural, as much as one can being dead, with mouth and eyes closed. But due to the fact that it was a warm spring day and the house not air-conditioned, I wondered how long the family would wait before heading for the cemetery.

I milled around, eating refreshments and trying to blend in. Time dragged by, as it is wont to do at these types of events. Boredom set in. Unable to resist, I returned for another look at our departed friend. His mouth was now partially open, the onset of rictus pulling his lips back. Whether precipitated by gravity or warm air, a small tuft of cotton now showed between the errant lips. Repulsed,

I backed away, reinstating my lifetime ban on open-casket anything. Someone else must have noticed, for soon the coffin was slid into a vehicle, and the procession commenced. Elder S and I biked along between cars, all the way to the cemetery. There it was discovered that the immediate family had made no arrangements for a formalized service. Since some of the branch members were packing hymnals, we gathered together and sung a hymn as the casket was lowered into the ground. One of our elders offered a prayer dedicating the gravesite, everyone in tears.

The following week we visited the Riveros couple, then ended up teaching them and the Coronels the first part of Charla D. It was the first time I'd felt impressed to tell investigators that the warm, calming feeling they were experiencing was the Spirit of the Holy Ghost.

These were the best of times for Elder Stephens and me. While other missionaries were out knocking doors or otherwise struggling to find people, we had five families to work with, all reading the Book of Mormon, and all of them praying about it. They were searching for the true church, and we were the missionaries helping them. The weight of this responsibility wasn't lost on me. I felt the need to work harder than ever to ensure they were all baptized.

DURING THE LAST PART OF AUGUST, I received a letter from President Parón, telling me the time had come to finish passing off my discussions. Accordingly, Southern's companion (Elder Gideon) set Thursday, September 16th, as the day for me to pass off F, H, and J. While I struggled with discussion memorization, some of our investigators were struggling with its content. One night we were explaining the commandments to Coronel and Riveros. My portion included the Ten Commandments, tithing, and the Word of Wisdom. I was nervous about presenting the latter portion, as it involved asking the investigators if we could help them rid their homes of tobacco and alcohol. I posed the question, and everyone but Roberto Riveros was willing to. Later in the conversation, Elder Stephens repeated the question, receiving a pack of cigarettes each from Riveros and Coronel. We promised them that if they would live the Word of Wisdom for three days, they would see a difference in their lives. At that point, it seemed as if Roberto was the only person out of the seven relatives who wasn't ready to be baptized.

That evening I indulged in self-deprecation, blaming myself for the discussion not being "spiritual" enough. If only I'd done a better job of memorizing more of the words and concepts. The scriptures admonish missionaries to "seek to obtain my word; then you shall receive the Spirit." As usual, I was more than willing to believe I had failed as a missionary. Like the deepening grooves in a rutted road, so was my conviction that regardless of how hard I worked, I would never quite measure up. It was a hard way to live.

CHARLA I AND THE BAPTISMS

THE DUE DATE LOOMING LARGE, I spent the morning and siesta of September 9th on Charla F. Though unsure how I was going to pass it off, I plowed ahead. And so it was that just before district meeting the following day, I passed off F. One of three albatrosses had flown from my shoulders. The district meeting that followed, though, was a mixture of relief and uncertainty.

Elder Southern was about to finish his mission and return to the States. He offered some parting words of counsel and wisdom, "a few of which were helpful," as I tersely noted in my journal that evening. I still held a measure of resentment for him. As a former assistant to the president, he'd held the highest position of trust and responsibility a missionary could have in the mission field. Yet he'd screwed around as much as he'd worked. I didn't understand his behavior or why it had been allowed to go on. But for my sake I cut him some slack. Maybe it was because I knew how hard mission life could be. Some of us were more extreme in the way we adapted to the two years of service. I had to assume he was doing the best he could, having overcome his own demons to enter the mission field. Regardless, I let go of my hard feelings toward Elder S so I could move on.

OUR INVESTIGATORS' STRUGGLES CONTINUED. Though Riveros and Coronel were MIA the following Sunday, we were able to spend some quality time with the Guidarelli family at church. Later we found out that while the

Coronels had to stay home and deal with a sick child, Roberto had been out boozing it up the night before. The following evening, though, while teaching H, we challenged the Coronels and Riveros to be baptized, and they accepted.

All in all, we were pleased with the progress the three families had made. Señor Coronel had been cutting down on his cigarette use, day by day. To help him out, we delivered a sack of candy to him as a substitute, only to find out that he had already quit. But he took the candy, anyway. As for Roberto, he promised to stop drinking wine.

ONE OF THE FRINGE BENEFITS of the impending baptisms was a delay in my final date to pass off Charlas H and J. I did spend most of the 17th studying H. But by mid-afternoon I was burned out and tossed in the memorization towel for the rest of the day. Besides, we had more important things to worry about. That evening Stephens and I accompanied Elder Gideon and his new companion, Elder Sorensen, as they traveled to the homes of Coronel and Riveros. They interviewed Señor Coronel and his wife, as well as their daughter. Then the ZLs spoke with Roberto and Elisa Riveros. Gideon informed us that the five were ready for baptism and that we had prepared the families very well. Stephens and I were overjoyed. I knew the Lord had blessed me, probably more than I deserved, in spite of my imperfections. But I knew that God wanted these people in His Church, and I believed it a privilege to be an instrument in His hands. I'd let him down so many times, yet he was still giving me the opportunity to help others, which in turn blessed me with forgiveness.

We traveled to the home of the Guidarelli's. Following those interviews, Elder Gideon said that the Señora understood the gospel very well and had a testimony. As for her spouse, Elder G said that "he doesn't seem to know jack." But the fact that he had a testimony and wanted to get baptized qualified him. Gideon and Sorensen went off to another room and prayed about whether the baptisms should be held the following day or postponed. The answer was to go ahead with the ordinance.

SATURDAY. Having paid their bus fare, we escorted the three families to the Godoy Cruz chapel. We gave them a tour of the building and the baptismal font, then held a short meeting to explain how the baptisms were to be performed. Elder Stephens and I accompanied the three men to the dressing room to don white baptismal jumpsuits. Their wives and Coronel's daughter were attended to in the women's dressing room by ladies from the Jugo Branch.

Stepping into a white, one-piece jumpsuit for the first time since my baptism four years earlier, I realized how far I'd come. Now it was my turn to baptize someone else. My thoughts bounced around between happiness and an obsessive, lingering fear that I might not be worthy to perform the ordinance. I forced my mind away from that distracting train of thought. I had sacred duties to perform. This was no time for self-doubt. *Think about these wonderful families. Stop dwelling on yourself. Be happy for them. Look at how the Lord is blessing you and them.*

I entered the small room where the font was situated and found a seat in the front row of folding chairs, next to our investigators. They looked happy and content, if a little nervous. There was an opening song, then a prayer. A talk on baptism was given, followed by a few words on what it means to receive the Gift of the Holy Ghost. Then it was time. I walked through a side door and down the white, tiled steps into lukewarm water that rose to my waist, pant legs ballooning. I faced the onlookers above. Señor Coronel came down and stood to my left, wearing a shy grin and a look of total trust. I raised my right hand and said:

> *"Having been commissioned of Jesus Christ, I baptize you in the name of the Father, and of the Son, and of the Holy Ghost. Amen."*

With my left foot planted in front of his toes—so he wouldn't slip—I pulled him back and down, under the water, as he held his nose. Then I pulled him back upright. According to the two witnesses standing at water's edge, one of Coronel's elbows had not gone under, so I had to perform the ordinance again. After he was upright, he wiped the water from his teary eyes and hair, and thanked me. I congratulated him and slapped his back. Then I pointed to the stairs. He headed up and away to the dressing room. As I stepped back to let him pass, my foot knocked the drain plug loose. Water began draining out and the crowd giggled, watching my offending foot try to fish the plug back into place. The problem resolved, I baptized Señora Coronel, then her daughter and Señor Guidarelli.

It was during that fourth baptism that a feeling a deep love and happiness for these people washed over me. The experience was new and it was wonderful. It made up for all the uncertainty and doubt that had dug away at me. After I made my way to the dressing room, Elder Stephens baptized the Riveros couple and Señora Guidarelli.

A person becomes a member of Christ's Church by being baptized. When Christ was baptized, the scriptures say that immediately afterward, the Holy Ghost descended upon Jesus in the form of a dove. The Holy Ghost serves as a guide to every baptized person, helping him or her recognize truth. The way the Holy Ghost is conferred upon people is by way of the laying on of hands, and is called "confirmation." We had baptized seven people. Now they all needed to be confirmed. I had never confirmed anyone before, but having studied the guidelines for doing so, I placed my hands on one of our investigator's heads and said something similar to the following:

"Having been commissioned of Jesus Christ, I confirm you a member of the Church of Jesus Christ of Latter-day Saints, and say unto you, receive the Holy Ghost."

I followed with a few other words, as a sort of blessing upon the person, then ended the prayer in the name of Jesus Christ. Having performed that first confirmation, fear was replaced by the same calming feelings of love that I felt during the baptisms. More than that, I experienced a moment of clarity: I knew I was where I was supposed to be, doing what the Lord intended me to be doing.

At meeting's end, Elder Stephens and I accompanied the families home on the bus, then returned to our place, worn out but satisfied with a job well done. The next Sunday all of our new members showed up for church, and we couldn't have been happier. This was the way missionary work was supposed to be.

IN ARGENTINA, the first day of spring is September 21st. Viewing this as a prime opportunity to meet people and proselyte, the ZLs suggested that we spend the day at a local gathering place: the plaza in downtown Jugo. There'd be a big celebration, families everywhere, lots of people enjoying the beautiful weather, everyone's spirits high. Gathering a bundle of pamphlets and copies of the Book of Mormon, we boarded a bus for the Centro. Unsure what to expect, I was looking forward to a new experience. How did people in this country celebrate spring?

The bus arrived at the plaza and we disembarked, ready to shake hands and introduce ourselves. First order of business would be to find a place to set up shop: by a park bench or at the center of the plaza commons?

And what would I use for an opening line? Entering the plaza proper, we looked around. We looked again. The place was empty. Well, actually it wasn't. We were there. It was everyone else who was missing. Evidently, we'd been the only ones interested in celebrating. We gathered our belongings and returned home. We said we'd try again later. But we didn't.

POST-BAPTISM SLUMP AND CHARLA J

As THE AFTERGLOW OF THE BAPTISMS FADED, the pace of life slowed. I became complacent. Tasks such as that of translating the English "Every Member a Missionary" program into Spanish were more like busy work than anything else. I became so frustrated one day that I went outside during the siesta and beat the ground with a mallet. Confiding in the journal about such Jekyll and Hyde behavior, I wondered what was wrong with me. I was having a hard time getting back on my spiritual feet. Part of me believed I had the right to rest up, which conflicted with the work ethic I'd developed. It was the perfect recipe for inner conflict. On top of that, I was again besieged with temptations and thoughts about sex. I was having a hard time coping. But I wasn't alone.

During the September 26th priesthood meeting, Hermanos Zoto and Paez started arguing about something trivial, matters made worse when other men started shoving their oars in. It seemed that the adversary was doing all he could to destroy things in the branch. The only plus that Sabbath was a good evening session with the Regules couple, to whom we showed four flicks. They were well received.

Several days later we shared dinner with the Riveros family. Things were going along nicely until Roberto started talking.

"You know, Elders—a few days ago I was going to renounce my membership in your church."

Your church?

"But then I changed my mind."

Well, that's nice.

"You know, I like reading the scriptures. But I don't like going to church. The meetings are boring."

In essence, he was going inactive—and he'd barely joined. Sort of a worshiper's remorse. But I couldn't say that I was surprised. We'd heard rumors of him starting to drink again. It reminded me of the parable of the seeds. Some fell among the rocks, where there wasn't much soil. The roots had no depth. When other seeds sprung up, the heat of the sun scorched them and they withered away. Had we failed Roberto in some way? We hadn't forced him to join the Church. It was his decision. But how could he have felt, seen and heard so much, yet wanted to walk away from it all? I couldn't understand him.

As for Regules, she enjoyed the charlas, though no one else in the home wanted to listen. Jaime, another investigator, was still meeting with us, but struggled with the idea of paying tithing. With the ushering in of October, I was having my struggles, as well. My journal holds the following entry from Saturday, the 2nd:

> *"I get a sick feeling inside, every time I think about the way in which this lack of self-confidence is holding me back from doing things the way I should be doing them. At times I want to cry out, scream- just to vent this frustration that builds up inside of me. I need to ask the Lord, starting tonight, to help me develop a better self-image."*

Tuesday the 5th I spent the entire morning studying Charla H, intending to pass it off before day's end. In the middle of the session the ultimate distraction arrived. Not a pretty girl, but a package from home. Mom had sent items I couldn't find in the local stores: bouillon cubes, three cans of tuna fish, three cans of sardines, one can of strawberry-flavored Nestle Quick, three packages of Japanese noodle soup mix, four packages of Kool-Aid, two sections of the Oregonian newspaper, and a one-pound box of Swiss Miss chocolate cocoa mix. Unpacking out of the way, I continued studying, and during the siesta passed off H. Only J, thirteen scriptures, and a final randomly-picked charla stood between me and freedom.

The outlook continued to brighten with success at the Giunta home, where a mother, her daughter, and the daughter's baby lived. So we could get through the lesson, Elder Stephens and I took turns teaching and taking a fussy baby out of the room. The only trouble we had was on the way home. My comp's bike chain kept falling off, so I had to tow him.

For P-Day our district went to General San Martín Park in Santa Fe. It was a beautiful place to spend time. I could feel myself relaxing amid the forest landscape, lush grass, and palm trees. We had a barbecue, played Frisbee football, took pictures of each other on a statue, and ended with a testimony meeting. I felt renewed as a result, reminded that this was the real reason for P-Days.

Saturday the 9th I passed off Charla J, the last big monkey on my back. This left ten scriptures to recite from memory, and a final pass-off. Then came Monday. A slip was drawn. Charla I it was. I started out strong, moving through Concepts 1, 2, and 3. Halfway there. Then my brain faltered and frustration set in. Unable to remember the second half of the discussion, I crashed and burned. It was devastating. As I went to bed that night I wondered if I'd ever be done with the damned charlas.

CHARLA I AND SELF-ESTEEM

WEDNESDAY, I STUDIED I, D, and G again and again. Since the charla choice was random, I wanted to improve my chances. Thursday Elder Sorensen held out the hat, from which I drew a slip. Charla I again. I sailed through it and G as well. It felt so good to hear Elder S say "Congratulations!" as I uttered the last phrase. Later I found out that Sorensen had filled the hat with slips, *all* marked with the letter "I". While thankful for his mercy, I was more grateful that the shame-filled ordeal was over. The way was now clear for me to study Church books and scriptures, guilt-free. At our mission conference the following Saturday, I was having an interview with President Parón and handed him the worn, tattered sheet of paper that showed all my charlas passed off and signed. He congratulated me, saying that things would go a lot better, now that that burden was out of the way.

At the end of October, I participated in a work session with Elder Sorensen. The opportunity to finally direct in my own area was a big boost to my confidence. But with every step forward, another slip backward was sure to follow. Whether or not it was self-sabotage or self-defeating behavior, I could never tell. All I knew was that I was being harder on myself than the Lord would ever think of being. In a letter home I remarked that,

> *"Still can't believe I'm 22. I feel and act like I'm still 18 or 19—but that's fine with me."*

But deep down, it wasn't fine with me. Since junior high I'd harbored the feeling that I was immature compared to others my own age. Physically I was a late bloomer. I hadn't grown to full height until I was sixteen. At twenty-two years of age I was only shaving once every five or six days, and then not much of a crop to write home about. I believed that this "little boy" image was due to my being pushed into first grade too soon, something I'd heard my mother say many times. All through the school years I felt more comfortable with kids one grade back from mine. Every time we were told to stand in line for team member selection, I was one of the last to be chosen. I took all of this as evidence that I didn't fit in, that I wasn't likable.

Eventually I took pride in my desire to be a non-conformist, and this preference for the solitary life grew and grew. Combine this with a thin-skinned, sensitive nature, a thinly-veiled contempt for authority, and a bad temper, and I had the perfect recipe for an industrial-strength case of low self-esteem.

Yet my work with investigators was still progressing. On the last Sunday in October, the Giunta's and another investigator family attended church. During sacrament meeting, Señor Coronel got to pass the sacrament for the first time. And Roberto, who had recently experienced a revival of his feelings toward the Church, received the priesthood. Despite how low I sometimes felt about myself, I felt blessed to have had a small part in helping our new members and investigators draw closer to God.

WITH NOVEMBER CAME THE BRANCH'S MOVE to a new building, across town in Guaymallen. The change seemed to revitalize the members, judging by their increased numbers. Giunta (the daughter) was still attending, as well, but was beginning to show the signs of mental instability that I'd noticed in the last couple discussions we'd had with her. During one portion of fast and testimony meeting, she asked Elder Stephens if he could see a "white thing" behind the head of a man who was speaking. She claimed she could see a light that followed certain people. Maybe she did have visionary powers, but from what source I couldn't tell.

During a weekly companion inventory session, Elder Stephens and I set goals for the coming week. But Elder Stephens also said he couldn't help but notice how bad I was starting to treat myself, that I put myself down too much. I told him that I knew this, but wasn't sure how to change my behavior. In the journal, I said that I hoped my children and grandchildren would never be saddled with this problem. It was a continual burden that I wanted the Lord's help with, but I didn't know what to ask for.

All through November, our seesaw relationship with the Giunta's continued. One session would be great, the next so full of family drama and strife that we wanted to give up and leave. One week the mother said she'd lost her faith in God; the next week it was her daughter's turn.

DURING THE MIDDLE OF THE MONTH Elder Stephens went off for a work session in Casillos, while I was assigned to work with one Elder Morera, from Buenos Aires. As Elder M hadn't passed off all his charlas yet, I was finally able to serve as the senior companion. Elder Morera was new to the mission, and as such had a few problems, one being a lack of humility. Another was his dislike for the mission rules. For this work session, the leaders had given each of us an evaluation sheet to fill out. On it was a goal to focus on then and in the future. Mine said: "Confidence in yourself to depend on the Lord."

We stayed in the apartment Tuesday morning, so Morera could pass off Charla I. The fact that his snoring had kept me up part of the night made the timing of the study session fortuitous. I was able to catch up on my sleep. At 11:30 a.m. he started passing it off.

TURKEY DAY AND A NEW COMP

THOUGH NOT AN OFFICIAL HOLIDAY in Argentina, Thanksgiving was drawing near, and the zone was planning a celebration, no matter what. At the ZLs' request, Elder S and I purchased two turkeys from a business across the street that sold chickens, pigs, and the like. We brought them back to our place. But since we didn't know how to kill them, it was up to the women. After the birds were hung from trees, Señora Mancuzo came over from next door with a large knife and slit their throats, while I looked on, grossed out. Afterwards we stuck one turkey in a pot of boiling water. The feathers came out fast and easy. Then we watched the Señora gut the bird, another task neither of us men was keen on.

Then we headed to Giunta's. The only person there was the daughter. Knowing beforehand that she was suffering from depression and anxiety, I had wanted to counsel her, and during the present visit I got my wish. I told her about my life, my parents' divorce, and the feelings of worthlessness that I sometimes struggled with. As we talked, I began to better understand her and her feelings. When we were finished, she appeared to be feeling much better. By the time we returned home, the Señora was cleaning up Turkey #2.

The dinner the following afternoon came off well. There was a talent show, where Elder Stephens read a poem he had written. Then I read an Ode to Indigestion, a short piece I'd cobbled together. I was surprised at the reaction, everyone laughing their heads off. Then we had dinner: turkey, rolls, mashed potatoes, gravy, corn, string beans, carrots, dessert, and some other stuff, though I missed the orange-and-cranberry salad my mom usually made.

Then came the portion of the program for which I was not prepared: transfers. After retiring to the chapel, the names of outgoing and incoming missionaries were read, along with their destinations. After each name was read, the crowd reacted with "oohs" and "ahhs." Elder Stephens's name was read. He was on transfer to

Bellville, a city near Temprano. Congratulatory applause followed. But when my new companion's name was read, the crowd reacted with scattered laughter and snickering. Elder Schieff was his name. Those sitting nearby offered me their condolences. I'd never heard of him, but apparently others had, and the prognosis was not good. As we rode home that evening, I wondered what in the world I was in for.

SATURDAY MORNING Elder Stephens finished packing, while I mulled over what the transfer meant. I'd heard a few things about Elder Schieff: that he'd been in the mission a month longer than I; that he still hadn't passed off all his charlas; that he had a hard time getting along with other elders. While that last item worried me, I looked forward to being the senior companion. I'd need to help him learn the charlas. I'd also be responsible for planning each day and setting up the appointments. My comp's things packed, we ate lunch, then hauled his stuff downtown. He left at 7 p.m., and I was sad to see him go.

On the bus trip back, Elder Schieff and I conversed, but he was uneasy. He'd answer questions, but wasn't long on conversation. Distracted, he looked past me and out the window, avoiding eye contact. Back at the apartment, he unpacked his bags in a fastidious manner.

I gave him the tour.

"There's the armoire, where you can put your clothes."

"Great."

"Here's the bathroom."

"Lovely."

"The backyard—"

"Whatever."

My new companion was unimpressed, even derisive, about what he saw. It irritated me, as if I was somehow to blame for not having demanded better living conditions. But I kept the thoughts to myself. Maybe Elder S was just having a bad day. But the following day it was me having the bad time:

> *"What am I going to do? I've just discovered that my companion is a neat-freak. He's been complaining about the glasses and the silverware not being clean. Now he wants to fix up the bathroom!"*

Elder Schieff was shaping up to be different from any other companion I'd worked with.

My debut as the senior comp was less than stellar. We visited a member to see if we could teach her neighbor, but the neighbor wasn't home. The appointment at the Celoni's to show flicks was preempted by a thunder and lightning storm that blew in from the south. We ended up back at the apartment, Schieff brooding and me wondering what to do next. But the next day was better. On our way to a discussion, a fellow at the train station waved us over. Inviting us into his office, he began asking questions about religion. I launched into an explanation about how Christ's authority had been restored, testifying several times that the Savior's Church was again on the earth. I felt confident as I spoke, and there was a good spirit in the room. I felt that I'd been guided in what I told him.

Next up was a visit to a branch member's home to talk to Señor Estrella. I tried several times to begin the discussion, but all eyes, including Schieff's, were glued to the Midnight Special television show. For a while I gave in, not wanting to risk a riot, but after forty-five minutes I began talking to Estrella about the pamphlets we'd given him. After a half-hour discussion, I handed him a Book of Mormon to read.

HAVING GIVEN UP ON TRACTING one afternoon, we were strolling through one of the poorer neighborhoods on our way home. Lots of dwellings, all adobe or brick, the yards packed dirt on all sides due to the señora tossing buckets of wash water out the door every single day. Grass hadn't a chance to grow.

At some point, we heard laughter coming from a nearby house. Schieff had some sort of radar, for he pinpointed the correct place in seconds. Instead of clapping out front, or knocking on the door, he went to the living room window and stuck his head in for a look, waving one hand and saying, "Hola!" Aghast at his brazenness with total strangers, I sidled up next to him. Inside was a group of folks young and old, watching *The Three Stooges*. Not content to leave after a minute or two, Elder

Schieff took up residence, arms folded and resting on the windowsill.

"Elder," I said, exercising my authority. "We need to go."

"Hold on," he said, shooing me away. "I want to see this," his face aglow with the kind of joy that only Curly, Moe, and Larry could provide. Five long minutes later Schieff waved "adios," everyone returning the farewell as if he were a member of the family. He was eccentric, but I had to hand it to him; he knew how to put people at ease.

What he didn't know how to do was put in a day's work. For every effort I made to get something substantive done, he parried it. Sleeping in late, feeling ill, wanting to cook things—whatever it took, he subverted my authority with techniques both subtle and overt. Not liking conflict, I went along to get along, all the while looking for an opening that would get us out and doing missionary work again.

WEDNESDAY, DECEMBER 1

(From note on Planning Card): "We stopped to look at the giant supermarket . . . What a waste of time. Cleaning our room."

THURSDAY, DECEMBER 2

(From note on Planning Card): "We left the pensión at 11:30."

SATURDAY, DECEMBER 4

Wrote letter to Parón. From note on Planning Card: "I just lost the key to the leaders' apartment."

SUNDAY, DECEMBER 5

No journal entries.

MONDAY, DECEMBER 6

"My companion knows how to cook without cremating, so this morning we cooked a bunch of doughnuts (or something like them). We have to take some sort of refreshments to a family night we'll be having with some investigators tomorrow night. The doughnuts were full of grease when we got done cooking them."

On Tuesday, we finally got back on track. Then, during a discussion with Elder Sorensen that morning, at his place, the subject of mission rules arose.

"How important are they?" our ZL asked.

"Very important," said Elder Schieff.

But from what I had seen, my comp was more concerned with the letter of the law than the Spirit that had inspired its creation. In my view, strict obedience was tantamount to living a lower law, while working by the guidance of the Spirit was of a higher order. We were at odds about the issue, and now we knew it.

Law or no law, I was having troubles of my own, dwelling on women to the point of distraction. The resulting guilt and remorse was causing the Spirit to withdraw from my life, like the static in mountain passes that blocks out one's favorite song on the radio. And of course, it was all my fault. I didn't factor into the emotional equation the fact that I was a living, breathing male in his early twenties whose hormones were merely doing their job. Unwilling to acknowledge this, I was paralyzed by guilt. What I needed was a balanced perspective. Though I was looking at girls a lot, it was something I needed to accept—not take personally or identify with—then stop dwelling on. The tendency to focus on the negative and beat up on myself was my version of the "thorn" that Paul talks about in 2nd Corinthians: that customized Achilles Heel all people are born with; an imperfection which, when overcome, can become one of the stronger facets of one's character.

Despite my feelings of unworthiness, the Work marched on. The Lamatas, a new family we'd started teaching, were doing well. We held a family home evening with them to which we brought "treats," for lack of a better word: those greasy donuts I'd tried to help Schieff cook the day before. Luckily, we were able to leave before refreshments were served. Another indigestion bullet dodged.

As for my comp's cooking, it was starting to interfere with the schedule. Elder Schieff took great joy in the culinary arts, said enthusiasm requiring expenditures of time and money, neither of which we had much of. Cooking required milk and eggs, which meant repeated trips to the store. And once something went into the oven, we were stuck at the apartment until it was finished cooking.

Unlike Elder S, I had no desire to learn the art. I was happy with our current setup: the señora cooked and we ate. If the offering was something I remembered from an earlier unpleasant occasion, I would hurl it out the side window and over the high wall for the benefit of neighboring dogs, who quickly removed the evidence. As for cooking, I loathed the act. Anything more involved than toast or the heating up of soup rarely went well. Eggs burned when I tried to scramble them. Meat blackened on the outside, yet remained bloody on the inside. Cakes burned, no matter how closely I followed the recipe. And then there were those damned instructions. Like the obscure backgammon rules on the back of every cheap foldup checkerboard ever printed, there was never enough detail.

THE HALFWAY POINT AND MALAISE

HUMP DAY ARRIVED, December 13th marking my halfway point in the mission field. We celebrated by going to the stake center for cake and root beer. It was the first RB I'd had in months, as it didn't exist in Argentina. A few days later I started receiving letters from a girl Elder Stephens knew in Utah. When I asked him what she was like, he said she was very nice, and had a great set of headers. Her name was Jane Smith, and her missives blunted the loneliness that was starting to afflict me. Maybe it was the proximity of the holidays—the fact that this would be my second Christmas away from home. Regardless, the only cure was to go out and serve others.

I reported to President Parón that we had zero hours teaching for the previous seven days. I attributed some of this to the new emphasis on working with Church members, as opposed to knocking doors. But the underlying cause was a growing discord between Elder Schieff and myself, mirrored by trouble brewing between some of the branch members.

We were all struggling, the latest Sunday priesthood class a prime example. Starting the meeting off with a bang, Hermano Zoto broached the subject of problems in the elders quorum. In short order, he and Hermano Cap de Vila were arguing. Having endured one too many of these verbal fisticuffs, I interrupted.

"Hermano Zoto?"

"Uh—yes. Elder Hiland?"

"Is there a lesson planned for the class today?"

"Yes," Zoto replied. Then he went to his pew and sat down. Cap de Vila shut his trap as well, and the lesson commenced.

Jugo

That night I dreamed about walking down a darkened street. I was looking at houses decorated with Christmas lights, reveling in the colors, searching for the darker and more pungent of the hues. It was a dream elicited by Christmas memories, juxtaposed with a most untraditional Yuletide in Jugo. Papa Noel appearing in a lot of store windows. My family and friends thousands of miles away. Tinsel on everything. Temperatures in the ninety-degree range. Real Christmas trees nowhere to be found, people opting for artificial ones that stood two feet high, covered with electric lights and bulbs. I longed to see a simple string of lights, all the same color. Orange. Or red. Maybe green. But especially blue. It was that darker color that spoke to me. By turns mystical and mysterious, blue evoked the same feelings as the more ethereal, serious, slow holiday music: "The Little Drummer Boy"; "Fum, Fum, Fum"; the darker of the *Nutcracker Suite* selections. I wanted to stand next to those warm bulbs and absorb the color, feel it . . .

FOUR DAYS BEFORE CHRISTMAS:

"While my companion is sleeping I'll write a few lines. We still aren't getting along very well. Maybe it's just me, but whatever the problem is, we just aren't of accord on a lot of things. I've never had problems like this with a companion before. Being at odds with each other slows the work way down. I still don't know what to do to keep from being aggravated with him so much."

215

The fact that we hadn't taught one single charla in over a month wasn't helping matters, my comp's crappy attitude about work being Suspect Numero Uno.

But as much as I resented his behavior, Elder S could be disarming. There was his affinity for The Beatles. In New Testament times, the missionaries were counseled to travel with neither purse nor scrip. Material things paled in comparison to the Lord's work. But for modern-day missionaries like me, music was one earthly possession that I was not willing to forsake. For years, my collection of listenable Fab Four tunes started with Rubber Soul. Anything before that was too "old." Elder Schieff convinced me to give some of his tapes from 1964 to 1966 a listen. From then on, I was hooked. So, we at least had that in common. It was a starting point.

As Schieff continued sawing logs, I recounted our adventure of the day before. We had traveled to the Guaymallen chapel to drop off a copy of the piano key I'd paid for. Having traveled all that way just to see if it fit, I put it in the slot. It didn't fit. Moments later a diarrhea attack hit, like an unforecasted tornado. Placing the key on the piano, I searched the restrooms in vain for bum fodder. Frantic, I rifled through kitchen cupboards, drawers and closets with the same results. Eventually I discovered some newspaper, angels, and cherubim circling it, and I ran for the Room. In my absence, Schieff manage to knock the key off the piano top, where it fell to its death in the bowels of the instrument, never to be seen again. Upon my return, I was given the bad news. We headed back to Jugo.

About the time I finished writing this, it was 10 a.m. Schieff was stirring. But before I could set the book down and speak to him, he fell asleep again.

OATMEAL REDUX AND THE CHRISTMAS BUS

FOLLOWING A HUMBLE BREAKFAST of oatmeal, we boarded the bus for a zone conference/Christmas party, my companion uncharacteristically subdued in word and deed. The conference was uplifting, the dinner afterwards a lot of fun. It almost felt like Christmas. Schieff, on the other hand, felt something else entirely, spending most of the time lying on a pew in the dark, deserted chapel.

Afterward, as we boarded the bus, he requested the window seat, "just in case." All the way home he resembled a zombie: green and staring straight ahead. As the bus rolled to a stop, I got up and he pushed past. Within seconds he'd disappeared. I disembarked and crossed the street. People on the other side of a large, deep ditch were pointing, staring at something and shaking their heads. As I approached the edge of the crevasse I could see Elder Schieff on his hands and knees, losing every bit of that breakfast oatmeal, and with extreme prejudice. After getting him a glass of water, he looked good as new. But once we got home, he crashed.

And so I sat, recording life in the journal while my companion slept the sleep of death. I noted, somewhat bitterly, that I seemed to have a natural born talent for neck adjustment. Elder S's would get out of alignment. The first time this happened, he asked me if I'd massage it for a few minutes. Then I was to spin his head quickly one way and the other. I was loathe to touch his greasy skin, let alone screw up and later have to explain to President

Parón and the elder's parents why he was paralyzed from the neck down. But after several requests, I took a deep breath and placed my hands on his neck. My feelings ran the gamut from disgust to fear to irritation. If it had been a girl's neck, the service would have been a pleasure. But a guy? Yecchh! I took his head in my hands and turned it one way, then the other, finally twisting his skull quickly to the right, then the left. No paralysis.

Around 5 p.m. my comp arose from the dead. We went out and gave a health blessing to a fellow who'd suffered a heart attack a few days earlier.

IT'S CHRISTMAS EVE. Elder Schieff is broke and I have 1,000 pesos ($5.00 US) to my name. Having spent what little funds remained on M-80s and firecrackers, we plan on joining the citizenry for the blowing up of fireworks. It seems that Argentines celebrate Christmas Eve like Americans do the Fourth of July. My guilt at having squandered precious funds is somewhat allayed by the fact that the real holiday celebrations are reserved for the Day of the Three Wise Men, on January 6th (a Catholic holiday).

This evening we're headed to a member's house for Christmas Eve dinner. But getting there is a struggle. We ride the bus to a neighborhood ten miles from Jugo. Then we walk ten blocks to the sisters' place. Then we walk all ten blocks back to the stop and wait for the bus. It isn't until the bus has taken us all over the city that we discover we've boarded the wrong vehicle. Finally, the driver stops, depositing us only five blocks closer to our destination. Once on the right bus, we make it to Hermana Piro's home.

9:45 p.m. We arrive and, after some small talk with the missionaries, sit down to dinner. The lady isn't the greatest cook in the world, some of the elders making faces after taking a bite of this or a mouthful of that. But we eat anyway. Despite the blessed presence of liters of pop, with which I wash down mouthful after mouthful of chicken, salad, potatoes, and candy, I soon have a world-class gut ache. After dinner we sing some Christmas songs and relax. I'm starting to feel better.

1:45 a.m. We say our goodbyes and head for home. Walking along, I look for an available bus, but there don't seem to be any running, the streets quieter than normal. It hasn't occurred to us yet that the dearth of transportation might have anything at all to do with the fact that this is the ass end of Christmas Eve—yea, verily, the dawning of Christmas Day. Having walked a very long fifteen blocks, we're halfway to our destination. Continuing what has become a sort of death march, we arrive back at the sisters' place ninety minutes later. I try to take my mind off the fact that we are probably doomed. We gab with them for nearly forty-five minutes, and all the while I ponder how nice it would be to crash there, mission rules be damned. But what little common sense I still have returns. No longer able to postpone the inevitable, we leave the ladies' comfy surroundings and make the long slog back to the bus stop.

3:00 a.m. Feet, legs and lower back worn out, we arrive at the blessed bus stop and collapse on hard benches not designed to provide more than three continuous minutes of comfort. I fall in and out of sleep, as does Schieff. Though early morning, it is also summer and sixty-five degrees. And still no bus arrives, us mystified.

4:30 a.m. Giving up on public transportation, we arise, stretch, and groan. Blurry eyes and legs leading the way, we commence walking to the ZLs apartment, twelve blocks distant, looking for refuge and relief. Arriving, we discover they aren't home. Hope of rescue abandoned, we're making our way back to the main street when a bus comes chugging up the street. Us nowhere near the stop, it looks as if all is lost. But the intersection lights change, forcing the bus to a halt. Little energy remaining, we run to the bus and crawl aboard. The seats are wonderful. My sleepy head sways this way and that with every turn, curve, and stop.

6:00 a.m. We arrive home and collapse.

SOMETIMES THINGS HEAL ON THEIR OWN, if allowed time to do so. For Schieff and I that time came the day after Christmas. We'd decided to have a companionship inventory session, during which I let him do most of the planning. We talked all morning about the problems we were having, hashed out a few issues, and got to know each other a lot better. In the process, I discovered that a lot of the conflict came from me. I let my pride get in the way. I wouldn't take constructive criticism from Schieff. And all the time we were letting tension and friction build, yet doing nothing to smooth things over. As a result, the work suffered. But we finally reached an agreement about how to get along with each other. It was a miracle.

With the grape season approaching, the December weather got warmer and warmer. Chicken egg-sized hail damaged vineyards and other crops. The days got longer and hotter—80s and 90s. Without access to air conditioning I was losing sleep every night. My weight had been dropping, as well, from 183 to 169. Yet I felt great, the sleep deficit having no effect as long as I stayed busy. And hard work strengthened my testimony of the Work I was involved in. This, in turn, was bringing new contacts and investigators our way.

SUMMER IN JANUARY, PEOPLE TO TEACH

As THE NEW YEAR BEGAN, Schieff and I were occupied with
charlas, post office battles, sacrament meeting talks and
service. During the first week in January we traveled to
a Jugo hospital to bless an investigator's baby. Upon arriving we found that the child was no longer ill. But two
other women close by asked that we bless their infants.
Though I'd never performed the ordinance before, the
look in these mothers' eyes told me it didn't matter.
They wanted God to heal their little ones. Consulting a
small guide I'd attached to the inner binding of my scriptures, I looked up "health blessings." Then I placed my
hand on one infant's tiny head and blessed her that she
would be restored to health, according to the will of the
Lord. Then we blessed the other baby. It was a beautiful
experience.

The temperatures continued to rise through the first
half of January, flirting with the 100-degree mark. Though
we left the windows open all night, I was still sweating to
death. One battle we were winning, though, was with the
mosquitos. A Raid citronella "spiral" was lit at bedtime,
the aromatic smoke keeping the flying critters at bay all
night. And speaking of blowing smoke, I started writing
to my parents about my impending transfer. I believed
that since the elders I knew were being moved to other
cities, my turn was imminent. Since transfers occurred
every five months or so, I was surely overdue.

As for investigators, we were not in short supply, Señora Lamata at the top of the list. We had been working with her for a while but not made real progress until she committed to baptism shortly after her mother passed away. Lamata's mother, who'd been paralyzed for thirteen years, had received a blessing shortly before her demise. During the prayer, she'd been promised that she would walk again. In a recent dream, Lamata had seen her mother dressed in white, walking under her own power. So, when we showed her a film about resurrection and life after death, she knew it was true—that it couldn't be by chance that she had seen the film, heard our message and had that dream, all three centering on life after death. The truth of our message was penetrating her conscience.

On this same day we interviewed Luis, a young Jewish fellow, in preparation for his upcoming baptismal interview. He was excited and ready. The rest of the week was filled with charlas and filmstrip presentations. On Friday night, we traveled to the stake center to watch a talent show. Schieff and I hung around, talking to other missionaries and observing the youth dance until 1:30 a.m.

On the advice of a branch member, we stood at a particular intersection to catch a bus that he guaranteed would get us home. But it never arrived. In order to avoid a repeat performance of the Christmas Eve debacle, we slogged our way to the bus terminal, one hour and fifteen blocks distant. We slept in the waiting area chairs until 5 a.m., when our bus arrived. Following an hour and a half of sleep, we left our apartment at 7:15 a.m. for conference. The only question I had later was how we survived the day with so little rest.

IN THE MIDST OF A PERIOD OF GOOD FEELING, I received a tape from my friends at home—the same folks I'd partied with before realizing I needed to be active in church again. While it was good to hear their voices, feelings of depression and loneliness engulfed me, much as they had during those party days some two years earlier. Memories of pot smoking, malt liquor, bad movies, bad music, and bad magazines paraded through my head.

I felt caught between two worlds, yet a member of neither. It took a while to shake the feeling, its timing leading me to believe that the adversary was doing everything possible to dishearten me. I was struggling again with thoughts about the fairer sex, but the more I tried to avoid pondering the sensual, the more the thoughts pressed in on me. I spoke to my comp. He told I was being too hard on myself. We read our patriarchal blessings to each other, after which I felt uplifted and relieved.

DURING AN EVENING DISCUSSION in the Lamata home, Señora Lamata's daughter Kristina and two other investigators were present. Partway through a discussion about the Godhead and the plan of salvation, Schieff became impatient with Kristina, as she wasn't paying attention. On top of this was a series of interruptions that kept derailing everyone's train of thought. It was as if an unseen force was trying to keep our students from understanding us. Two and a half hours later we finished presenting everything. But instead of believing that a lot had been accomplished, Schieff and I were agitated and out of sorts. We hadn't accomplished what the Lord had required of us. Schieff asked Kristina how she felt about the LDS Church. She said that she hadn't felt the Spirit yet. Furthermore, she told us that she'd decided to follow her father in his religion. It appeared that Señora Lamata was alone in her desires to repent and be baptized.

Deciding it was time to petition the Lord's help, we asked the other two investigators to leave the room. Señora Lamata prayed first, crying as she spoke. Then it was my turn. I felt the Lord's spirit as I asked Him to touch Kristina's heart. Then Elder Schieff prayed, asking the Lord to "please keep the man of the house outside until we are finished praying." I was unsure what he meant by this. Then it was Kristina's turn. I felt shivers run through me again and again as she asked the Lord to tell her which was the church of God. It had been a while since I'd seen someone exercising such faith. She began to weep. No sooner had she finished and we were standing on our feet than Señor Lamata entered the room. Unlike my comp, I hadn't heard the man's truck pull up earlier. All in all, the evening was a great spiritual experience for which I owed Elder Schieff a debt of gratitude.

The following day Señor Lamata signed the permission slip, though Kristina was still holding back, afraid of the things that would happen after she was baptized. I sat with her and we talked for over an hour about her problems and fears. I knew the Lord was guiding me, and I felt a strong love for Kristina and her family. Sunday, Kristina and her mother, along with Olga Recabarren, Olga Broll, Iris, and Señora Regules attended church with us.

TRUE CONFESSIONS AND THE NEEDLE

FOLLOWING A MIDWEEK VISIT to the Lamata's, we headed out of town to General Ortega. The route included a section of dirt road riddled with rocks and potholes. I was carrying a tape recorder, Schieff the Singer projector. Near Olga's house my comp hit a bump and lost his grip on the handlebars. I heard the crash and turned in time to see the Singer flying through the air. Though Schieff didn't break anything, the palms of both his hands were cut up good. Once we arrived at Olga's place, Elder S cleaned up while we awaited Olga's arrival. I plugged in the Singer. By some miracle, the bulb was still functioning. A half hour later the lady of the house arrived. Thirty minutes after that, here came Olga's husband. We showed "Christ in America," but there were so many mosquitos present that I couldn't sit still. Bugs were flying up my nose, into my ears, through my hair, on my arms and neck. But despite my constant slapping, Señor R understood and enjoyed the film.

Then I began teaching Charla C, but within minutes, friends arrived. Excited at the prospect of more investigators, I carried on, but was interrupted ten minutes later with the news that the last bus for town was about to pass by. Since Elder Schieff's injured right hand had gone stiff on him, he couldn't ride his bicycle. We had to pack and run.

A couple days later, during a visit to the ZLs place, I pulled Elder Barton aside. We retired to the garden for privacy.

"Elder Barton, I'm feeling awful."

"What's the matter?"

I explained my pent-up feelings of guilt and remorse. I asked him about the nature of repentance. It was those sex thoughts again.

"Before I went on my mission," he said, "I attended college and graduate school. But I had some real problems during that time. When it was time for me to leave on a mission, I had to go talk to S. Dilworth Young (one of the Church's general authorities).

"After I explained everything that I'd done, I waited for his response. Elder Young looked at me and said that it sounded like I'd paid the price."

"Then Elder Young took the Stake President's report (detailing my problems), and tore it into little pieces.

"'You know, Elder Barton—these sheets of paper— we don't keep these.'"

"Elder Young went on to tell me that my sins had been forgiven. That by confessing them to him, I had done the last thing necessary to receive the Lord's forgiveness.

Elder Hiland, the Savior has already paid the price for your sins. It is up to you to make that Atonement effective in your life."

Though I found Elder B's words to be of great comfort, I was still anxious.

That evening, Señora Lamata, Kristina, and Olga Broll passed their baptismal interviews. Schieff and I were ecstatic.

Saturday arrived. On the one hand, I was excited about the impending baptisms. On the other, I felt unworthy to perform the ordinance. As the morning hours passed, the suspense became unbearable. It was a hell of an ordeal I was putting myself through, and looking back on it now, I wonder if I shouldn't have just kept the problems to myself. I knew how to pray to Heavenly Father and ask forgiveness. But I had gotten myself into a position where I valued the relief that came from confession over the possibility that maybe, just maybe, I wasn't the crappy person I saw in the mirror—but actually a son of God, with good intentions and talents and abilities that no amount of failings or imperfections could wash away.

In the end, I talked to Parón. After the interview, Elder Schieff and I had the privilege of baptizing and confirming three wonderful women into the Church of Jesus Christ. That night we got home late. At 11:20 p.m. I closed my journal, having finished the day's events and feeling blessed that all had come to a good end.

THE FOLLOWING MONDAY I was again at Elder Barton's place. Evidently, good advice wasn't all he dispensed. It was time for my scheduled gamma globulin shot, and Elder B was the man who'd be administering it. Since these elders were not trained professionals, questions always popped up in my head prior to the shot. What if Elder Barton misses the "target?" What if he doesn't get all the air bubbles out of the syringe? What if he hits a bone?

"Well, Elder Hiland!" he said, rubbing his hands together, like this was going to be fun for at least one of us. "Ready to get your shot?"

"Oh yeah. Sure . . ." I said with as much sarcasm as I could muster, a bit of the old fear fluttering into my midriff.

"Well, let's get it over with," he said as I handed him the packaged syringe I'd purchased earlier at the pharmacy. Then I removed coat and shirt, irritated with myself for allowing my nerves to skitter around at the sound of Barton tearing open the packaging.

"So, how's life treating you, Elder?"

"Okay."

"Which arm's it going to be?" I offered one. He pulled the drooping garment sleeve up, out of the way, his manner a little rough for someone about to perform a medical procedure. Then he grabbed a good two to three inches of the muscled part of my upper arm between his thumb and fingers.

"First, I'm going to get it loosened up a little," he said as he kneaded the flesh back and forth and up and down and around. While he continued the small talk, I had to admit some measure of gratitude for the massage, if for no other reason than its delaying of the inevitable.

"So," I said, as he twisted the skin this way and that. "Where did you learn to give shots, anyway?"

"Oh, mainly here in the mission field. On missionaries like you."

Up went the red flags. I gulped but said nothing.

"Yep. Trial and error, trial and error."

As he joked, I tried not to look at the bouquet of needles stuck into a dartboard near the door. I just wanted this to be over. Then the kneading stopped.

"Okay, Elder Hiland. Hold still and don't move an inch. I have to do one more thing."

But before I could ask or react, he half-turned away, wound up, and backhanded my arm as hard as he could.

"Hey!" I yelped. It hurt like hell for a few seconds. He approached with the alcohol-soaked cotton swab, my arm buzzing with the heat of mild trauma. Quickly rubbing with cold cotton, Elder B returned with the syringe, held it up to the light, tapped the chamber a couple times, then stuck the needle into my numbed arm. The man was a genius.

MOVIE NIGHT, BAPTISMS, THE HARVEST QUEEN

OVER THE NEXT COUPLE DAYS, we spent time with the Lamata family, as well as branch members and another person preparing for baptism. But Elder Schieff was getting restless.

"Elder Hiland," he said one day, a local newspaper in his hands.

"What's up?"

"How about we go to the *movies?*"

"Well, I don't know," I said. After the *Doc Savage* debacle, the sound of any word related to the theater made me flinch. "The rules say we're not supposed to."

"But it's *Sleeping Beauty*. The *Disney* version."

I tried to hold out for some safer form of entertainment, but Schieff persisted.

In the end, we took the afternoon bus to a theater in Santa Fe. It was a double bill, the other feature being *In Search of the Castaways*, a film I hadn't seen since I was a kid. It was a good thing I knew the basic story line, because trying to understand the dialog in Spanish was the pits.

"You know," I said to Schieff, "It's sort of ironic."

"What's that?"

"The timing. I started my stay in Santa Fe with a trip to the theater, and here I am, back at the movies again."

The difference was that this time I felt good when I left the cinema.

On the 26ᵀᴴ there were two more baptisms: Jorge Montana and Luis Waschman. The former was the son of inactive parents, the latter a fellow we were finishing up discussions with. He'd been wanting to be baptized for several months.

The next day we attended a birthday party for Elder Barton at the sisters' apartment. Though Carnaval had ended some days earlier, the kids were still throwing water, one girl stalking us all the way to the sisters' front door, a bucket of the wet stuff in hand. After the party, we were standing around talking when a storm blew in, sky darkening and cold air rushing about the house. Then there was a THUNK, followed by another. Hailstones the size of golf balls were coming down, bouncing as they hit the ground. As I stood there, listening to the stones smack the thin cane roof over our heads, I marveled at the forces of nature. I was also grateful we hadn't left the party sooner, or we'd have been caught in the heavenly crossfire.

With all the success I'd been experiencing as of late, I believed that my time in Jugo was coming to an end. I'd been anticipating a phone call from the leaders every Friday for the last four weeks. Since it had become a distraction, I was trying to think about other things, with a modicum of success. But I didn't really want to leave. Jugo had become my home. I was friends with a lot of the members, and was working well with my companion— that guy no one could supposedly get along with.

MARCH 3ʳᵈ.

"Dear Mom: Well, it's late Thursday night and this is the end of a disastrous week. We didn't really get anything of worth accomplished. We didn't teach one discussion or visit any investigators. The ones we were going to see and teach moved across town this last Monday, and they didn't leave us their new address. To top that off, I received another good case of Montezuma's Revenge today . . .

"It's kind of ironic to have hailstones right in the middle of the grape harvesting celebration. This is the time of year when the grapes are being picked for wine and other things—and the people are celebrating it by electing queens (between sixteen and twenty-one years of age); and they have final judging at a big amphitheater at the base of the mountains. We're going to see this contest, as a zone.

"Well, I'm the oldest one in the zone. Out of the twenty-six missionaries here, I'm the only original now. I guess the Lord wants me here for some special reason, or I would have been transferred a long time ago."

SATURDAY AFTERNOON, Elder Barton, the sisters and I traveled by bus to Parque San Martín for a hike up the hill to the Amphitheatre. The walk was beautiful and it was great to be in the woods again. But we were not alone. Policemen and soldiers with guns and dogs were stationed in gulleys, tunnels, on the hillsides, and just about everywhere else one could think of. While it was nice to know there was so much protection around, it also made me a little uneasy. We emerged onto a road, then hiked uphill a mile to the entrance. Once inside we claimed our seats.

The amphitheater was situated in a bowl-shaped area between several hills. As I looked down past the stage area I could see parts of the city of Santa Fe between the gaps. Having gotten there early, we had lots of time to kill. Though I'd brought my camera, there was only so much I could photograph, our area of movement restricted. It wasn't like I could take a stroll along the fence line, unless I wanted lots of pictures of the local constabulary, or possibly some interior shots of a nearby jail cell. We missionaries could take pictures of each other, but that happened every time we assembled, so the novelty was gone. This left the mountains, the stage area, the haze-blanketed cityscape, or other people. Opting for the latter, I gave up after the subject of one shot turned his camera on me. I took a seat on the flat concrete, talked to other missionaries, watched the stage for any sign of movement, then more talk, then the stage, and on and on. Two and a half hours later the showed started.

We were treated to fireworks, lots of fancy light displays built into the stage floor, and various ethnic dances, all in an effort to represent the history of South America and Argentina. After an hour and a half of this the queen was chosen and crowned, a process which took another sixty minutes. By that time, we'd all had enough entertainment. My butt was numb, the attention span long exhausted, thirst and hunger and sleep beckoning. We left early, but gained no advantage. As the ZLs coordinated taxi rides for each group of missionaries, the increasing size of the departing crowds, with their accompanying clouds of dust and noise, made for total chaos. I got back to the apartment at 1 a.m. The following day I celebrated seven months in Jugo.

A FALSE ALARM AND THE REAL THING

MONDAY, MARCH 7 WE WENT TO THE ZLs' apartment to drop off our weekly reports. Elder Viktor then said that Elder Zarate and I needed to go to the terminal to pick up some papers from a couple elders who'd just arrived in Santa Fe on transfer. After accomplishing said task, I stopped by the downtown area for a few minutes before returning to the apartment. No sooner had I stepped in the ZLs' door than I was told to be packed and ready to leave for the city of Coronel Diaz no later than 6 p.m. If there was any change, Elder Viktor said he'd call me by 4 p.m.

So off to Jugo Elder Schieff and I went. I was packed and ready within two hours, despite a few interruptions along the way. Having received no phone calls to the contrary, we headed for the bus stop at 5 p.m. The first bus couldn't take us because I had too much luggage. We caught the next one. Arriving at the terminal with no time to spare, I checked my bags in at the lockers and went looking for Elder Viktor. But he found me first.

"Well, Elder Hiland, I've got some bad news for you."

"I know," I said, sarcastically. "I'm not leaving today."

"Yes, you're right!" Elder V said, his smile belying a lack of concern that pissed me off.

"You've been misinformed. The bus didn't leave at six. It left at 5 p.m."

He blathered on about not being able to make the call, due to some meetings they had to attend. I felt like a second-class citizen.

"You've been rescheduled to leave at 7 a.m. tomorrow. Your new companion will be Elder Doyle."

Schieff and I made one last trip back to Jugo. I could only hope no more mistakes were made before I headed south. I was scheduled to arrive in Coronel Diaz at noon.

CORONEL DIAZ

THE BUS LEFT JUGO AT SUNRISE, olive orchards and vine-yards giving way to wheat fields and rangeland. The mountains receded, then disappeared during the five-hour trip southwest. Unable to sleep, I stared out the window, more meditative than looking at anything in particular. I thought about the people I'd left behind—friends, acquaintances—those whose lives I'd touched and those who'd affected me. And I wondered what lay ahead.

Five hours and 175 miles later the bus entered the outskirts of Coronel Diaz, population 12,000, and the smallest town I'd served in so far. With no hills or mountains to interrupt a view of the horizon, Coronel Diaz was a twenty-block wide, twelve-block deep bit of civilization in the middle of nowhere: the city furthest south in our mission for proselyting. It could also be the coldest, though at the moment pleasant fall weather was still in the air.

After exiting the bus, I was escorted by one of the leaders to my new pensión. As we walked along, I recognized the same barren look I'd seen in other towns:

squarish, white-washed, dull pastel buildings; few grassy areas; streets lined with severely pruned trees that surrounded tile-covered plazas and stucco-fronted offices. Within ten blocks we'd arrived at my new home: an older brick residence with tall, European-style doors. I was introduced to Elder Doyle, from Wyoming. With a slight paunch and curly hair that was battling premature balding for cranial real estate, he looked older than the average missionary. He seemed pleasant enough, though, and down to earth. But I wondered what life with him was going to be like. He had only six weeks left. After I got settled in, we went out to meet some of the members I'd be working with.

Over the next few days, a clearer picture of Doyle began to emerge. For one thing, his working style was laid back. I began to detect signs of trunkiness in him, suspicions that were soon confirmed. He was counting the days. He also liked to reminisce. Once I joined in, we'd talk at length about what we did before becoming active in church. The parties, the girls. Blah, blah, blah. This tended to drive thoughts about missionary work out the window and down the street. And as soon as I started telling him about my favorite movies, I was doomed.

He loved the Old Testament, Elvis, and country-western music. And bashing with Jehovah Witnesses. And making fun of my classical music. One day I turned on some *Swan Lake*. Before I knew what was happening, Elder D was pirouetting and hopping around like an overweight, but determined, ballerina. At first, I thought it was funny, but the fact that he was performing in his underwear was sort of off-putting. And since he wouldn't stop until I turned off the tape recorder, I grew irritated with his intolerance. But we barely knew each other, so I let it pass.

Something my new comp did like was *maté*, a green, weedy-looking herb that, along with wine, was the national drink of choice. Served boiling hot in a gourd-like container that fit in the hand, it was sipped at one's peril through a straw-sized metal tube. I concluded, even after six cups, that it tasted like boiled weeds. Having been an inveterate coffee drinker some three years earlier, I longed for cream and sugar to cut the bitter taste.

DURING THAT FIRST WEEK, I met the new district leader, Elder Aldin, and his comp, Elder Diarmid. Due to Coronel Diaz's diminutive size, our district was composed of only four elders. The fact that the town was at the end of the road, and an hour's bus ride from the ZLs in San Rafael, meant that we were left to our own devices as to how to accomplish the Work. Sure, we were to abide by the mission rules, but that did nothing to allay the feeling that I was living in the equivalent of a frontier town.

GETTING ACQUAINTED, TEACHING

SUNDAY, I GOT ACQUAINTED with our meetinghouse. Located on a street corner a few blocks from downtown, it was a long, grey, one-story building with two narrow, shuttered doors opening onto the sidewalk. There was no lawn, only a gravel driveway on the right side that led to a back parking lot. At the side of the building was a baptismal font. Consisting of concrete steps that rose to the top, then ran down the other side, it was our only alternative to a river rumored to be nearby, and like that river, the font was full of dead leaves and tree branches. I wondered how the water for a baptism was heated, and suspected there might be some wood chopping in my future.

Soon enough I met Don Lorenzo. He was a stroke victim, the left side of his body paralyzed. Bedridden, he lay near the only open window in his small room, a prisoner of his afflictions. Unable to speak, he used hand signals and guttural throat sounds to communicate. Don was not LDS, but was interested in our church. Other visits we made that day included ward members and investigators from all over our area. By evening I was exhausted. I figured we'd walked fifteen miles, my legs and back unaccustomed to all the non-bike exercise.

Tuesday, we taught two charlas, the first one to a new contact. In an effort to change things up, I gave the Joseph Smith story in my own words, and discovered all over again why it was better to stick to the memorized form. In an effort to do things the easy way, it turned into a mess. Like trying to paraphrase the scriptures, something vital is lost in the effort. It may be interesting to listen to, but it's not what was intended. The second charla, taught that evening to a lady named Bujaldon, went a lot better.

The next day I sat in a barber shop writing letters while Doyle got his last Argentine haircut. He'd reached the point where the Lasts were occurring with increasing frequency, the ultimate still to come: at the airport, experiencing his last minute in the country. I tried to focus on letters home amid distractions: Beatles, Elvis, tango music from a local radio station, piles of magazines on the table, like *Gente* (the Argentine version of Life), comic books, and my favorite, the novellas. The latter was a way to watch an entire movie without having to sit through two hours in a darkened theater. Reproducing hundreds of shots from a particular film, without somehow violating copyright laws, snatches of dialogue accompanied every photo. I worked my way through several films that were playing in the US, realizing I'd never have to waste time on them once I returned home.

Later on, we taught two charlas, one of them to a lady named Irma Fernandez. She was a humble, quiet woman who lived with her daughter in a small house on the edge of town. We were so impressed with her that we challenged her to be baptized on March 26th. She accepted, such was her desire to join the Church. All she lacked was some instruction.

I finished the day tired and somewhat ill. My stomach having been upset for three days in a row, I foresaw a trip to the doctor in my future, the prospect of which was more troubling than the malady. As for things medical, we did go to the hospital the following morning for group blood tests, though I knew not why. What I did know was that when my turn came, the nurse shoved that damned needle about an inch into my finger. It hurt like hell.

Friday morning we taught another charla, then gave two investigators copies of the Book of Mormon. This was followed by a couple more discussions. On the heels of a successful baptismal interview with Señora Bujaldon, we went to the church and cleaned the leaves and trash out of the font. Then we stuck a hose into it and went home, as it would take all night to fill. The following day Bujaldon was baptized. While I was happy for her, I was also glad I wasn't doing the baptizing. That water was cold, and I hoped that the next baptism would utilize our fire-building and water-heating services.

THE BUS RIDE TO MORAL OBLIVION

SUNDAY THE 20TH I had an epiphany about what I deemed inappropriate thoughts. All I had to do when a girl came into view was not avoid looking. It was what I did after the look that was important. If I talked about her for a few seconds, it would be better than spending the next fifteen minutes dwelling on her face and figure. It seemed like a viable plan.

The next morning, I left Coronel Diaz at 7:30 a.m., bound for Palacio and document renewal. Worried about how much rest I wouldn't get, among other things, I neglected to break the conversational ice with the fellow sitting next to me. For the following ninety minutes, I said nothing. By the time we arrived at the San Rafael bus terminal, I was beating myself up for being such a coward. What sort of missionary was I, anyway? I had a chance to share my beliefs with a stranger, things I knew to be true, things that made me happy. But I held back because I was afraid.

I hung out at the leaders' pensión all morning. At 12:30 p.m. I boarded a bus with two elders and a sister. Four hours later we arrived in Santa Fe, then took off again at 6 p.m. I read, then napped, then woke up and read some more. Soon it was dark and I had to flip on the tiny overhead reading lamp. Since cell phones wouldn't be in general use for another twenty years, and buses didn't show films, I was limited to the scriptures, Church books, and the *Reader's Digest* magazine I was currently reading from cover to cover. Sleep eventually returned, though only in twenty-minute intervals, interspersed with long stretches of insomnia. I was too tired to be miserable, my countenance taking on the look of a well-dressed zombie.

At 2:25 a.m., and in a daze, I looked out the window. We were passing through Temprano, streets well-lit even at this ugly time of the morning. I wondered if Elder George was still serving there, sleeping soundly in a warm, comfortable bed. I thought about the friends I'd acquired there, but sadness washed over me. For as close as I was at that moment, I'd probably never see any of them again, at least in this life. The realization that I no longer belonged there was sobering.

I drifted off to sleep again, then awoke and continued reading the *Digest*. An article about the genocidal Pol Pot regime in Cambodia got me so riled up that it drove sleep away. How could the world stand by while the communist Khmer Rouge murdered 1.2 million people? It validated my lifelong hatred of communism. It was a cancer spreading across the world, under the direction of the Father of Lies.

After countless stops along the Milk Run from Hell, we pulled into Palacio at 6:30 a.m. The rest of the morning was a blur. Somehow, I made it downtown with the others by 8:30, and took care of the documentary red tape. Then we were off to the mission home for some relaxation and chatter, before getting loaded down with books and packages to deliver to the zone. Then we were on our way back to the terminal.

Faced with the prospect of another interminable bus ride, I sought a seat on the back row of the bus. I could stretch my legs out and hopefully get some solid hours of shuteye. The bus pulled out of Palacio and it grew dark inside the vehicle, the evening light fading fast. At some point a figure worked its way along the aisle, heading my way in the gloom. It was a woman. A pretty woman. And she took a seat next to mine.

At first, I was uncomfortable about her close proximity—it was a female, after all, and I was a missionary. And being that there were no arm rests between us, her warm body was constantly bumping against mine—from the side, of course. After an hour or so, the lights went out. And it was when I closed my eyes that I started to relax and feel that body continue to move against mine. Despite myself, I was now hoping that the bus would keep taking sharp turns, swerve, whatever else it took to keep the jostling going. It felt wrong yet right, this surrender I was experiencing. I wasn't thinking about sex, per se, yet I was aroused, though fighting it every pulse beat of the way. I reveled in the closeness, and wanted it to go on forever. And for several hours it did. I would close my eyes and bask in the warmth, wondering what she was thinking, and if she was purposefully leaning against me. I couldn't tell if what I was feeling was wrong or right, but the anonymous contact with a mature woman overloaded my emotional circuitry. I realized how lonely I'd become, how starved I was for the bodily contact that only a woman could provide. I forgot who I was. I forgot my purpose for being there. And for a while I just didn't give a damn.

By the time our bus pulled into the next depot in the bleak, early hours, I was a mess. My clothes were disheveled. I hadn't slept a wink. The party was over. I disembarked, holding my suitcoat and bag in front of me in embarrassment. One of the sisters looked at me and asked if I was feeling well.

I sat in the San Rafael terminal, waves of guilt washing over me. And despite their familiarity, I'd never gotten used to the awful feelings they induced. I pulled out the journal and started writing. It was a rant about the sorry state of morality in Argentina— as if this soapbox effort would absolve me of guilt. The only part of the entry that seemed credible was the final sentences:

> *"The temptations seem to come at a faster and more frequent rate. Each time I resist them, I receive great blessings. Each time I don't, the fall seems harder, and closer to hell."*

I snapped the book shut. Who was I fooling? Though I believed I could let it go, I was in a rut. And it seemed that the only way out was to dig another, deeper rut right next to it—a moralistic foxhole from which I could reach over and castigate and berate myself in an effort to become clean. I'd change my thought patterns. Yes, that was what it'd take. Then the bus arrived and I forced myself to think about something else before the guilt could continue consuming me.

A well-dressed man entered the bus and commenced strolling up and down the aisle, selling a cure-all ointment. Several applications and your health problems would go away. Though I didn't want to buy what he was selling, I admired his intestinal fortitude. Two weeks earlier we'd shared another bus ride with him. "Buy my ointment while you still can," he'd warned us. "I'm leaving for

the south and won't be back this way for several months."
Now he was telling us that he'd be gone for six months. I
hoped that this time he'd keep his promise. But beyond
that, I wondered if there was a quick cure for anything.
That One-Time Solution.

For the next few days I chastised myself for encouraging such a strong emotional response to that female
passenger, for my lack of self-control. But I might as well
have asked the sun to not rise in the morning, or the
clouds to stop raining.

DON LORENZO, A DIAGNOSIS

WE VISITED DON LORENZO every four or five days. He enjoyed the talks immensely, even if they were one-way
conversations. According to his doctor, Don's health was
improving. Since his only son wouldn't see him, I attributed the man's improvement to the visits we and other
Church members were making. This time around we
showed him "Christ in America" and "Man's Search for
Happiness." They made him cry. Before leaving we gave
him a health blessing.

FRIDAY, MARCH 25TH

*"Dear Mom: Right now we're in the middle of the grape
harvest—called the Cosecha—and everywhere you can
see large trucks heaped with loads of green, red, and
purple grapes. My mouth waters every time I see one of
those trucks go by. This town is also heavily populated
with gauchos. As with all traditions, the gaucho image*

seems to be dying out. The gauchos you see nowadays are usually no younger than fifty-five."

During our next Don Lorenzo visit, Elder Doyle pushed him to say a few words: "Pablo," "agua," and "años." After he said the words he began crying. I wasn't sure if it was from joy or frustration. But otherwise he was in good spirits. He enjoyed the messages we shared and had faith in them. At one point we sat him up, but had to lay him back down after a few minutes, as his back was hurting. We were optimistic, but blindly so. How he was really faring health-wise, no one seemed to know.

Due to my complaints about not feeling well, Elder Doyle talked me into seeking medical advice. At the hospital clinic, I told the doctor about my weakness, constipation, blood in the stools, and nausea after eating. He had me lie down. He probed my stomach with his hands, listened with a stethoscope. Mumbling about a vitamin B deficiency, he prescribed a two-week regimen of five pills a day, sixty drops of a dark, foul-looking liquid in a bottle, laxatives, vitamin supplements, and anti-spasmodics.

"And you'll need some *inyecciones.*"

"Some what?" I asked, afraid that I actually understood what he'd just said.

"You need six injections."

Crap. I hated shots.

"And you'll need to receive them every other day."

Holy crap, that was a lot of needles. And my reaction wasn't lost on the good doctor.

"It would be better to receive the injections than risk us having to go in and look for the problem, wouldn't it?"

Go in? Look for the problem? Suddenly a half-dozen shots didn't seem like such a big deal when compared to a crap shoot like exploratory surgery. The sting was lessened by the fact that I could have Sariah, a shapely—no, well-endowed—young nurse in the Church branch administer the injections. Resigned to my fate, I used the last of my funds, and a 2,000 peso contribution from my comp, to purchase six syringe kits and medication. I sought out the lovely Sariah that very morning. The only thing left was deciding the area of injection. Based on the amount of dermal real estate available, Sariah determined that the gluteus maximus was the best candidate. The shot administered, it would then be up to me to remember to turn the other cheek, so to speak. No sense getting stuck in the same side every time.

A cure for the medical problems having been procured, the struggle with the spiritual continued. I was getting burned out about the Work. Several of our investigators were preparing for baptism, yet I had a hard time getting excited. I blamed this attitude on a lack of prayer and scripture study, ignoring the fact that I had been physically ill for several days in a row.

Then there was the matter of my companion. With twenty-seven days left, he was the very essence of trunkiness. He acted like a tourist on his last day in the country: at the hotel desk, ready to check out, taxi waiting. Doyle's conversations about "what I'm going to do when I get home" had a toxic effect on me. When he talked of traveling, I would reminisce about the old days, my thoughts no longer on the Work. Having been distracted for the last few days was causing me anguish. I felt like I was drifting further and further from my responsibilities as a missionary. I wondered if there was some way to help my companion keep his mind on the task at hand, when my best efforts should have been directed toward my own well-being.

Thinking it would make me feel better, I did some whining to Parón, via the weekly letter:

"Well, we're doing fine. We have a lot of people to teach, but we haven't had much time to visit them. The trip to Palacio used up all my money, and I lost three days of work in my area—but what can we do? The documents have to be renewed, right?"

NEEDLEPOINT AND SHORT WAVES

ON MONDAY THE 28TH, Sariah gave me Shot #2. Wednesday was Shot #3. With Friday came #4. Amidst all this medical treatment, Irma Fernandez was baptized. The shy, quiet woman from the end of town had progressed in her prayers and reading and studying. When the right time came, the Lord answered her questions and she stepped into the font on the first Saturday in March. I felt it a privilege to have been involved in her instruction.

Then came the Sunday shot. Fear of the needle gone, I was lackadaisical about the whole affair, even emboldened. Doyle and I went to the church building.

"Elder Hiland," Sariah said, as she stood behind me, the sounds of gloves being snapped on, a plastic package crinkling.

"Yes?"

"Lower your pants, please."

Following an "Okay," I undid my belt and let gravity take my pants all the way to Mother Earth.

"Uh—Elder Hiland," Doyle said, looking sideways at the spectacle, "She didn't ask to drop your pants. Only to *lower* them."

Standing where she was, the lovely Sariah couldn't see my smirk. But she did have a front-row view of my ass, partially covered by a white shirt tail. And at that moment I just didn't care.

I OWED MY DOCTOR A GREAT DEBT. I was gaining weight and feeling strong again. And though scheduled to see the doctor on Tuesday and Shot #6 from Sariah, I decided I'd had enough. Why bother when I was on the road to recovery?

During the evening our district of four visited Lino Casado, a shortwave radio operator. For a while he tried contacting a missionary in Colombia who Diarmid knew. But after a couple hours he gave up. There was too much interference. For the next two hours Lino sent messages across the United States, trying to contact anyone related to myself or the other three elders present.

Nothing seemed to be working until 2 a.m., when he found a guy in Pennsylvania by the name of Clayt—the same fellow who'd helped Elder Doyle with a phone patch to relatives a while back. Clayt called my mother from the eastern seaboard. Once the operator got through, I could hear the phone ringing. My heart was beating hard. Mom picked up on the second ring, and was more than surprised. At a loss for words, I managed to talk to her for a few minutes before the line was cut off. Two minutes later the connection was re-established and we spoke for a bit longer. It was so good to hear her voice after a year of letters and the occasional tape. As Mom was saying goodbye, the connection broke up and she was gone. But it was healing balm for my soul. Home was real again. It was still there.

Three days after my decision to forgo further medical treatment, I noticed two lumps underneath the skin near my throat. Unnerved by their sudden appearance, I scheduled another hospital visit to have blood work done.

ELDER DOYLE'S PROWESS with the Old Testament encouraged me to investigate that portion of the scriptures I'd been avoiding since my Methodist days. Though it was horribly complex—especially Samuel, Kings and Chronicles—I found it helpful to make an outline and synopsis, chapter by chapter. In line with this endeavor, I joined the district for a trip to the cinema to see *The Ten Commandments*. My third visit to the movies proved to be the charm. No one was concerned about whether or not we should go. It was a guilt-free expedition to view Hollywood's most ambitious attempt at a biblical epic. And though it suffered from some miscasting—Edward G. Robinson? Anne Baxter? John Carradine? —and was doctrinally off-base at times, I enjoyed the diversion. Nothing like a plague of locusts to take your mind off of your troubles.

DIAGNOSIS #2, A SANITY-CHALLENGED LANDLADY

TO SAY THAT THE MONDAY VISIT to the hospital was entertaining would be a flat-out lie. Unsure what was going on with my body, I wanted answers. Instead I got a blood test, thus heightening the suspense. Wednesday morning the neck lumps were larger. I could feel them when I swallowed. Off we went to see one Dr. Jafalla.

"Now, about your white blood cell count . . ." he said as he went over the hieroglyphics on my lab report. Apparently, I had 11,000 leukocytes instead of the standard-issue 6,000 to 7000.

"I'm going to examine your glands." He felt around in my groinal area, then under my armpits.

"No swelling there." Grabbing a clipboard, he scribbled some notes, then filled out a prescription slip.

"Here. This is for some vitamin pills." The same ones I'd been taking.

"I want you to come back in a month. We'll take some more blood. If the tests come back positive, we'll need to do a biopsy on those lumps in your neck."

Holy crap.

"And regardless of what we find then, those lumps will need to come out."

Expletive deleted.

As if that wasn't enough, I was broke. Out of the $8,050 I'd received from the mission home, I'd repaid Elder Doyle the $7,000 I owed him. The rest of the money had gone somewhere for expenses. Since my companion was going home in ten days, I couldn't touch him for more funds. On top of this, we were scheduled to change apartments soon, since the present landlord was charging too much for rent. But on the bright side, the new place, belonging to one Señora Moreno, was a better bang for the peso. Though we'd be paying a little more, benefits included a huge room, washed clothes, hot water, a kerosene heater, breakfast, lunch, telephone access, and a toilet that actually worked.

Later that special day, we visited Sariah and gave her the glad tidings.

"Guess what?" Elder Doyle said. "We found a new place to live."

"How wonderful," said Sariah, clapping her hands. "So, where is it?"

"At the home of a Señora Moreno. It's really nice. It has a—"

"Wait a minute. You say her name is *Moreno?*"

"Yes." Doyle told her the address.

"*Elders.* I have lived there before. There's something bad there. Don't move in. Please."

"Bad? In what way? What's the problem?"

"I won't go into the details. Let's just say that there were problems there, a while back."

"*Problems?*"

"She has some mental issues."

"Well, that's just great," I said, as we pedaled away. "Now what do we do?"

"We don't move in, that's what we do."

TROUBLED BY DR. Jafalla's sinister diagnosis, I sought a second opinion that evening. Visiting Physician #2 at his private clinic, I handed over the lab results from Dr. J.

"Remove your clothing, please."

This had to be entertaining for Elder Doyle, I thought, as I stripped down to my birthday suit.

"Okay, let's begin." The good doctor poked and prodded and generally felt around before returning to his clipboard. "I see you've been circumcised," he noted, as if that had anything to do with anything.

"Are you Jewish, or Jehovah's Witness?"

"Huh—what?" I said. Doyle was definitely looking entertained.

"Elder Hiland," my comp said. "He wants to know if you're Jewish or a Jehovah's Witness."

"Oh, no. I'm a Mormon."

"I see," the doctor said, scribbling something else on his page. I sat there feeling stupid, and wondering when I could don my apparel.

"As for your lab results," he said, pointing to the blood analysis, "there are a few mistakes here."

"*Mistakes?*"

The doctor didn't respond. Then—

"You will need to take twenty drops of laxative this evening. Then you must collect samples of your feces and urine. Bring them to the lab tomorrow morning."

Unfamiliar with the finer points of feces and urine collection, I queried further.

"So—how will I know when to get up and collect these samples?"

"Don't worry, Mr. Hiland," he said, looking over the top of his glasses. "You'll know."

Elder Doyle was smiling.

Armed with that cryptic answer, I paid $1,500 to Physician #2, said funds borrowed from my comp. Upon returning home, I located a two- by three-inch glass jar with beveled edges. In an earlier time, it had held cold cream or jam or jelly or some other pleasing thing. Now it would soon be put to a less dignified use. Placing The Jar on my nightstand, I downed the Twenty Drops and set my clock. I fell asleep that night wondering where we would be living, come the weekend. We might be able to move into a house the Branch President owned. But similar to my pending bathroom encounter, whatever happened next was going to be messy.

ATOMIC LAXATIVES AND HITLER YOUTH

AT 3 AM I AWOKE WITH A START, remembering what was on my biological dance card at this forsaken hour. For a few moments, I didn't feel that bad, just sort of full. But the motion of sitting up was like a trembling finger poised above the rocket launch button. I threw aside the covers. I grabbed The Jar. I ran for the can. Everything thereafter was a blur, my guts boiling like a pressurized kettle as I scrambled to place the receptacle on the little shelf-like ledge down inside the toilet before it was too late- and then assuming the position amid fears about how to accurately aim for a target so small. And then not caring as I exploded . . .

It was all over, literally and figuratively, within seconds, but the work was only beginning. Following a heavenly cleansing shower, there was a hell of a mess to clean up. As I swabbed the porcelain decks, I cursed Dr. #2 and his methods. I was sure he hated Americans—so much so that he didn't tell me about any of the fecal collection devices that must surely have been available for use. Let the Yankee clean up his own mess! *Number Two, indeed,* I muttered, musing on the physician's nickname. Looking back on it now—after having earned the Diaper-Changing merit badge while raising three kids—I did remarkably well. And by comparison, the urine collection portion of the program was a walk in the park. Or restroom, if you will. The cab ride later that morning to the doctor's office was a subdued affair, compared to the previous session. I was relaxed, sleepy, and grateful the ordeal was over. My comp, on the other hand, looked troubled; the urine sample container had developed a leak and . . .

During the day, someone contacted a German lady who had a room for rent. It would cost a bit more than Moreno's place, but sounded like a nicer setup. A bit smaller, but sans any psychotic baggage. She was informed that we were ready to move in, and the die was cast. We loaded up Brother Yllanes's pickup the next morning and headed for the German's place. But upon arrival, she said that a girl was still occupying the rental room. The deal was off. Forming a huddle, we made plans.

"Now what do we do?" someone moaned. Then came, "This really bites," followed by the perennial favorite: "Crap."

"Well, why don't we move into Moreno's?" I asked. After all, how bad could it be? It wasn't as if we hadn't dealt with neurotics before. We told the driver to take us to Moreno's place. She was overjoyed at our reappearance, asking if there was anything she could do for us as she handed over the door key, then left. Everything moved in, I started unpacking. I could see the possibilities in our luxurious surroundings already: a huge room, washed clothes, hot water, a kerosene heater, breakfast, lunch, telephone access, and a toilet that actually worked. As for those silly stories about our new landlady? Surely gossip, nothing more.

WE STOPPED BY SARIAH'S HOUSE to give her the good news.

"Guess what?" Elder Doyle said.

"Yes?"

"We found a new place to live."

"How wonderful," Sariah said, clapping her hands. "So, where is it?"

"Señora Moreno's. It's really nice. It has a—"

"No! *Elders.*"

"Yes, Sariah?"

"Elders. How could you? I told you already—she's a *bad* person."

"*Bad?* You said that before, but you wouldn't give us any details. We had to take you at your word."

Sariah looked at her mother, and they both spoke at once: "Señora Moreno was committed to a psychiatric ward for four months. She was accused of having sexual relations with her tenants."

Committed. Psychiatric ward. Sexual relations .

"Well, that's just great," I said as we pedaled away. "Now what do we do?"

"We don't move in, that's what we do."

Instead we called Brother Yllanes and the district leader.

THE TALENT SHOW at the branch meeting house that evening was a big success. A lot of investigators and other non-members attended, everyone having a good time. I even participated in a sketch. Elder Doyle, in full gaucho dress, served as the emcee and hammed it up. He read gaucho poems, eliciting much laughter though unsure why. Later he was told that some of the verses described the act of flatulation, and in most unflattering terms.

After the show, Elders Aldin and Diarmid helped us pack up our stuff. I looked around our new digs with no small sense of loss: the huge room, washed clothes, hot water, a toilet that actually worked, a kerosene heater, breakfast, lunch, and a telephone. All slipping through our fingers forever. What-Could-Have-Been being replaced by What-Was-Not-Going-To-Happen. We waited nervously until midnight, hoping Señora Moreno didn't show up and ask what was going on. Yllanes arrived and we were out of the apartment in two minutes, heading to his place for the night.

The following day, Elders A and D went in search of an apartment. Stopping by the German's place on the off chance that she'd reconsidered, she told them the room was now open. We moved in at noon, feeling blessed. The quarters were small, a living room converted to a bedroom. There were two beds, a sofa, a chair, a nice armoire, and sheepskin rugs. Services included breakfast, lunch, and laundry service. I got the bed under the window, Doyle sleeping below locked windows through which one could see into the kitchen. As for our new landlady, she was a big, gruff, German woman who could be very nice yet get stern at the drop of an attitude. Over the next day or two she told us of her days as a Hitler Youth. Her description of that time was bleak and terrible. Eventually she came to South America and made a new life for herself. During those first few days she treated us to homemade strudel and we got to meet one of her blonde Aryan granddaughters.

SICKNESS, HELP, AND SOLITARY REFINEMENT

IN THE HEALTH DEPARTMENT, the growths on my neck were getting more painful every day. Having traveled to San Rafael with Elder Aldin in preparation for an upcoming district conference, we waited at the ZLs' place until they got home. I began to get nauseous, my stomach aching. The only thing that helped was lying flat on my stomach, so the sick feeling could subside. I got a few hours' sleep that night, but was dragging around the following day, the conference talks unable to hold my attention.

After the priesthood session, I met with President Parón and explained my health and personal problems to him, prepared to sell my projector and shaver, I was so broke. He gave me 10,000 pesos and some advice about avoiding bad thoughts. I left the interview feeling much better. By evening we were back home and I got to spend my first night in the new apartment. It was good.

The following week the doctor noted that my neck lumps were starting to shrink. It appeared that the medicine was finally having the desired effect. That evening our DL and the ZLs visited Don Lorenzo with Doyle and me. We sat him up in a chair and sang several Church hymns. He loved it all, waving his hand back and forth like a choir director.

IT WAS THURSDAY THE 21ST, Elder Doyle with one day to go. But he wasn't making it easy for me. If we were visiting members, small talk was the order of the day. If the Work needed to be discussed, I had to initiate the discussion. My companion's mind was elsewhere. But regardless of how cavalier he was acting, my comp was feeling the effects.

"You know, Elder," he said, "I feel like I'm walking in a dream."

Maybe he was starting to realize that he didn't want to go home as badly as he'd originally thought.

DESPITE THE INFUSION of cash from Parón, I sold the Singer to a sister missionary for 10,000 pesos. As for final visits, we stopped by Don Lorenzo's place so Elder Doyle could say goodbye. Don was continuing to improve. He could move his left leg and shoulder a little, the paralysis having waned. At 6 a.m. Saturday morning, Elder Doyle waved goodbye, climbed the steps and disappeared into a departing bus headed for Palacio and the mission home, the first leg of a long journey home. I'd enjoyed our time together, except for the trunky last couple weeks. He worked hard at times and had developed a strong bond with the people in Coronel Diaz.

The other elders accompanied me to my pensión, then left for their area. I sat down and looked around the room. Aside from bus trips for document renewal, this was the first time I'd been without a temporary or assigned companion my whole mission. I savored the aloneness, the singularity of my existence. Besides, my new comp would show up any minute.

With nothing else to do, for the moment, my thoughts turned to the recent past. It had been fascinating to watch how Elder Doyle changed during those last few days. When I first arrived, he was always talking about home, what he planned on doing after he got there, how great things would be. But on that last night and following morning, he seemed stunned. It made me realize how special mission life was. What I chose to do with the next seven months and three weeks was totally in my hands. On the verge of getting a new companion, I could start over with a clean slate. Set new goals. Say new prayers. Really show the Lord that I wanted to work.

That evening I went with the other elders to teach a discussion. Afterward they brought me home and left. It was so quiet. Peaceful. I fell asleep that night, wondering when my new companion would show up.

OF BOWELS AND MIRACLES

ON THE SECOND DAY, I woke up late, my alarm clock still in transit from Jugo. During church, we were assigned sacrament talks. Then it was back to solitary refinement, reading, sleeping, memorizing discussions, and preparing as best I could for the upcoming week. I was starting to enjoy the time off.

ON THE THIRD DAY, I slept in. During the afternoon, we visited Don Lorenzo. He understood everything we taught him. Later that day I scribbled in the journal:

> *My new companion still hasn't arrived yet. I don't know where he's at, but I wish he'd arrive. I'm tired of working with the other two elders as a threesome. It limits me to only half a day's work possible in my area.*
>
> *I received a package from Elder Schieff today. It contained my alarm clock, which I sorely needed, and five letters.*
>
> *The sisters from my group are going home around the second week in June. That's only a month and a half away. As Elder George once stated, "The farther along you get in the mission, the faster the time goes."*

The latest journal entry made, I headed for bed, grateful my red clock was back in the fold. Maybe now I could start getting up early again.

ON THE FOURTH DAY the German spoke.

"Mr. Hiland, we need to talk."

"Okay . . ."

"The toilet keeps clogging up."

"The *what?*"

"It clogs. Yes. This is no good."

I nodded my head, but was unsure if I had heard her correctly.

"So here." She handed me a bag made of nylon netting. "You go in that—then put the material in this can," as if this poop-handling task were no more trouble than switching television channels. As I nodded in disbelief, she continued.

"Then I will throw it in the garbage, okay?"

"Uh . . . sure."

Having done *her* duty, she trundled off. I stood there gazing at The Bag, wondering about *my* duty. How would I pull this off? Writing about the conversation in my journal, I wondered if she should get the house outfitted with larger pipes. I also wondered if my landlady's strudel had been left in the oven too long.

> *"No companion yet. Maybe he arrived during the siesta today. That would explain why Aldin and Diarmid are forty-five minutes late coming to pick me up.*
>
> *"I've been memorizing my charlas for the last couple of days. It seems that I've forgotten most of the questions and scriptural references, as well as a few of the longer and more difficult concepts of the charlas."*

A short time later Aldin and Diarmid appeared, sans my new companion. Before we fired out, someone used the toilet.

Our threesome visited with a branch member to talk about missionary work, then ended up teaching a Charla C on the spot to some friends of his. We followed that with a discussion at another home before I was returned to my cage. There was a note lying on the table:

> *"Mr. Hiland, please comply with your 'word.' Once again, this afternoon, the toilet was plugged after your visits (from the other elders). If and when I find the toilet plugged Friday, the apartment will terminate!"*

War had been declared.

ON THE FIFTH DAY we visited members and taught a couple discussions. All was quiet on the German front. At 11:57 p.m. I struggled to stay awake, trying to record the day's events. Still no companion.

ON THE SIXTH DAY, Elder Hiland got cross. We visited members all morning, me getting more irritable with every successive hour I had to spend as Elder Third Wheel. My mood was not helped by listening to a lengthy tape from the ZLs, in which they foisted on us some lame attempts at humor. My temperament took another nosedive during a visit to an elderly woman who was a member of our branch. Her Catholic caretakers did not appreciate our presence. But despite a spate of grouchiness, I was in the mood to bridge-build.

"Hello," I said after we shook hands with everyone. "We're representatives of Jesus Christ and-" I was interrupted by a fellow who tipped the scales at 350 pounds, if he was an ounce.

"If you are who you say you are," he told me, "heal my leg!"

Taken aback by his surly attitude, I looked at said appendage. It certainly looked like it needed something.

"But that's not the way the Lord works," I said.

"Hmmpphh."

"The power of the priesthood that I hold is from God. Healing and blessings happen according to the Lord's will, not ours."

But the portly fellow and his relatives were having none of it, while the poor member lady sat there, speechless. Due to the toxic combination of my irritation and their haughtiness, we got nowhere. The discussion ended with both sides beating a hasty retreat, the result being a bitter taste in the mouths of all concerned.

The afternoon went better. We taught Don L the first part of Charla C. Unable to speak, due to his condition, he cried during the discussion. Before leaving we taught him how to pray. Later we taught a Señora Lucero, but she had trouble understanding us so we had to go slow. Following that we taught a married couple part of D and showed them the *Man's Search for Happiness* flick. I ended the day scribbling in my journal at 1:20 a.m., wondering why I was still without a comp.

ON THE SEVENTH DAY, we taught Don L about Christ's visit to the Americas and showed him the flick. Then it was on to Lucero, followed by another visit to the couple we'd taught the day before. Things were going great until we found out that they weren't actually married. This brought our plans for baptism to a screeching halt. They would need to talk to a judge or lawyer about getting separation papers started before the baptism could take place. Another potential Church member frustrated by the aftereffects of strict divorce laws and the common-law-marriage. Our last charla for the evening was with Don L's nurse, in the home of Señora Miranda.

And on this day Elder Fineas arrived. Out over a year, he seemed pleasant enough. I hoped for the best.

TEACHING AND THE GERMAN'S HEATER

MONDAY MORNING, as I wrote in the journal, I could hear Elder F swearing when his shower water turned ice cold. In what was becoming a daily event; the German told us she was low on gas—propane, that is—so we wouldn't be able to take any more hot-water showers. As for conditions generally, my companion disliked things even more than I. And he'd only been in town three days. We were both ready to leave as soon as the next month's rent was due. It wasn't just the fact that we were paying $30 more a month than the other elders. It was the German's increasing belligerence, an attitude that left us wondering what was provoking it.

That weekend we traveled north to San Rafael to attend the baptisms of the Soria family. Though there was a font in Coronel Diaz, the cold weather would have been bad for Señora Soria's heart. The service went well, except for Elder Aldin's deteriorating inseam. Being the baptizer, his exertions caused the white baptism pants to tear a little more with each dunk. He had to hold his pants together during all the baptisms. Then we took turns confirming the family members. While saying the confirmation prayer for Sylvia, I forgot to confirm her a member of the Church and had to start the prayer again. Though embarrassed by such a mistake, I felt a good spirit. And as with all the people I had previously confirmed, I felt a love for these people which is hard to describe. During the prayer, I wanted to bless them with all sorts of good things, but had to concentrate instead on speaking the words the Lord wanted them to hear.

WITH TWO MONTHS in Coronel Diaz accrued, time was flying. Things were going well. We had solid investigators to teach, as well as a lot of success encouraging branch members to help with the Work. At one meeting in the Lopez home I had to compress the contents of a forty-five-minute discussion of D into a ten-minute presentation, for a large group of people. Before showing the *Man's Search* film, I handed out pamphlets and set up appointments to teach several people in the coming week.

In the following days, we showed more films and taught more discussions. At one meeting there were thirty-two children, a couple of adolescents, and five adults in attendance. I had to do most of the work, as Elder Fineas was suffering from diarrhea and stomach problems. But I could see that the Lord was blessing us with more people to teach, and I loved it. It was the best work on earth.

MAY 10TH. Upon our return to the apartment, a small electric heater we'd been using was wrapped in paper, a note taped to it: "PROHIBITED—DO NOT USE!" The weather turning cold and us needing a heat source, I had ignored the German's demands that we stop turning on the heater. The fact that she knew we'd been using the device made me realize she'd been going through our apartment while we were out. Though I was willing to help conserve resources, this latest shot across the land-lord-tenant bow was too much. I unwrapped the heater and placed it on top of the armoire. The following morn-ing, upon our return from a trip downtown, I went to the kitchen to ask the German a question. The heater was resting on top of a cabinet.

"What's *that* doing up there?" I asked, my BP shoot-ing for the stars.

"You did not keep your word!"

Struggling to hold back a stream of corrosive ver-biage, I grabbed the heating device and carried it back to our room as a most surprised and angry landlady looked on, speechless. Our plans to leave the following week vali-dated, I wondered what she would say when she discov-ered that I'd plugged the toilet.

Yet the Work went on. That afternoon we taught Omar about the law of chastity, and invited him to be baptized on May 21st. The only hitch was that he'd need to get written permission from his mother, then approval from the mission president. That evening we taught C to another crowd of people in the Lopez home, four families this time around, three of which I was able to set up appointments with. I was starting to enjoy teaching large groups. I noted in the journal that I had 216 days left.

Thursday the 12th I was trying to record the day's events while on board a crowded, noisy, swaying bus, bound for San Rafael, some sightseeing, and a zone Conference. Hours earlier we'd had a big fight with the German. It was definitely time to move out. The question was, where? For the moment, anywhere would be better than the apartment. Elder Diarmid was across the aisle, talking to Fineas about life at BYU. Elder D had an interesting take on that Utah university, having been kicked out of it after several rounds of practical jokes that included putting the president's car up on blocks and walking around the campus, spraying coeds with streams of pressurized water.

I sometimes dreamed of attending the "Y," but given my poor performance at college over the last couple years, attending a big school with high academic standards was a veritable crap shoot. I had no idea what I wanted to do with my life, unlike some of my contemporaries. Going to school would be a waste of time and money, regardless of the number of marriageable women roaming the BYU campus.

OF TOSSING AND BEING TOSSED

IN PREPARATION FOR A RECREATIONAL TRIP to Valle Grande, I stayed with Elders Thurston and Sewell. We talked late into the night, Sewell regaling us with stories of near-death experiences and the like. Laughter was abundant. Continuing his self-appointed role as chief storyteller, Elder Sewell steered the topic of conversation to illness. Some eight hours earlier, both elders had consumed large portions of pasta. And though Thurston was comfortable, his companion's gastrointestinal tract seemed unwilling to allow entry or passage of said Italian dish. Sewell's digestive jury was still deliberating about which direction to send the load of pasta that had taken up residence in his stomach. Hence, our storyteller's decision to air the Barf Tape.

The subject of said recording had been suffering the ravages of an extended bout of stomach flu, microphone in trembling hand as he recorded himself puking. As an added feature, commentary was provided between bouts of retching. At first revolted, I started giggling at the idea of someone recording such an event for posterity, or a medical examiner. Then I was off to the races, laughing harder than I had in months.

After a particularly violent yakking episode, the voice on the tape quieted to a whisper, the Elder trying to catch his breath. Then came a thin, reedy voice:

"Happy Barfday to me . . .

"Happy Barf—day to me (an audible gulp followed).

"Happy Barfday—ungghh—Happy Barfday—" followed by gagging and a moment of composure-regaining silence.

"Hap-py Barf-day to—BLEAUUGGGHHH!" the microphone cast aside as the poor guy ejected unwanted foodstuffs via the North Door. I was rolling on the floor, laughing so hard I thought I'd gag. The tape ended abruptly, and after a few more laughing jags, we all went to sleep. Worn out from the merriment, we'd stayed up too far into the wee hours.

Around 5:30 a.m., we resurrected ourselves and were out the door, shambling our way towards the bus station, along dimly lit, pre-dawn streets. The air was chilly, rain threatening. A trip anywhere seemed like a lousy idea. And despite the few hours of valuable rest he'd gotten, Elder S looked like hell, yet determined to make it to Valle Grande. Several blocks into our sojourn, Sewell mumbled something, then lurched from the sidewalk to the center of the street, bent forward with back arched as pasta sprayed from his mouth. Neighborhood dogs, alerted to the noise, began barking their encouragement.

My first reaction should have been distress. But giddy from lack of sleep, I started giggling. Elder Thurston, conversely, was not giggling. There was a strange, faraway look in his eyes. He glanced at his companion, swayed a bit, then dashed into the street and folded in the middle before launching his own stored meal to the pavement. I fell to the sidewalk, convulsed with laughter. After a few minutes, the companionship finished purging. Once the elders got their breaths back, we marched on to the bus terminal in silence.

We arrived at the station, the sisters being the only other missionaries present. By the time the Valle Grande bus arrived, we were still the only missionaries present, so the bus left without us. The sisters returned to their apartment, and would be mad at the leaders for the rest of the day. Curious as to why no one else had shown up, I went to the leaders' place and knocked. Receiving no answer, I walked in. They were fast asleep. I grabbed a blanket, found a clear spot on the floor and conked out. Sewell and Thurston returned home to their sickbeds.

The following afternoon, our district was hanging out at the new apartment, telling jokes and having a good time. We weren't making that much noise, but the German seemed to think so and yelled at us; then said she was calling the police. I thought she was bluffing. Then I heard her calling someone on the phone. A few minutes later it rang, and we could hear her giving directions. Freaking out, we set a new world's record for packing, then hauled everything outside and stood around, racking our brains for some way to get ourselves and our belongings away from the German's place ASAP. She stormed out the front door, insulting us and, in general, radiating a very ugly spirit. She tried to draw us into an argument with her, but we didn't take the bait.

Unable to bear the suspense any more, I went next door and asked Señor Ramirez to call a taxi. Who would arrive first: the police or our ride? As we were waiting, the German reappeared to inform us that she'd flushed the toilet again to see if it was plugged. Before we could learn what she had discovered during her lavatorial inspection, the taxi came and we got out of there fast. We ended up in the other elders' apartment, filling their room with boxes and luggage.

THE CALM BEFORE THE STURM

WITHIN TWO DAYS we'd found a much nicer place to live. Owned by an older couple, it was quiet, had decent water pressure, access to a refrigerator, a kitchen table for meals, and a toilet that didn't clog at the drop of a meal. That issue settled, we went out to work, visiting Don Lorenzo and the Peralta family. With the latter, we were trying to get the father of the family to sign a permission slip so his wife could get baptized.

The next night we rode our bikes out to the Peralta home with the slip, but they were gone. Since we were on the road, we decided to visit the Tellos. Though positive we could get there via Road A, my route took us in the opposite direction. We traveled three miles before I realized it was the wrong street. We headed back to town, where we took Road B another three miles to Tellos. Afterwards we took Road C to return home, my legs shot from the exertion.

I BEGAN A WORK SESSION with Elder Aldin, the district leader. We visited members, saw investigators, and had a good charla with Señor Soria and his family. He was that fellow I'd felt impressed we needed to start teaching. The Spirit was there and they felt it. Since he didn't know how to read, his wife would have to help him with the assignments we gave him. For the next few days we taught a lot of charlas and accomplished much with the Sorias, Aliagas Omar, and Don Lorenzo.

Sunday, May 22: "Well, these last few days have been routine: get up late (7:30 a.m.); get dressed; go heat up some milk; eat breakfast consisting of bread with marmalade on it, hot chocolate and a Postum-type drink; fire out at 9 a.m.; buy tomorrow's breakfast; go to the other elders' place to see if we got any mail; go visit members or investigators for a few hours; lunchtime— we eat at the other elders' place; afterwards, talk to them for a while in their small room; back to our place; study, shower, etc., until 3:30 or 4:00 p.m.; fire out; visit members and teach some charlas; at 9:30 or 10:00 p.m. return to the apartment; eat something; study a little; fire-in; personal prayers; hit the sack."

Around this time, things started going downhill between me and Elder Fineas. The last few companions had been easy-going. But my new comp was a different breed altogether. The tolerance I thought I was showing him was not being returned. The harder I tried to get along, the worse things became. Without warning he'd get nasty or snappy in his responses to me and the other elders. Maybe he wanted to look macho, and sarcasm was the key. I wanted to talk to him about the issue, but was afraid he'd get defensive and angry. The cold, rainy weather cast a pall over the town. It looked to be a long winter.

HOW NOT TO IMPRESS CHURCH LEADERS

ON THE 24TH I RECEIVED ANOTHER SHOT from the lovely Sariah—this time of gamma globulin, and in the arm. Later in the day our DL and his comp told us of their great plan. It was called a "sting," referring to a big surprise. The idea was to fill the chapel with 200 people for a special meeting to be called "The Master's Touch." Four converts would bear their testimonies, telling about their conversion to the Church. There would be a choir number, followed by a testimony meeting. Elder Aldin promised there wouldn't be a dry eye in the house.

In line with this idea about a "sting," Elder A had had business cards printed up with the words *"Coronel Diaz knows how to Sting. Do you?"* in the center. Below that it said *"With love,"* nicknames for each of us concluding the message. Yes, the card was irreverent, what with those clever nicknames, sans the "elder" designation. But the intent was to invite people to listen to us, to see that we were a force for good, that we were fun-loving and all that. Though unsure who to give the cards to, I thought they were kind of cool-looking—a novelty in a world that needed some shaking up once in a while. And if there was one thing Elder Aldin wanted us to do, it was shake things up.

During the week, we boarded a 5:30 a.m. bus for the long trek to the Santa Fe area conference. Area meetings were a big deal for us missionaries—especially the leadership. A lot of training took place. Usually there was a high-level member of the Church—a general authority—present to look things over and ensure that the missionaries of the Church, from the mission president, assistants, to the ZLs and on down, were progressing, and that policies and programs were being followed correctly. This time around it was Robert Smith of the First Quorum of the Seventy who presided, giving talks and providing needed instruction. His keynote address was three hours long, the main subject being the best ways to teach and proselyte. That part of the program finished, Elder Smith descended from the podium while several missionaries prepared a slide presentation about President Parón.

I was grateful for a break from the long talks. What I wasn't so thrilled about was Elder Smith choosing to sit next to me. It wasn't that I disliked him, but what do you talk about with a man who has traveled all over the world and rubs shoulders with the top leaders in your church? The weather in Jugo? The price of maté? The latest diarrhea cures?

At first, I considered just keeping my trap shut and enjoying the slide show. But no. I just had to pipe up.

"Hi," I said to Elder Smith. "I'm Elder Hiland."

"Nice to meet you," he said grabbing my hand in a firm, leader-like grip. Unsure what to say next, I went for the low-hanging fruit. I handed him one of our district's "business" cards.

"Here's one of the cards we use to introduce ourselves to people," I said, proud of its message and look. Simple, yet cavalier. Elder Smith looked the card over.

"What does this word 'sting' mean?" he asked, traces of a scowl forming on his face. Trying to keep things upbeat, I attempted an explanation. The man was not impressed. But I gave it one more try.

"So, what do you think of it?"

Elder Smith gave the card another glance, then—

"*Le parece mal.*" In English this means, "I don't like the looks of this."

At that moment the lights went down, signaling the start of the slideshow. Elder S was distracted for the moment, his attention directed to the screen. I sat there, feeling like a jackass. I'd betrayed my fellow elders. It was the *Doc Savage* movie debacle all over again. I could see it now: Smith would call us into an empty room immediately after the meeting.

"Okay, brethren," he'd say, pacing back and forth in front of us. "We have a serious breach of protocol on our hands." He would then hold up the Sting card.

"I would like you to explain yourself, Elder Hiland. How could you have the poor taste to hand out these *things* to the public?"

"But—" I'd begin to say, before Smith cut me off.

"You're a disgrace to the mission, a slap in the face to the missionary effort."

After that meeting, Parón would call me into his office, then send me home, disgraced.

Elder Smith was still looking at the screen. I waited for him to say something, but he seemed to be ignoring me. Maybe he'd think things over and hand the card back. Then I could steal away and destroy the evidence. To my horror, he tucked the card deep into his portfolio pocket, forever out of my reach. Taking advantage of the darkness, I inched to one side, then snuck off to a distant, darkened pew. So much for my encounter with authority.

CONTENTION, SUCCESS, DISAPPOINTMENT

THE FOLLOWING WEEK, Elder Fineas and I challenged Soria to be baptized, worked with an inactive family, taught more charlas, and showed films to interested parties. We were getting the work done. But my companion was on a slow boil. One day, as we were crossing the street, I darted in front of a motorcycle, despite my comp's wishes. After we made it to the other side, he started in with me.

"Hey! Watch where you're going."

"I looked both ways and decided it was safe to cross."

"If you're going to get all ticked off when I try to protect you, then I just won't worry about it anymore!"

"I'm not mad," I said, though I was headed in that direction. "I just think I can watch out for myself."

Now it was his turn.

"Companionships exist for a reason. Companions exist so that we have protection and stay out of trouble. But I'm not going to worry about it anymore, because you get so damned ticked off when I try to help you!"

Now I was pissed. We walked along in angry silence while things cooled down. After we visited a member, though, the bad feelings were gone.

"I'm sorry," I said. "I guess I was being proud. Thanks for watching out for me."

"It's okay. Everybody has their disagreements." After a bit more silence he continued.

"You know—besides Elder Breck, you're the elder I've had the best relationship with." It made me wonder what the *bad* relationships had been like, and I shuddered. Apologies shared, we moved on, for the moment. And the timing couldn't have been better. We needed to be in good spiritual shape for the charlas that evening with Soria and Aliaga. The discussions went well, especially with Señor Soria, who, despite his inability to read, was progressing well.

The Master's Touch program the following Sunday was a great success. Though we only had one hundred people in attendance, we still filled the chapel. As I looked across the room, I realized that all our hard work had paid off. Many inactive members showed up, as well as several investigators from across the district. I conducted the hymns, and during the testimony portion of the meeting I helped set the tone for those who followed me. When it came time to speak, I felt the Lord guiding me. It was a wonderful experience. Afterward, the members came up and shook our hands, thanking us for the program.

That evening I relaxed for the first time that week, reading Church magazines for a couple hours straight, reveling in the knowledge that I could bring about change for the better when I really put my mind to it. What I couldn't figure out was how to help Elder Fineas. Before crashing for the evening, we talked. He told me about his family, how they were not unified, leading to feelings of hatred and resentment among various family members. The wounds ran deep, and seemed to be affecting the way my comp treated others. The following day I was still thinking about what Elder F had told me. And though he divulged deep feelings, he didn't seem willing to change. Fortunately, Elder Aldin answered my prayers by taking Elder F aside for a private chat. As a result, my comp returned in a better mood.

DUE TO ALL THEIR PRAYING and studying, the Soria's were receiving solid testimonies of the truth, their interviews scheduled for Thursday morning. The baptisms were to take place Friday afternoon. In preparation, we spent part of the day cleaning dirt and leaves out of the font. Then we began filling it with water. During the Thursday morning interviews, we found that though Señora Soria was ready for baptism, her wine-swilling hubbie was not. On top of that, he was indecisive about being baptized. Elder Aldin told him to make up his mind by 1:30 p.m. on Friday. And so the wait began.

Friday morning Fineas set up things in the driveway next to the church. We cleaned out two 55-gallon drums, then started filling one with water while we went in search of firewood. Upon returning, we noticed that the barrel was leaking. Too late to fix it, we got both fires going and put the two barrels on top of them. Then we left for lunch. Later we cleaned up, got dressed in our suits, and raced over to the Soria home to pick them up. Señora Soria informed us that she had just come down with tonsillitis. Furthermore, her husband's boss had picked him up to finish a job. I couldn't believe what I was hearing. I wondered how we could have been so spiritually out of touch that we weren't prompted ahead of time. Saying farewell to Soria, we returned to the church and extinguished the fires. Putting the firewood away and dumping the barrels, we trudged home, defeated. But the day wasn't a total loss. That evening we taught two quality charlas, one to the daughter of the Rosales family, the other to Señor Ramirez, whose wife was a member of the Church.

Talks with Soria continued Saturday morning. In the process, we discovered that it was a good thing he hadn't been baptized. Still drinking wine, and with a sketchier understanding of the Book of Mormon than we'd been led to believe, he needed more time. Later we had another charla with the Rosales girl and fixed a date for her baptism. But as with so many other good prospects, marital problems reared their ugly head. Since she and her husband were married—but about to separate—we had to get his permission for her to be baptized. We went to his house and talked to him about signing, but he refused. Saying thank you and goodbye we left, determined to find another way.

That evening we rode all the way out to Tellos house, but no one was home, our fourth failure with them that week. From there we traveled the dark and bumpy road to Peralta's house. Though winter was at the gates, the weather was beautiful, a warm wind blowing from the south, the stars bright. The countryside was peaceful and celestial. At Peralta's home, we were again making a request for the spousal signature. Though we showed him the slip and explained what it meant, he was hesitant and uncertain. Then a thought came to me.

"Well, Señor Peralta," I said, "if *you'd* like to get baptized, we don't need your signature or your reasons for not wanting to." Dead-set against being dunked, the reverse psychology scared him. He signed the permission slip, along with a short statement about why he wouldn't be getting baptized any time soon. It was a major victory for us, given that the other elders had tried and failed to get the fellow to sign.

Monday evening, we went to the Rosales home to teach her the second part of C. There stood her soon-to-be-ex, ready to sign the paperwork. That out of the way, we proceeded to the next charla.

TESTS OF FAITH AND MORTALITY

AS THE DAYS PASSED, preparing our group of investigators for baptism was becoming a test of faith. Some were progressing, but others were not. Some, like Soria, were out of town. The result was a feeling of inadequacy, triggered by a lack of faith that the Lord would help us with these seemingly "impossible" people. While I couldn't pinpoint the trouble, I knew that some of our important contacts were slipping away. Time was running out.

We spent the June 20th P-Day inside the apartment, writing letters and listening to music on our tape recorders. I was convalescing from a cold. Snow fell for two-and-a-half hours straight, the temp hovering around thirty degrees. That afternoon we visited members, courting hypothermia in the process. It was the coldest weather I had experienced in Argentina. Finishing a journal entry at 10:40 that evening, I noticed snow falling again. The following day would herald the official start of winter.

The next morning, we trudged through two inches of fresh snowfall and slush to Peralta's home for a review of the plan of salvation. The dirt streets had turned into slimy mud pots, walking a challenge. Conditions conspired to destroy my only remaining pair of shoes. Water-soaked and caked with mud, they weren't long for this world. That evening we visited with Ramirez. He told us that he didn't believe he was ready to be baptized on the 25th. The fact that he wasn't praying didn't help matters. We also met with Señora Rosales.

Thursday evening, we met with Graciela Rosales for another good discussion, but noticed that she looked very sick. Though I thought about giving her a health blessing, I held back for some reason. We said a prayer with her and left for home. But at the street corner a block away, we turned around and went back, giving that poor woman the blessing she deserved.

So, WHAT DID WE DO on Friday, June 24th, the day before the planned baptisms, you might ask?

Well . . .

Aldin and I went to the Post Office and bank. Then we walked out to Peralta's for her interview. Then back to town to visit with an investigator.

Lunchtime.

Then to the Arias home to talk to another investigator. Then off to Sariah's home, where I gave my first baptism interview. It wasn't difficult at all, though I took an hour for what should have only been a twenty-minute effort. Then we were off to the Rosales home, where Aldin gave her the baptismal interview. Graciela passed with flying colors, and looked much healthier. Then we were off to the Cuello home, where I interviewed the father of the house for baptism. Then I ran to the Mansilla house for what turned out to be a great interview. Then I ran across town to the chapel. Diarmid was there, rigging up a pump system to heat the water for the font. He and Fineas had figured out a way to circulate water through a pump while it was being heated by the fire. Then we went to Soria's. Then we picked up our clothes. Then we went back to the chapel. Then we went to the other elders' apartment. Then we went home.

Yet, in the midst of all the activities of that day, there was one we missed. During the afternoon, Sisters Miranda and Castro had been trying to contact us. Don Lorenzo was in the hospital and Miranda wanted us to give him a blessing. Since we couldn't be found, she returned to Don Lorenzo's bedside and offered a prayer. As she finished it, his body gave a jerk and he was gone. He was suffering no more.

BAPTISM, SICKNESS, AND MIRACLE

SATURDAY AFTERNOON I WAS CHOSEN to baptize eight people. During the last-minute preparations, we discovered that there wasn't enough white clothing to go around. Then we found out that the box of clothing the ZLs had promised to send was not going to arrive. But the members banded together and found what was needed, saving the day.

The water was luke-cold, but not freezing. What worried me was the water level: a mere four inches above the knee, when it should have been near the belt line. And so we began. I baptized the first woman twice, her knee coming out of the water the first time. I had to baptize the Cuello girl three times, and a couple other persons twice each. The last person to be baptized was Señor Ramirez, the fellow who thought he wouldn't be ready but was. Señor R tipping the scales at about 250 pounds, I was wondering how I'd get him all the way under. The first time I accidentally pulled one of his arms. The following effort was successful, but I almost fell on top of him in my effort to pull him back out of the water.

After the confirmations, everyone went home, us elders staying behind to clean up and take advantage of the hot coals for a late dinner. In a celebratory mood, we barbecued steaks, drank pop, and ate potato salad, cookies, and alfajores. It tasted especially good, considering that I hadn't eaten much all day. It was a great end to an even greater day. I'd seen people get baptized who, a week earlier, had seemed hopeless cases. We had to exercise a lot of faith, and do some pushing, for it all to happen. But in the end, many people's lives were blessed, families made a little more whole. The one sour note amid the happiness was the missing Soria family. What was to be done about them?

As for our barbecue, tradition dictated that a pair of shoes be sacrificed to the flames. This time the sorry footwear was my own, the shoes that had caused me so much pain during the last few days. Of course, that left me without, so Diarmid loaned me his. They were a couple sizes too small, and about four blocks from our place I couldn't stand the pain any longer. I removed the borrowed shoes, walking the rest of the way in wet-stockinged feet. Perhaps this is why I came down with a cold the following day.

And the timing couldn't have been worse. We had to travel around town, filling out registration forms for all the people baptized Saturday—a job Aldin was supposed

to have taken care of before the ordinances were performed. As we walked from house to house, my teeth got
to chattering. Still sick with a cold, I was nearing exhaustion. By the time we got home, I was so tired I could hard-
ly stand, my leg and back muscles spent. The following
day, though, my illness had lessened to a mere head cold.

During the next week we focused our efforts on the
Sorias. Day after day we visited them and taught Señor
S about the importance of living the Word of Wisdom,
meaning no more *vino*. By Sunday we knew we'd prepared them as best we could. We had to leave the rest in
the Lord's hands. Starting the afternoon with prayer, we
made preparations. I built a fire to burn tar out of the
barrel we were going to heat water in. Then I built two
more fires. Once the barrels had been filled, we moved
them over the flames. Then Fineas and I walked across
town to the Sorias, only to find that they weren't home.
I felt sick at heart, but had to keep exercising faith that
things would work out. We went to our apartment, then
returned to Sorias and left a note before heading back to
the church.

As we neared the chapel doors, I looked up the street
and saw a man coming along the road on his bicycle. It
was Soria. What was he doing?

"Señor Soria?"

"Hello, elders." He was oblivious.

"What are you doing? Do you remember what day
this is?"

"Oh yeah. I'm getting baptized, right?" I wanted to slap him.

"Yes. Where is your wife? Is she ready?"

"I don't know," on both counts.

We went to his house, but she wasn't there. He offered to go look while I waited. He returned twenty minutes later.

"Well, Elder—she can't get baptized. She has a bad headache."

I knew it was just an excuse. There was something else going on, and I could feel it. I wanted to talk to her, but we had to get back to the chapel and tell the members about the baptism. Once informed, they started setting up for the service.

Brother Yllanes took Soria and me to the house where Señora S was hiding out. I'd been praying that the Lord would help me find the right words to say. Something that would convince Señora Soria to come to the church and be baptized. Telling the men to wait, I entered the house and shook hands with Soria's wife. I could see the fear in her eyes by the way she carried herself. She told me she was dead-set against being baptized. But as we continued conversing, she relaxed. Letting the Spirit dictate what I said next, within minutes Señora Soria realized that she needed to follow through on her original decision to be baptized. We got into the truck, the Sorias up front, I in the pickup bed for a cold ride back to the chapel. Once there, Elder Aldin interviewed the couple. Meanwhile, we readied the hot water. As the service began, we started pouring the water through a screen. A branch member and I ran buckets of water from the three barrels to the font, finishing just in time. Then the members all moved outside to watch as Elder Fineas baptized the couple. It was a great way to end a long, hard day.

CRISIS, TRUCE, AND A TALK IN THE DARK

As of late, Elder F had been getting harder to live with, his main problem being the way he snapped at others when they asked him questions.

"Of course (*Stupid*!)."

"That's what I said (*Stupid*!)." That sort of thing.

We'd talked about this before, and he knew he was doing it, and he tried to stop. But he kept sliding back into the same old ditch, like a wagon wheel on a muddy road.

Frustrated because my companion wouldn't share with me what we were going to do that day, I recorded my feelings in the journal. I ended that portion of the entry with the desire to just put up with the bad behavior for the time being. After lunch, we were in the apartment, studying. When it came near to fire-out time, I asked again.

"Elder Fineas, what's the plan for this afternoon?"

"I don't know," he said, shrugging the shoulders.

I waited a bit, then—

"What are we doing today?"

No response. I was getting pissed.

"What are we doing today?"

"*We're stopping by the Garcia place*," he said in a low, menacing way, then stared at me as if I were some sort of idiot. In all the time I'd served in the field, not once had I contemplated violence against a companion. But at this moment I was seconds away from punching his smug face.

"What are we going to do after that?" And so it went. I would ask and he would answer. He acted as if I was supposed to already know the schedule—the one he hadn't told me jack about.

"Why are you looking at me like that?" I said.

I was furious. Plopping on the bed, he looked at me with mock humor.

"Well, how do you want me to look at you?"

"Whuh?" was all I could manage. I was torn between fight and flight. Was the next step physical violence or an offensive stream of swear words from Dan's Private Collection? But Fineas beat me to it.

"What would you like me to do? Kiss your ass?"

I was so shocked I didn't know what to say. We sat there, staring at each other, the silence deafening. Nothing else existed outside that small room. Then I softened.

"Elder, what's wrong?"

He said nothing, staring at the wall behind me. No movement. Just the Stare. He was starting to creep me out, and I didn't know what to do or say. Was I witnessing a nervous breakdown?

"How do you feel right now?" I said.

He'd answer slowly with two or three words, then clam up again. Having withdrawn from the situation, he looked to be in a trance. As the minutes passed I started to see a little of myself in him. So, this was how Schieff felt when I'd rebuff his efforts to help me. Things went on this way for a good hour and a half. I'd tell him things or ask how he was feeling. Then—

"Why do you keep all this stuff inside?"

"It doesn't help to let it out."

"Why?"

"Because the same damned thing happens all over again, whether I keep it in or let it out."

While I understood his point of view, I couldn't find the right words to help him. At an impasse, we went out to work, saying little to each other the rest of the day. It wasn't necessarily anger, more of a truce or ceasefire. But I felt like I'd been stabbed repeatedly with a dull knife, Elder F's words coming back again and again. The ugly looks, the vicious lashing out. What the hell was wrong with him? I wanted to talk with Elder Aldin in the worst way. But how to do it without alerting my comp?

As the week came to a close, we hadn't much to show for our efforts. It was the post-baptism slump, and we were living examples. Early one evening I finally had a chance to speak to Elder A. I felt like a bomb ready to explode. He was surprised by Fineas's behavior, and understood how frustrated I was feeling. But like me, he didn't know what he could do to help.

So the hours and days passed, my companion and I engaged in an uneasy agreement to get along. I conducted baptism interviews for the other elders' investigators. We held family home evenings with the Sorias and others. Cognizant of the fact that I had only five months left, I struggled with feelings of remorse about all the time I'd supposedly wasted. But recognizing the emotional trap I was setting for myself, I thought about other things, refusing to fall for the old "unworthiness" trick again. I felt good about who I was and what I was doing. In an effort to keep positive vibes going, I started listening a lot to Tchaikovsky's *Swan Lake* ballet suite. It was music I loved, and I believed the Lord approved of it as well. The classics always put me in a meditative mood, moving my thoughts to a higher plane. Hearing a beautiful melody caused a surge of profound emotion, and I was grateful for the genius that had inspired its composition.

But appreciation for said genius wasn't shared by my companion. The ugly incident of the "trance" well behind us, we one P-Day morning argued about the tapes we wanted to listen to. I had the Beatles, Linda Ronstadt, Elvis, James Taylor, and Cat Stevens. Fineas had The Moody Blues Greatest Hits. I'd been listening to the same Moody Blues tunes for weeks and weeks. If I had to listen to much more, something bad might happen. In the end, my solution was to go to another room to write or read.

ONE EVENING AROUND DUSK we stopped by the domicile of Señor Otin—a man of few words and negligible conversational ability. He invited us inside his gray adobe dwelling, a residence that had never seen electricity. Everything about him was at half-speed as he invited us to sit at a table. We hoped that this would be the evening we broke through his mental barrier. The results of this charla would determine whether we kept teaching or dropped him from the pool.

As we began the discussion, the only available light came from the guttering wick of a kerosene lamp with barely enough fuel to cover the bottom of the bottle. We spoke of the Book of Mormon, then asked him some questions. The response was feeble. We talked about modern prophets and Joseph Smith. His answers were in the form of questions. How could we get through to him? The longer we talked, the smaller the flame got, making it difficult to see the flip charts we were pointing at. Yet on we taught, believing that by sheer force of will, the Spirit would touch him.

After a lengthy spate of doctrine, we were sitting in gloom so profound that we could no longer see each other's faces, let alone the scriptures or our visual aids. Through it all Señor Otin said nary a word. Not a peep. Awakened to the futility of it all, we said goodbye. Stumbling outside to fresh air and light, we decided that someone else would have to try and get through to Otin—when he was willing to put forth some effort.

ON THE WINTER DAYS WENT, our time spent visiting members, giving baptismal interviews, performing baptisms, and attending home evenings. During the first week of August we began teaching Walter Santander, a young fellow who was interested in the Church. He appeared ready to move forward with baptism.

During a trip to San Rafael, I got to see Elder Stephens again. While we were getting caught up on the news, two young men approached. The older of the two started asking us questions about the Church, his manner that of a basher. We retired to a classroom and the discussion began. The guys informed us that they were from a local fundamentalist church; then the older fellow started up in earnest. He asked a question, then tried to trip us up with our own words.

Steering the conversation one way, then another, the fellow presented himself as some sort of authority on the scriptures, the younger man a trainee. The pace of the talking heated up, as did the rhetoric. The tipping point came when he pointed at a photo of the President of the Church, calling him a false prophet. I couldn't take it anymore. I bore testimony to him about what we knew to be true. With that he gave up, and the two of them left, the leader in a huff, the younger man stalling long enough to ask when we could meet with him to begin the charlas.

A MAD DOCTOR, SOFTBALL, AND AN
UNDERSTANDING

FOLLOWING THE AUGUST 9TH DISTRICT MEETING, we stopped by
the home of one Dr. Moscoso. Fineas wanted to be reim-
bursed for a Bible the doctor had purchased from him.
Once inside his shuttered home/office/laboratory, the
middle-aged, black-mustachioed physician led us toward
the back of his residence. Classical music emanated from
unseen speakers—one of those dreary/dreamy British
pieces by Delius, full of sun-drenched meadows, as Sir
Beecham's orchestra went on and on, little climaxes followed by quiet sections before swelling and subsiding, no
sign of resolution in sight.

"I want to tell you something," Dr. M said in a con-
spiratorial tone, and in English. "Come here," his finger
crooked and pointing. "Into my office."

Ensconced inside more secure confines, he continued.

"I am afraid to talk to you in Spanish. You see, the
communists are after me."

"Really" was the best I could manage.

"They could be listening in at this very moment. They
use electronic wave—tape recorders, you know . . ."

He gave us a moment to let this sink in, then—

"There are a lot of communists living in Coronel Diaz"
he said, starting to get worked up. The music droned on
somewhere.

"They work through the drug pushers, you see— the
Spiritualist churches—those dirty filthy Negroes . . ."

His face was a mixture of fear and anger, though it was unclear which emotion was winning. Then he grabbed a piece of paper off his desk and began scribbling out his dialogue, just in case. Certain that the physician's trolley had slipped off the tracks, Elder F and I were ready to make a run for the door. I tried to focus on the British meadows of unending background music, but could not. Unfortunately, our guest soon tired of writing. Placing the pencil and paper on the desk, he reached deep into his suit coat, pulling out a screwdriver, then a file.

"Know what these are for?"

Collective shrug.

"Self-defense," he said as he slowly waved the utensils in front of him, then put them back in a suit pocket. "And you know what else?" he asked, as I wondered how to escape without getting hit by friendly fire.

"I can throw acid at people that try to attack me."

Violins and cellos were building to a crescendo. Wondering where other family members might be who could break the tension, or possibly distract their patriarch while we beat feet for the nearest exit, I tried to humor him.

"Well, that's pretty interesting, Dr. Moscoso, but we need to go . . ."

He came from behind and grabbed me.

"Here's what you can do when they try something," he said, pulling my head back before I could react with anything more than a mix of that same anger and fear he'd displayed earlier. Then, distracted by something after a few interminable seconds, he relaxed his grip and let go.

"Er—Señor Moscoso?" I said. "We need to go." Without awaiting an answer, we shook his hand and were out the door faster than you could say "dementia."

Saturday the 13th, our district took a truck ride out to a Japanese colony in the country. We'd been invited to play a game of softball with them. It felt so good to be at the plate, swinging a bat, and out in the field, chasing a ball around in the grass. After the game, we were invited to the community hall for tea and crackers. We had some good discussion, though it was tough to get used to hearing Japanese people speaking Spanish.

Tired of the little flare-ups still erupting between Elder F and myself, we discussed the issue and called a truce. I wouldn't bug him about that damned Moody Blues music if he'd stop needling me about things. You would think that a couple of Christian men could quickly implement the gospel enough in their lives to overcome such petty squabbles and bickering. But I was learning that some problems take time to work out—that if a miracle were to effect an instant solution, opportunities to learn lessons would be lost. Such an opportunity came on my 23rd birthday, when I walked into the apartment. There on the bed was a shawl made of llama hair. Fineas had bought it for me.

As the month of August wound to a close, we stayed busy teaching Walter and a lady named Aibar. We also had chances to counsel members of the Branch about problems they were having with church attendance, their testimonies, and any other issues we felt we could help with. One of the things we couldn't do was get Señora Aibar to commit to baptism, even after two months of hard work. She knew the Church was true. She believed in the scriptures and our message about the Restoration. But she was afraid of the unknown.

So, when Elder Tower, the ZL's companion, came for a work session, he could see that Señora Aibar needed some prompting. He told her that he'd come all the way from San Rafael just to talk to her. Then he challenged her to be baptized the following day. Suffice it to say that Señora Aibar wasn't the only one shocked by Tower's bold challenge. But she accepted his invitation, as did Walter when we taught him later that same day. So it was that twenty-four hours later, following the Ritual of the Three Barrels, I was in the font, baptizing two more people into the Church of Jesus Christ.

BUDDHISM AND THE MERCY KILLING

We were scheduled to teach the Baqueros, a reference from someone in the branch. For some reason, I was getting bad vibes about the pending visit, but kept them to myself. We rode three miles out of town to a store. We asked the owner if it was called Triangulo. He didn't know where that was. Three miles further down the road we came upon another store. That owner told us that Triangulo was back towards town. In reverse we went, griping all the way. Eventually we found the dirt road mentioned in the directions. Pedaling through thick sand and across a washboard surface, we came to a farmhouse also mentioned on the map. We parked our bikes, then made our way along another sand-infested road to the Baqueros.

During the ensuing discussion, it came to light that due to his Buddhist upbringing, Señor Baquero didn't believe God was an actual man. He said that we are all merely animals. The look on his quiet wife's face demonstrated that she didn't feel the same way. The fruitless discussion at an end, Señor B offered us a ride to town. Tossing our bikes in the back of his car, we rode along as dust poured in through the windows. We arrived home covered in a thick layer of grime.

After getting cleaned up, we taught an investigator, then decided to call it quits and walk back to the apartment. Conversing little as we trudged along, I saw something moving around on the street ahead. It was a dog—a full-sized greyhound. He'd been hit by a vehicle and left for dead. Lying on his side, the dog's eyes darted back and forth, his breath coming hard and fast, the skin around his mouth puffing in and out. Leaning over the animal, I told Elder Fineas that I saw no blood anywhere, and being a dog lover, took this as a good sign.

As usual, Elder F popped my balloon.

"Look at his hips."

The dog saw me taking an interest and wagged its long thin tail. The hips did look strange, half collapsed and moving the wrong way. A shining lumpy pile of something yellow and green was trailing out of its rectum. Lifting its head to get a better look at us humans, the animal tried to stand, its wobbly front legs extending but getting no assist from the back two. It collapsed in a wasted effort, a whine starting in its throat. I looked around for help, trying to ignore the possibility that it was a lost cause. Veterinary services in Coronel Diaz were reserved for animals that made an economic difference, not brutes like this specimen who contributed nothing but unconditional love to all it met. My comp said little, standing there staring at the poor mutt.

"We've gotta do something," I said, trying to be the leader.

"Elder, his hips are *crushed*. There's nothing we can do."

He was right. In unison, Fineas and I walked away, avoiding something we didn't want or need to do. After all, it wasn't our problem. Let the owner do the dirty deed. But the more I thought about the situation, the more conflicted I became. The fatalist in me said we must've come across the accident scene for a reason. Past experience held me back from whatever our duty might be. But I turned and went back to the animal. Whining, it again tried to lift itself up, tail wagging, the picture of optimism.

"We've gotta do something," I said. Grabbing its stiffening front legs, I drug the dog to the curb, hoping it wouldn't panic and bite me.

"Well, at least it's out of the way now," I said. But we knew it wasn't enough. Maintaining his silence, my comp crossed the ditch and started looking for something. Understanding what he sought, I joined him. Our search yielded a large stone about a foot across. Heavy enough to do the job. Elder Fineas carried it over to the dog and assumed the position, even as the animal's tail wagged and thumped again and again on the pavement. Elder F lifted the rock above his head. The dog continued to stare.

Unable to watch, I walked toward our pensión, a mere hundred feet away. I waited for the thump, but none came. Continuing to distance myself, I snuck a look. My comp was still holding the rock up. I kept walking. A few more seconds passed, and no sound. Then there was a hollow thud, like a melon hitting the pavement. I stopped and waited for my companion to catch up, looking back at the still figure, thankful there was distance between us and the dark, spreading pool of life oozing from the dog's body.

"That's the grossest thing I've ever done," Elder F said.

"Yeah . . ."

We walked to the apartment in silence. At the dinner table we worked our way through the meal, eating little and saying less. And that night, sleep didn't come easily. As Elder Fineas lay in his bed, sawing logs, I tossed and turned, wondering where he'd found the strength to drop the rock—and what it was that'd held me back. Me, the guy who'd been putting up with Fineas longer than anyone else in the mission. And during that night of sleeplessness I realized that somewhere along the line I'd stopped forgiving Fineas for perceived insults and slights. I was the one poisoning the well. And as I thought about my actions, I realized I had to change.

FLIGHT PLANS, TRANSFER

FRIDAY, SEPTEMBER 2ND, I received my flight plans. If anything was liable to set the Big Countdown Clock to ticking, this was it. A mere thirteen weeks between me and civilian life. The end of an era. But it wasn't real yet. Putting the paper away, I tried to forget I'd ever seen it.

The next evening, we returned from a successful charla with Señor Soria. Flicking on the room lights revealed unfamiliar bags lying on the bed and floor. The name "Elder Birch" was inscribed on them. Unsure where the wayward elder was at the moment, my heart beat a little faster. I was finally leaving. A new town. And even better, a new companion. But where? And how soon? Once Birch returned, I got the news.

"Elder Hiland, you're going to La Guerra. It's a little resort town near the city of Palacio."

"Wow," was all I could manage.

"It's a beautiful place. Lots to look forward to."

"That's good."

"But there are some big problems in the branch." In the next breath, he told me my new companion would be one Elder Fallon, but had nothing to say about the man. Once we settled in and found the new elder a place to sleep on the floor, we talked for a while, then everyone conked out.

The next morning, I packed for a couple hours, but was unable to fit in everything. Fineas would have to ship the rest. All the while I was trying to process the fact that

I was on my way out. The other elders got ready to leave for church, but I said I'd be staying behind. I didn't like goodbyes, I told them. Once they were gone, I breathed a sigh of relief. No messy farewells or tears or hugging. And I finally had a couple hours to myself to think and relax. But with that idle time came questions: What would Elder Fallon be like? For having been there a while, Birch had nothing to say about him. And what of that remark about "troubles in the branch?"

When the guys returned, one of them said I'd missed out.

"Man, those people really love you. You should have heard what they were saying . . ."

Though I shrugged it off, I knew that I'd made a terrible mistake. I'd worked with these people for months, developed bonds of love and trust with them—and this was how I repaid them? But what was done was done.

With no pending appointments we could attend to, we sat around all afternoon, listening to Elder B's taped dramatizations of the Book of Mormon. But after a while those got old. I resorted to underlining biblical references in the scriptures with a colored pencil. Three-and-a-half hours of taped dramatizations later my brain was fried. I was ready to get on a bus and sleep.

That evening we were joined at the terminal by Elder Phelps, on transfer northward. We approached the bus for my 9:45 p.m. departure. Fineas was speaking to Elder B about sports and other things I didn't recall him ever mentioning to me. I could tell he wasn't going to be shedding tears any time soon about my transfer. He was already acting like a new man, as if he'd been released from prison. As I was about to climb the bus steps, I turned and apologized to Elder Fineas for not having gotten along better with him. We shook hands and he told me to take care of myself.

As I settled into my seat and thought about it all, the two elders walked off together, while Phelps got seated next to me. Our bus pulled away from the well-lit station, onto a darkened country highway, soon rolling across unfamiliar farmland toward Palacio.

La Guerra

LA GUERRA

THE BUS ASCENDED, WINDING ITS WAY through the mountains outside of Palacio. By turns bored and apprehensive, I looked out the smudged windows at densely packed hills covered with scrubby vegetation. Musing about the unknown, I pondered my spiritual condition. Yes, I was still thinking about girls a lot, but to not do so seemed a fight against nature I would never win. Feelings of unworthiness came and went, along with the usual self-indictments for not speaking with people on the bus about the gospel. Other concerns nipped at my brain: What would the town look like? Would my new companion be cool, or a pain in the butt? Was La Guerra a small branch? If so, how small? Who would be at the bus station to greet me? When would trunkiness hit?

At one point, I caught a glimpse of a beautiful lake. Then the trees blocked my view. But there it was again, and we seemed to be going toward it. The thought came to me that I was entering a place of beauty, and that I should enjoy it. Then the thought passed, but with it so did my misgivings. A sense of the ethereal had come and gone, as if to remind me that whatever happened, I would get through it.

Soon enough our conveyance rolled down from the mountains and into the city terminal. I descended from the stuffy bus at 10:30 a.m. to cool, dry weather. As for the anticipated greeting party, there was none. But I needed to be patient. They'd show up. I strolled around, looking at the small shops and kiosks that surrounded the station. Then back out front, where I saw no one but civilians, most of my fellow passengers having been spirited away by family, friends, and taxis. I paced. Maybe they'd been detained. Well, I could wait a bit longer. But after twenty minutes that patience evaporated.

I retrieved the apartment address from my paperwork and asked the ticket office for directions. Pointed in the general direction of downtown La Guerra, I gathered my overcoat, luggage, and whatever else I was still lugging around at this stage of the game, and set off down an unfamiliar street, good and pissed. Where the hell was Fallon—or the district leader? For that matter, where the hell was I?

I walked on, arriving at first one wrong address, then another. After some thirty minutes, I stopped in front of a whitewashed, two-story, stucco-covered building, a motel-style sign jutting from its roof. As there was no front porch, I made my way to the side door and knocked. A short, middle-aged woman appeared, a sour expression on her face. I introduced myself. She cheerlessly pointed up a flight of stairs and walked away. Hauling my tired body and assorted baggage up the steps, a landing, then another short flight, I stepped into a hallway and walked through an open bedroom door. There sat my new companion.

"Hey, I'm Elder Hiland."

"Hi, I'm Elder Fallon," he said as we shook hands. "Welcome to La Guerra."

I plopped down on the empty bed near the door. Elder F was a tall, lanky guy, his short-cut blonde hair being phased out by premature balding. He seemed pleasant enough.

"Boy, I had a hard time finding this place."

"Huh."

"Any idea why no one was at the station to greet me?"

"Nope," and a shoulder-shrug.

I felt myself heating up a little at the lack of concern, but I was new here. I didn't know Fallon yet. Give it some time. I let Elder F talk. He gave me a tour of the room, which offered a nice view of the surrounding houses, rooftops, and nearby hills. There was the outer hallway which ran some thirty feet to a window with a scenic view of the city and the Pampas beyond.

Downstairs I was introduced to the landlady, her thirty-something son, George, and an older fellow who looked like the in-house slave. None of them seemed to like me very much. As for meals, the lady of the house would supply us with one or two each day, the sample portions I saw looking rather skimpy. Her only other duty was to clean our room.

Preliminaries out of the way, I was ready to go out and meet some of the Church members. Maybe look over the town while we were at it. But Fallon needed to go to Palacio and pick up a pair of contact lenses he'd ordered. Though this was a P-Day type of activity, I said nothing. Maybe it was an emergency situation. So onto a bus we went. At Palacio we caught another bus downtown, then walked for what seemed like ten miles before heading back. For some reason, my companion wasn't able to secure the lenses. My legs and feet were shot by the time we returned home. Going to bed that night with many questions unanswered, all I wanted to dwell on was how beautiful the area was and how good it felt to be horizontal.

ALFAJORES, A NEW CHAPEL, COCA

THE NEXT DAY we took a walk downtown, our path taking us through several blocks' worth of residential housing, the properties simple but well-kept. Then we passed a long line of businesses, the first of which was a restaurant whose kitchen exhaust fan blasted hot greasy air at my head. We got to see the Big Clock, an oversized timepiece surrounded by flowers that served as a tourist attraction occupying the middle of an intersection. Jaded traveler that I was, I was wowed for about thirty seconds. From the little that I'd seen so far, this was a tourist town. Full of things attractive to strangers, but pedestrian and obnoxious to the locals.

By this point in my Argentine journey, the cities—especially large ones like Palacio—had ceased looking much different than the towns back home. I'd seen the gauchos, eaten most of the European-style food, and become accustomed to weather that was nearly identical to that of Portland. Even the reversal of seasons no longer offered surprises. But there was one thing I hadn't yet experienced: Havana alfajores. And La Guerra was an exclusive distributor of the little gems. As much a novelty as Coors, White Castle, and Krispy Kreme products had at one time been, west of the Rockies, so were Havanas to LDS missionaries. And as customer bases went, there was no group more loyal to a dessert product.

Having made our way to the sacred environs of the small, nondescript Havana store, we entered. Throughout my time in Argentina, I'd eaten my way through several alimentary phases; Choc-Choc bars, Aguilera and Toblerone chocolate, shortbread cookies, and fresh-baked croissants. Unlike Havanas, the aforementioned treats were everywhere. But a box full of Havanas was no sooner purchased than consumed. And to heighten the allure, this outlet store appeared to be open infrequently, adding to the mystique of the quest. So, it was only fitting that I should be treated to my first authentic Havana. I don't recall if the filling was dulce de leche or chocolate sauce, or what color the delicate tinfoil wrapper was.

But after all the pale imitations I'd endured, this hockey puck-sized confection was good. Real good.

Playtime over, we visited one of the members, then went to the construction site. One of my wishes during the two years had been to be in a town where a new chapel was being built. And the location couldn't have been prettier. Situated on the edge of Lake San Roque, the building looked majestic, its spire visible for miles. Bearing a coat of light-yellow paint, the cinder block structure was close to completion, though there was a lot of finish work remaining. I was hoping to get the chance to work on the building before my mission ended.

That afternoon, Elder Fallon took me to Coca's house, at the base of those hills visible from our bedroom window. After introductions, we tried to teach a fellow named Estanislavo, but upon commencing the charla, he steamrolled us with a string of questions that only demonstrated how much more interested he was in his point of view than ours. Having worked with his type before, I steered the conversation to a hasty conclusion. We thanked him for his time and parted ways.

Coca, on the other hand, was a joy to spend time with. She was a stout Arabian woman who'd been in the branch a long time. Unmarried, but with a teenage daughter at home, she was outspoken, blessed with a loud laugh and a boisterous, if not risqué, sense of humor. She was also a breath of fresh air. After we got acquainted, she gave me a crash course on the La Guerra Branch. The place was a rumor mill. As a result, many people had gone inactive. The branch president wasn't immune to the Wagging Tongue Syndrome, either. One of his counselors wasn't attending church. The other had a smoking problem. In Coca's view, this was a battle between Good and Evil, Saints vs. Hypocrites, and she wanted me to know she was on our side. Unfortunately, the gossiping she accused others of was her M.O., as well.

That night I retired to bed both enlightened and troubled. The Señora was weird: bothersome enough to have driven former missionaries to other locations before returning, having discovered that lodgings were even more expensive elsewhere. There was Coca's dark description of the branch. And lastly, the fact that my companion seemed to spend an inordinate amount of time at a single woman's house. What would tomorrow bring?

STORM CLOUDS AND THE VACATIONING ELDER

WHAT TOMORROW BROUGHT was the next installment of Contention 101, courtesy of one Brother Rosales. Second Counselor in the branch presidency, he had an axe to grind with President Beltran. He was mad at his leader for a variety of reasons, top of the list being Beltran's participation in, and instigation of, rumors and gossip. By day's end I was getting a little depressed.

On top of this I discovered that my companion— the one person I should be able to rely on for spiritual back-up—didn't give a damn about anything of a religious nature. Instead he spent the days reading novels. No scripture study. No charla reviews. No daily or weekly or even monthly planning. Just novels. Given that our district leader was a forty-five-minute bus ride distant, and me with no phone access, I was on my own. Maybe there were a few members in the La Guerra Branch who weren't yet at each other's throats, but from what I'd heard so far, this little congregation was going down the tubes in a big way.

FACING AN EMPTY SCHEDULE on Friday, we went to the chapel site and helped mix cement for the roof tiles and cinder blocks. I loved every minute of the hard labor. In the afternoon, it was off to Coca's, then across town to visit an investigator who was more than three sheets to the wind. Unable to communicate with him, we dropped his name from our contact list until such time as he was willing to stop boozing it up.

Church services were being held in a small house, the most diminutive I'd attended during my mission. Sacrament service was conducted in the living room. Other meetings were held in the kitchen and former bedrooms. As a way of introducing me to the branch members, I was asked to speak on the importance of example, that being the same talk I'd given months before in Coronel Diaz. And although there was a good turnout—probably thirty—the small number of active members caused me to wonder why this town had been chosen as the site for a new chapel.

WE TRAVELED TO PALACIO for a zone conference focused on faith, works, and the importance of a positive
attitude. It was exactly the uplift I needed, after the six-
day dose of negativity that had sapped my strength and
resolve. Less motivating was Parón's request to remove
all recorded music from our tape collections that wasn't
classical or Mormon Tabernacle Choir. We were to box
up said tapes and ship them to the mission home for safe-
keeping. So, the musical pendulum had swung back. In
early '76 we were to avoid listening to rock or any other
music not conducive to the Spirit. Later we were to let
our consciences be our guide. Since some consciences
had been remiss in their duties, it was back to square one.

I planned on handing over my excess tapes at stake
conference, the following week. Then I changed my
mind and took them to Coca's. While there I had her
give me a haircut. After lunch, we walked an hour out
into the country to visit a member and her daughter.
We passed through dense brush, up and down gullies,
the lake and the surrounding mountains always in view,
beauty all around us. It was my first good look at the scenery, and reminded me of some M.C. Escher drawings I'd
seen. Ethereal and otherworldly, the views were a balm
to my soul.

And balm was needed in abundance. We hadn't
taught a charla in a week, and I laid the blame on Elder
Fallon. The only thing he'd accomplished since I arrived
was polishing off the latest novel he'd borrowed from a

branch member. That and getting plenty of rest, since he never arose before 8:45 a.m. As for being trunked out, he was past that, his mind never having left home, for all I could tell. It was like working with a greenie. I had to do all the leading, a task he eschewed, yet expected me to take on. I wanted to have a good sit-down with him in the hope that he'd start working, then dismissed the idea as a waste of effort, given the short amount of time my comp had left.

P-DAY AND THE DEATH MARCH

STAKE CONFERENCE AND SUNDAY MEETINGS came and went, and suddenly it was Monday again. Being P-Day, it was time to do some real sightseeing. At 11 a.m., Fallon, Coca, and I took the bus to a spot outside of town, where we disembarked and walked toward the hills. The weather warm and sunny, I got my best look yet at the Lake. Such beauty. We entered the hills, following a dirt road that wound and climbed into the canyons, then descended. Splintered mica and quartz littered the path and the surrounding slopes, and I stopped every so often to pick up a piece for examination. The brush and plants in full bloom, the air was lush with a sweet, vegetation aroma. I drank it all in, having not been on a nature hike since my time in San Martín Park.

We arrived at our lunch destination, the San Roque Dam. While there I got my first look at the Embudo. Designed to channel water from the top of the dam to a stream bed downstream, it looked like a giant funnel, set in the middle of the water, about two-hundred feet from the dam wall. At least one-hundred feet across, and black as night in its bottomless center, it was one of the most forbidding things I'd ever seen. The idea of something accidentally falling into that abyss and descending through the grinding turbines gave me the creeps. Tossing a few large rocks into it and watching them disappear forever in the darkness sent waves of vertigo through me.

After crossing the dam, we took a road to the river bed, looked around for a bit, then hiked a trail back to the base of the dam. There was a pool there, the residue from those times when water was released from a large pipe above us that projected from the dam's wall. It was quiet, a good time to sit and relax and reflect. But the clock was ticking. We were scheduled for a home evening at 8 p.m. We started hiking back up at half-past four, and since we were pressed for time, my companion decided it would be faster to take the road that ran toward Palacio, to the southwest.

The walk along the road bordering the lake was as beautiful as any I'd seen. Meadows of thick, lush grass hugged the shoreline, waving in the breeze as we walked along under late afternoon sun, the air balmy and fresh. There was something about this place that pulled my mind toward the infinite; as if the weather had always been balmy, the grass forever undulating in the breeze, the lake a constantly rippling, bluish-green.

We talked little as we strolled along, just taking in the views. But as the journey got longer and the sun dropped closer to the horizon, I began to wonder where we were. Coca had removed her shoes, sore feet covered with blisters, and she was complaining. Within a few more miles we saw a small town at road's end. As we approached the signs saying "Welcome to Bialet Masse," we discovered that we had traveled fourteen kilometers away from La Guerra, not toward it. It was now 8 p.m., and the fact that we were thirsty and hungry mattered not to the fruit and souvenir stands now closed for the day. Our only hope was the bus, so we sat and waited. Sometime around sundown it picked us up, returning us to La Guerra at 9:30 p.m. Then we ran to Versaci's to apologize for being ninety minutes late, and to reschedule.

RUMORS, CONTENTION, A GOOD CHARLA

SEPTEMBER 22. I noted in my journal that due to the problems the members were having, we would need to resort to our least-favorite activity: door-knocking. In a well-functioning ward or branch, the members would be providing us with people to teach—their friends, neighbors, fellow employees. But not in La Guerra. The situation was bad enough that like the officers in Wouk's classic book *The Caine Mutiny*, smoking first counselor Nakayama was trying to persuade inactive second counselor Rosales to go with him for a visit to President Zobell and request that President Beltran be removed from his position in the branch.

Then there was Pinnock, the missionary work coordinator and construction supervisor for the new chapel. He too was engaged in his share of gossip and backbiting—that is, when he wasn't busy trying to dispel rumors about him fooling around with Monica, a twenty-year-old woman in the branch. American by birth, Brother Pinnock had fled the States years earlier with children from a previous marriage. After marrying an Argentine woman, he'd been offered a paying Church job as Construction Supervisor. And though he was a busy man, there was something a bit off about him—as if he were living on borrowed time, in relation to his status as a member of the LDS Church. The fact that he couldn't seem to shake the Monica rumors didn't help matters. He could be funny and engaging, but something about him didn't add up.

During the afternoon, we visited two member families new to me: a totally inactive fellow, and a family named Rosenthal. The latter of German-Jewish descent, they were semi-active and very prideful. Their irritation with the branch was apparent, though of indeterminate origin. Following those less than efficacious visits, we went to the Versaci home. There we spoke with a fellow who reminded me of Korihor, a man in the Book of Mormon who resembled the anti-Christ. Though I initiated a civil discussion with him, discourse went downhill fast. He would be speaking in a normal tone, then wax blasphemous.

As Fallon refused to engage in conversation of a religious nature, I was on my own. I asked Korihor a few questions:

"Where do we come from?

"Why are we here?

"Where do we go after this life ends?"

The man couldn't answer these queries, choosing to fire back with attitude and rancor.

"I must tell you," I said, "that the answers to these three questions are vital to our eternal happiness—that if we don't get them answered before we die, we've wasted our time here on earth."

That being another unpopular statement, he responded with vitriol. I lost my patience with Korihor, hitting him with a few verbal fusillades, which really got him worked up. In the end, I was left feeling that I may have overdone things. But sometimes one has to take a stand, especially when the other party becomes disingenuous, verbally abusive, and disrespectful. After all, this was the second go-round for this fellow, the previous set of elders having dropped him once their cup ranneth over with bile.

Unbeknownst to me, the Versaci boy was listening to the whole thing. He'd heard the questions I'd posed. He was impressed with my stated belief about the importance of learning the answers to those three questions.

Before we left for the evening, he asked us to return and teach him the Purpose of Life charla the following day.

WE TRAVELED TO COSQUÍN for a district meeting, where I met our DL, Elder Chuparro. He was enthusiastic and energetic, telling us about a new mission program having to do with group meetings. It sounded like the perfect thing for the beleaguered members in the La Guerra Branch. Before leaving, Elder F and I told Elder Chuparro about the troubles with the branch presidency. Ending the day on a positive note, we enjoyed a family home evening with the Versaci's. The non-member father participated, a good introduction for him to one of the more important programs in the Church.

As promised, we taught his son, Luis. Held at Coca's place, it was a combination charla: part Restoration and part Purpose of Life. I felt the Spirit's presence during the meeting, despite constant interruptions that were part and parcel of life at Coca's. She kept us well supplied with crackers and Café Malta, the munching of which became a persistent distraction. Luis's interest showed me that he could soon be ready for baptism. The only trouble was that I had to do all the teaching, which irritated the hell out of me.

"Elder Fallon," I asked on our walk home, "why wouldn't you help me teach Luis?"

"I'd rather not talk about it."

Well, bully for Elder F! I was pissed off, and continued to needle him, but he wouldn't budge. How does one respond to "I just don't want to," in all its variations? Lost for a rational response, I clammed up. But the resentment was building. The nerve of this guy, refusing to do the one thing we were all called to do for two years. I was coming to the conclusion that since he wouldn't pray, study, teach, or proselyte, he didn't have a testimony of the gospel. I wondered what in the wide world he was doing in the mission field, but came up with no answers. "I can't baptize people by myself!" I wrote in my journal that evening.

CONTACTS, A CLOSE CALL, AND THE HOLY GHOST

MONDAY AGAIN, which meant only one thing: a trip to Palacio in search of the Sacred Contact Lenses. Traveling to the city that morning, we shopped for souvenirs and enjoyed lunch with a very pretty twenty-year-old LDS dentist. Then it was back to the streets for another quixotic attempt at securing Fallon's lenses, which were again not ready. I was starting to believe that they either did not exist, or this was yet another way for my companion to get out of doing missionary work.

Leaving the optometrist, we passed through a charming part of town inhabited by prostitutes, bars, and crazed loners. At one point a mid-thirty-ish woman approached us.

"Hello," she said, hand outstretched. "Are you fellows Mormons?"

"Yes, we are. I'm Elder Hiland," I said, extending a hand. "This is Elder Fallon."

"Very nice to meet you," she said, her manner a little too forward. Then followed a series of questions about the Church. As she asked them, she seemed clingy, desperate to hold our attention. Something didn't feel right about her. Fallon, on the other hand, was enjoying the exchange.

"Well, we can talk for a while, if you like."

I didn't like. All I wanted to do was get away from her.

"Here," she said, holding out her keys. "Let's go to my place so we can talk more."

Then she was ahead of us on the sidewalk, pointing to a gate up ahead, a block away. Fallon said, "Sure. We can talk."

As she walked ahead, stopped, then beckoned, I wondered how far my comp was willing to follow. We came to a gate. She unlocked it. Alarm bells were going off in my chest and head. *No, this is wrong.* And though I didn't know why, I believed we needed to leave ASAP—that this woman's intentions were less than pure. But through the gate we went, my dumbass companion traipsing along, ready for the next step. As she turned to look and beckon and make sure we were still following her, I called to Elder F.

"Elder? Elder Fallon."

"Yeah. What?"

"Let's go."

"But we can't. She's invited us in to talk. I think we should be courteous."

We were spread out along the alley now: Mrs. Crazy at the front door, fumbling with her keys. Elder Fallon close by her. Me some thirty feet down the alley, glancing toward the safety of the street. As she opened the front door I yelled at my comp.

"Elder Fallon!"

"What?"

"Goodbye."

"Huh? Wha—"

"I'm leaving." And then I was on my way out the gate. Elder F stood there for a few seconds, looking back and forth, then joined me.

"That was weird," I said, hoping he agreed.

"I don't know about that. She seemed very nice."

"Yeah," I managed. Then we were on our way to the bus terminal. Or so I thought.

"Elder Hiland? Let's stop by a friend of mine."

"Where? Here?"

"He's nearby. A nice guy. Used to be a member of the Church, but he's been excommunicated."

Great.

"Okay," I said, curious though wary about the prospect of another encounter with someone my companion thought safe to visit. We ended up at the apartment of a heavy-set fellow. Friendly and accommodating, he lived in an ornate, well-kept place. As it was close to the dinner hour, he fed us and we spoke for quite a while. Before the visit was over I knew why he'd been excommunicated: he was gay. At first uncomfortable with his admission, I finally relaxed, disarmed by his gentle, pleasant manner, his intelligent way of speaking, and his courteous nature. All he wanted to do was visit with friends. And behind all the talk I sensed deep loneliness.

Before leaving, we related our story about the Beckoning Woman. Our host revealed that the woman had serious mental and emotional problems; that she'd been inviting men to her apartment for quite a while. We returned home at 9:15 p.m.

SICKNESS, AN INFLATABLE TENT, AND BALM FOR THE SOUL

AS SEPTEMBER WOUND TO A CLOSE, so did I. After two nights in a row of fevers and little rest, I came down with a cold. Anxious as I was to get out after sitting in the apartment all day, we accompanied Pinnock for a look at the latest in proselytizing: the Airetorium.

During my time in Argentina, I'd had encounters with Catholics, Methodists, Jehovah's Witnesses, Evangelists, and born-again Christians. Even a witch or two. But I'd never seen a ministering technique quite like the one the Seventh-Day Adventists were using.

Set up near the center of town was a large, inflated tent. It didn't help matters that they were displaying a name different than their own—as if the real one might scare away otherwise curious truth-seekers. Judging by the size of the crowds—somewhere in the neighborhood of 200—the inflatable tent was quite the draw. Once inside the door flaps, you were greeted by people sitting behind a table. If you were a return customer, they checked out a personalized Bible to you. If you were new, they registered your name, and then loaned you a Bible from their library. Either way, you then went into the main section of the tent, where you would hear about the evils of drinking and smoking, along with a host of other topics straight from the Holy Bible.

If you stayed with the program for several weeks, you got to keep the tome. While it seemed like a hard way to score a free book, I felt a twinge of envy. Up front was one Mr. Rando, preaching to a large crowd every day, while we, the only two "authorized" ministers in town, sat in cheap folding chairs, wondering how to increase our teaching pool from one family to two.

STILL TROUBLED BY A CHEST COLD, I attended the weekly district meeting, at which the ZLs encouraged us with inspiring talks about the sacred nature of our callings and the importance of recommitting ourselves to the Work. I again spoke with Elder Chuparro about the problems the La Guerra branch was having, and then felt compelled to discuss Fallon. Elder C said that though he was willing to talk to my comp, it would probably be a waste of time, after which he dropped several small to medium-sized bombshells: 1) It took Fallon two to three months to adapt to a new area; 2) President Parón would rather leave him in La Guerra for the rest of his mission; and 3) My companion had been in La Guerra for more than a year.

THE SAND-LIKE QUALITY OF MINUTES, hours and days slipped through the hourglass as my struggle against the spiritual vacuum that was Elder Fallon drug on. The following P-Day found us on a bus to Cosquín, then on foot along a dirt road across flatland and though orchards to the mountains. Blossom perfume was thick in the air, everything turning green. It added up to a beautiful, though lengthy, hike to the top by way of almost one hundred curves and switchbacks that wound around and through progressively deeper canyons.

Ninety minutes later we reached the summit, a viewpoint from which one could snap pictures and partake of over-priced food at a souvenir shop, and where I spoke to a shop employee about the Church. She said she wanted to hear more, so I made note of it. We then resumed our climb, the ascent getting steeper and more shale-covered with every yard and twist. A half-hour later we were at the top, where a crucifix and an astounding view greeted us. I could see the small and large Sierras, Unquillo, Río Ceballos, Palacio, La Falda, and Cosquín. The beauty of the vista left me speechless.

As for the Work, things were slowly progressing. By the end of the week we had acquired two new investigators: the souvenir stand lady and one Tania Canto. On the home front, things were regressing. Though the señora and her son George would be gone from Friday until Monday, our current interactions with them were unpleasant. They treated us with disdain, being outright rude and disrespectful at times, though for what reason I could not tell.

CONTACT LENSES AND A NEW INVESTIGATOR

SATURDAY, OCTOBER 8. We worked at the chapel for ninety minutes, clearing materials away from the front of the building so Pinnock could begin laying the last of the sidewalk tiles. Sunday at church, President Zobell announced that Pinnock had been released as the branch missionary director, no replacement mentioned.

Then came Monday and time for Trip #3 to Palacio for those damned contact lenses. We visited a shoe store so I could buy a comfortable suede pair. Fallon, inspired by my purchase, began looking for shoes as well. But it wasn't easy, his size twelve-plus about as easy to procure as contact lenses. Twelve stores later he found the right shoes. Given the amount of walking we were doing these days—our bikes sitting idle, due to hilly La Guerra—it was best to have good shoes. We stopped by the Palacio Zoo, the post office, and the apartment of Fallon's gay friend. He cooked an excellent dinner, and afterward we talked for a long time. It felt weird to try and relax, knowing that we should have been on the bus back to La Guerra. But trying to adhere to the mission schedule had become impossible with Fallon around. I could push and coerce for only so long, after which I reached the point of diminishing returns and dissipated energy.

Our friend loved to talk, whether or not anyone was listening, and since the conversation was centered on him and other non-religious topics, my mind wandered. The place was ornate in decoration and profuse in quantity. Artwork was everywhere. The host was obviously well-heeled, but it wasn't apparent what his profession could be. Though unwilling to interrupt the conversation between Fallon and him, I longed to leave. Strains of Debussy's ethereal, atmospheric *Nocturnes* whispered from a wall speaker next to my head, offering a break from the tedium.

After what seemed like forever, we said our goodbyes, the fellow handing me eight bottles of Jugo de Uva on my way out the door. I was heartened by his generosity, but we'd stayed too long. Not arriving home until 1:45 a.m., it was 2:30 before I finished recording the day's events and hit the sack.

TUESDAY, WE FINALLY MET with Tania for an afternoon discussion. The topic was the plan of salvation. Though it went well, I had to teach the whole charla sans companion, Fallon being a dumbass, not lifting a finger to help out. After Tania left for home, I let Fallon know how irritated I was with him, that I didn't want to do all the work from now on. His reaction was negligible, non-committal. His only desire—to go home—was the one thing I couldn't help him with, though I wanted to. Maybe I could fight fire with fire, as the San Rafael ZLs had done a couple months earlier. Faced with two elders who would rather sit on their butts than do missionary work, the leaders restricted them to their apartment for five days straight. After forty-eight hours, the elders were climbing the cement walls. After seventy-two more they were more than willing to go out and work. But since this was my companion's M.O. already, he'd probably welcome the ploy.

AMIDST MY EFFORTS to move the Work along, the Adventist's inflatable tent was gaining ground. In mid-October, we made another visit. In attendance were Tania, some of our former investigators, as well as Pinnock, Perez, Rosenthal, and the Gardenas, all branch members.

At our own Church meetings the following day, we taught Tania and her daughter about the organization of the primitive church, the subsequent apostasy, the Restoration, the commandments, and baptism. I challenged Tania to be baptized October 29th. She wanted to but would have to clear the air with her parents, who were giving her a hard time about investigating us and the Big Tent. They told her that if we tried to visit her at their home, they would kick us out. Though I proclaimed in my journal that "We'll see about that!" I wasn't interested in a confrontation. I merely wanted them to understand what we were teaching their daughter.

TAKING A BREAK from the Contact Lens trip to Palacio, the following Monday was spent climbing the hills around the Pan de Azúcar (Sugar Bread) mountains. Our group included Elder Chuparro and his companion. For a change, we hitched a ride up in a member's Jeep-like truck. The beauty of the area refreshed me and I sorely missed my camera. And although I enjoyed wild driving once in a while, our driver made me nervous when he opened the truck hood and showed us a growing crack in the vehicle's steering column. On the return trip, I rode in the open pickup bed, positioning myself by the edge so I could leap out, should our driver's fast, erratic driving finish off the steering column and send us sailing off a cliff.

Though I was dragging the next day due to a fever, sinus headache and three hours of sleep, we met Tania at the chapel. I taught her about the commandments and the need for a living prophet.

Teaching continued during the week, while she struggled with her divided loyalty between the Adventists and the LDS Church. Which one was telling her the truth? The Adventists said that Saturday was the Sabbath, while the Mormons (and the majority of Christendom), worshiped on Sunday. Though we could present a convincing case for the latter, it was up to Tania to ask the Lord in prayer for an answer. Due to the fact that she was progressing so well, we were considering moving her baptism date to October 26th, so Fallon could attend.

As for my companion, the question of his departure date had been resolved. Mid-week he received his flight plans, which stated he'd be heading for the Palacio airport on October 27th. While surprised at its being earlier than he'd expected, he was pleased to be escaping from a life he'd come to loathe. On the plus side, the news meant that I'd be getting a new companion, and soon.

In order to help Tania, we spoke with the Ramos couple about her and how she was progressing.

"Tania is doing well. She's attending all the charlas and seems sincere in her desires to know the truth."

"That's nice, elders. We're glad to hear about your success."

"Something that would really help her a lot is the support of Church members like yourselves. You have testimonies. You know the Church is true."

"Elders, I don't believe she's ready for baptism," one of them said.

"What are you talking about?"

"It's not right for you to push her into something like this. She needs more time."

"We're not pushing her into anything," I said, irritated at this couple's uninformed opinions about our teaching methods and intent. They hadn't been present at any of the charlas. How could they know about her progress? Had I wanted to, I could have asked them why they thought they were in a position to judge, given the fact that they hadn't been to church for ages.

But since the Ramos family was new to the Church, I decided to err on the side of mercy and forgive them for their attitude. We'd have to look elsewhere for the help we needed.

As EVIDENCE THAT MIRACLES DO OCCUR in these latter days, Contact Lens Trip #4 was successful. Among other stops, I visited a bookstore that was selling Rotring pens. Featuring capillary-sized tips, they looked to be a joy to write with. Now I could more easily annotate scriptures and other books I was studying, the resultant lettering so small.

MY COMP PACKS, TANIA PROGRESSES, MY COMP UNPACKS

WITH FIVE DAYS TO GO, Fallon spent a good part of the day packing, things he couldn't haul home being set aside for sale. It was the most animated I'd seen him. Watching Elder F go about his business sparked feelings of trunkiness, despite the fact that I'd made a commitment to not let this kind of thing get to me. The fact that going home seemed so unreal helped hold the distracting mindset at bay, though. I could stave off reality when I really wanted to.

Later that day we returned to the Ramos home, my hope being that they'd listen to us this time. I told them that Tania was ready to be baptized. Would they reconsider helping Tania, not pushing but encouraging her? Instead of arguing with us, they agreed to help, an unexpected change of heart that surprised me. That evening, thunderstorms and rain brought relief, a welcome end to the hot weather streak we'd been enduring. Breathing in the cool, moisture-laden air reminded me of how much this part of the country was helping calm and soothe me. It was a gift from Above.

Tania attended all the Church meetings the following Sunday. After teaching her about the true meaning of baptism and the purpose of the Holy Ghost, she said she wanted to be baptized. I was happier than I'd been in weeks.

DUE TO OUR NEWLY DEVELOPED HABIT of alternating between P-Day excursions to Palacio and the mountains, it was time for a trip with Coca, via bus and a lengthy hike to a monument called Indio Bamba. Located in the middle of hilly countryside, it was a tranquil place to spend the day. After lunch and some Frisbee tossing, we descended the hill and walked back to town along the edge of the highway.

That evening I received a letter from Parón concerning my request that either I or Fallon be transferred out of La Guerra:

> *"Elder Fallon is a special case. He has never taught a charla and probably never will. The only thing you can do at this point is be a good example to him. Get him out of bed at 6:30 every morning and try to set the standard while you are out working. It's probably too late to help him improve; please be patient a little while longer."*

So that was that. And while it was disappointing news for me, more was on the way for Elder Fallon. Arriving during our latest discussion with Tania, Elder Chuparro told my companion that his flight plans had changed. He'd get the new set at the October 31st zone conference—four days after he'd been promised he'd be going home.

"I can't believe they're doing this to me," Elder Fallon said, later that day. Struggling to not say "That's just too damned bad," I found it impossible to sympathize with my companion. Appalled by his words, attitude, and behavior, I found Fallon's current predicament well-deserved. His plans had been upset. He'd been inconvenienced. Well, so had I. It would've been funny, had it not been so pathetic.

His bad attitude resurfaced on the 27th, while I was teaching Tania a full-length discussion at the chapel. Though the charla went well, it could have been much better—but only one of us was teaching. I was fighting off anger and frustration as Fallon sat there like a lump, impatient and asking me to hurry up and finish. I was done with him and wanted him to leave. Despite all of this, Tania continued to progress. She even caught a bit of the missionary spirit, inviting a couple friends to church.

A NEW COMP ARRIVES, TANIA IS BAPTIZED

ELDER SCOVILL ARRIVED Saturday, October 29th, at 2 p.m. Never was I so glad to see a new comp. He was energetic, optimistic, and down-to-earth, his sense of humor—any sense of humor—a welcome change from the dour atmosphere that had taken hold.

"Well, guys," Elder S announced, "it looks like we'll be working as a threesome until Fallon leaves on November 5th."

November 5th? This was not what Elder Fallon wanted to hear. Whether or not he complained about it, it was evident to Scovill that my comp had issues. And for the next few days, the three of us would have further issues to deal with: cramped sleeping quarters, an over-booked bathroom, and other awkwardness. Elder Scovill didn't help matters, needling Fallon about things like his shoe size: "Man, those look like skis," to which Elder Fallon replied irritably.

The zone conference on the 31st did offer Elder Fallon and us some relief, though. He was told that his new departure date would be November 3rd. As for Elder Scovill, I could tell that we were going to get along just fine.

WEDNESDAY THE 3RD started out rainy and cool. Following a waffle breakfast at the stake president's house, we prepared for Tania's baptism. Meeting Pinnock at the new chapel, we traveled with him in his truck to the present one, where we loaded up chairs and hymn books. We returned to the church site and set up a meeting place next door, in the new house Pinnock hadn't moved into yet. I went to a back room and changed into white baptismal pants and shirt.

Due to lack of time, I hurriedly planned and scribbled the meeting program on a piece of paper, then walked to the front of the room and began the service. One of the members had helped Tania get dressed, and she looked nice sitting there, all in white, smiling. After the opening hymn, prayer, and talks, we walked down to the lake shore, the rain having stopped for a few minutes. Barefoot, I had a tough time stepping around and on top of unseen rocks and pointy objects, but we eventually struggled out far enough that the water was waist-deep and pleasantly cool. Then I baptized her, feeling at peace about the entire service. For her part, Tania was very cooperative. She appeared happy and content with her decision to join the Church. As the rain began to fall, we made our way back to shore.

After changing into dry clothes, I resumed the service, taking a few minutes to explain what confirmation meant. I called Tania forward and Pinnock confirmed her a member of the Church, telling her to receive the Holy Ghost into her life. Then we sang another hymn. Sister Zobell offered the closing prayer, and we were done.

Later on, I hung around at the apartment, relaxed as I always was after a big event like a baptism had finally come to fruition. Watching Elder Fallon pack his bags for a second time, I found it hard to believe he was leaving, a fact made more poignant with the knowledge that in several weeks I'd be doing the same thing.

NEW SIGHTS, A NEW ATTITUDE

AND THEN ELDER F WAS GONE. There was peace in the valley. All was right with the world—or as right as it could be in a place like La Guerra. Elder Scovill and I did a little sightseeing. We walked up to a water tower on a hill at the edge of the city. Then we descended the back side of the hill to a path on the other side of the highway. This led us into a sticker-filled, brushy area that we had to fight our way out of to reach the lake. We emerged onto a shore populated by tall, wispy, poplar-like trees that cast long shadows across deep, waving grass. The beauty astounded me, and my gratitude to God for sending me to this place couldn't be adequately expressed. That evening we taught Tania more about the gospel. She was doing well.

Another day, Scovill and I walked out to the San Roque Dam. After eating lunch and chucking rocks over the railing, into the spillway, we decided to get overhead pictures of the Embudo. Ascending the steep terrain across the street from the dam's edge, we were soon several hundred feet above the road, my fear of heights growing with every foot of altitude we gained. Elder S having made sixty-five parachute jumps, he had no problem walking up to the very edge of the cliff and gazing down at the dam's funnel. I was on hands and knees. But despite the terror, the view was astonishing.

Soon we descended, Scovill scrambling downhill with the agility of a mountain goat, me with the grace of a wounded water buffalo. When the passenger boats arrived, we took one back to town, enjoying the beauty the lake had to offer. And for once I was able to record that beauty. I'd purchased a Kodak Instamatic camera and was photographing every hill, lake scene, tree, and piece of mountain vegetation I could.

CHANGES IN THE BRANCH, TANIA'S BOMBSHELL AND MR. RANDO

DURING OUR TIME WITH TANIA and other investigators, the Adventist tent droned on, drawing crowds and attention. Pinnock informed us that the Rosenthal family had been baptized into the SDA church on the 12th, another woman from our branch taking the plunge the following day. As for other changes, the stake president announced that President Beltran had been released, Brother Elded to take his place.

The new week began with souvenir hunting, lunch, and a trip to the river, where I posed for a photo, standing knee-deep in water, and in my good clothes. After weeks of no teaching hours or new contacts, we stopped by Tania's house. She told us about the inflatable tent and that she was still attending. She'd even gone on a Sunday picnic with them, instead of coming to the church she'd been baptized into. She invited us inside, where the conversation turned to polygamy, making me suspect that the Adventists had been talking to her about more than the proper day for Sabbath worship.

Then Tania's brother showed up. We talked to him about the Church for a while, and discovered that he was quite interested. We scheduled an appointment to speak with him and his wife. We also found out that some pamphlet boxes we'd set up around town were being visited on a regular basis. We ended the day speaking with President Elded about ways to increase missionary work in the branch. Finally, some progress.

After a few days of encouraging events among the branch members, we met Tania on the street.

"The Adventists have me convinced!" she crowed. I felt sick inside. It was really happening. We were losing another person to the inflatable tent. Hoping we could convince her otherwise, we went with her to her house and sat down for a discussion. Just as we were getting somewhere, her parents showed up and spoiled everything. It was as if Tania was destined to fall away, like those seeds that land among the rocks and never get a chance to sprout. She needed fellowshipping.

"Well, elders, I'll see you at church Sunday, okay?"

That was something, though a trifle weird.

Sunday, we spoke with her at the chapel for ninety minutes. She was now a regular attendee at the Tent, and getting confused. She liked our church, but she liked the

SDAs better. That was where her daughter wanted to be, so that was where she'd go, as well. Though our counsel helped, she needed to pray about the situation and understand for herself where the Lord wanted her to be. That was something we hadn't the power to do.

As we were walking her home after church, a fellow rode past on his bike, then stopped and engaged us in conversation. It was Señor Rando, the Inflatable Tent's ringmaster. The dialogue started out civilly, but turned into a bash. We threw scriptures back and forth for some fifteen minutes. He knew the scriptures very well, but had a tough time explaining where his priesthood authority came from, or how his church was first organized. Eventually, he cut the conversation short. He had to go. While unsure what Tania thought of the exchange, I was sure it did nothing to build our esteem in her eyes. We'd failed the test of a good Christian: tempted to contend, we'd succumbed. The only upside to the afternoon was the fact that the man painting the new chapel wanted to start taking the discussions in December.

FINGERPRINTS AND EARTHQUAKES

REQUESTED BY A POLICE OFFICER on the street to present ourselves for fingerprinting, we arrived at 5 p.m. on the 22nd.

"This will only take about ten minutes," we were told by a man at the front desk. We each took turns having all our digits rolled into the black ink pad, then pressed onto small squares on an identification sheet. As we were wiping our fingers clean, we were told, "Sorry, but we need another set," so back to the pads we went. Then again. And again. After the fourth set and as many apologies, we were asked to report to the Intelligence Division. Wondering why we hadn't been told about this before, we acquiesced and went where we were told. It was 6 p.m.

Seated in a small cubicle, we answered questions for a fellow at a typewriter. Who are you? Where are you from? What are you doing in La Guerra? The questions went on and on. There were queries about Church doctrine, our interrogator gaining curiosity the more we talked. I was wondering when it would end and looked at the front doors leading out to the street. Freedom seemed near at hand, though I knew what would happen if I stood up, said I'd had enough, and walked out those glass doors. And it wouldn't involve further questioning—more likely a basement cell, a car battery, and some strategically-placed metal clips.

So we sat and talked and talked. What's this business about polygamy? What's your church doing in La Guerra? Soon more officers appeared and the questions multiplied. But at some point, the interrogation ended. We gave our interviewer some pamphlets and were excused. Before leaving we saw Tania's brother there, as well as another fellow we had taught in the past. It didn't dawn on me then that there might be a connection between our previous encounter with him at Tania's place and the fact that we were soon asked to visit the police station. Tania's bro did say he wanted to talk to us again on Sunday, at church, but we weren't sure what about. With that, we were out the door at 8 p.m., breathing freedom into our lungs once again.

ONE MOMENT I WAS ASLEEP, the next I was looking at the clock. 6:35 a.m. Something had woken me up. The bed was shaking.

"Elder Scovill!"

"Huh—what?"

"Look out the window."

"Huh—what?"

"Look out the window? What do you see?"

Thinking I was nuts, he looked out the window.

"What about it?"

"Do you see anything moving?"

"What are you talking about?"

"It's an earthquake. Can't you feel it?"

By the time he answered, I was half-dressed and down the stairs, then out the side door. I was standing on the front lawn when Scovill arrived. "Thanks for waiting," he said. Most of the neighborhood was outside in robes and PJs, watching and looking for something they could feel, but not see. The sign atop our building shook a lot, then a little, the tremors lasting a steady five minutes before subsiding. The crisis over, we filed back inside, then scurried out again five minutes later as more temblors arrived. At 9 a.m. the ground was still shaking, intermittently. The radio announced that tremors were present throughout the valley, Palacio, Chile, and other parts of the world.

We spent the better part of the siesta working at the chapel alongside President Elded. We moved large piles of ceramic roof tiles from one place to another, shoveled dirt and leveled the ground in front of the building. It was good, hard work, and I earned the blisters on my hands. Additional tremors during the afternoon prompted me to implement security measures. I stacked a pile of brass peso coins on one of the tables, another on top of the clothes closet. Hopefully, the sound of falling coins would alert us during the next quake.

We continued to spend time with Tania, the latest occasion being a home evening at the Versacis'. She had a good time, but was still hanging with the Adventists.

The ground-shaking continued: twice during the Thanksgiving dinner at Coca's, twice during the early morning hours of the 25th, and early on the 28th, my bed vibrating long enough before sunrise to leave me wondering if this was it, the Big One. But the stacked coins remained stacked.

As for my own unrest, it was coming in the form of apathy. With three weeks left, I'd lost the desire to work with the members. The idea that the last part of one's mission could be the best was not my reality. Instead, I was struggling to maintain the desire to study the scriptures, pray, or teach. And once the spiritual maintenance slacked off, those old feelings of unworthiness and doubt rose to the surface like existential pond scum. My spiritual batteries were not getting recharged.

A BURN HEALED, A SHOCK RECEIVED

FLIGHT PLANS ARRIVED the last day of the month. According to the schedule, I'd arrive home December 17th, at 2:23 p.m. I was starting to feel a bit trunky.

During the first week of December, Elder Scovill's sunbathing ways caught up with him. It started one Saturday evening with some slight itching on his back. But the more he scratched, the more the burn itched. By the time we arrived back at the apartment, my comp was close to hysterical, the itching sensation like a combination of poison oak and mosquito bites, stinging nettles thrown in for good measure— then multiplied by one hundred. An itch for which there is no scratch. Desperate, Scovill jumped in the shower, the cold water doing nothing but aggravating his condition. He had me smear lotion and creams on his back, but to no effect.

As he laid there on the bed, squirming and groaning, I wondered about giving him a health blessing. No sooner had the thought crossed my mind than he asked me for one. I sat down by the bed and anointed his head. Then I performed the sealing of the blessing. Within ten minutes the itching stopped and didn't bother him again. But the hot weather wasn't done with us. It made us weak during the day and sleepless at night. The siesta was the only time we could catch up on rest.

ON A P-DAY RUN TO PALACIO to pick up a package from the States, we were pulling into the Palacio terminal when I saw Pinnock's truck travel past. With him in the vehicle was Monica Morales, the scarlet woman we'd heard so much about. I didn't dwell on it at the time, though I wondered what his wife would have said about the situation. We retrieved my package from the Adouana, then headed for La Guerra two hours later. I saw many things on our trip. The hills. The trees. The clouds. The sky. And Pinnock's truck parked alongside the road by a restaurant, Monica Morales lying against him in the front seat.

"ELDER!" I shouted. Passengers were staring at me.

"What?"

"Look out the window!" Maybe suspecting there was another quake astir, he looked.

"There," I pointed. "See Pinnock's truck?"

Though he didn't get as good a look as I, he knew he'd seen something fishy. All the way home I wondered if I had really seen the two of them together. If so, the implications were terrible. That afternoon there was another small quake in Coronel Diaz.

SHOCKS AND AFTERSHOCKS

ON THE 8ᵀᴴ we traveled to Cosquín for a three-branch activity, but not many members showed. Near the campground and the river was a man-made dam. Four of us strolled over to check it out. There were waterfalls there and it was hot, so after we walked across the top of the dam a couple times, we did some wading. Then Elder Cooper and I went underneath one of the smaller waterfalls and got soaked. It felt so good in that heat, and was something I'd always wanted to do. After everyone else arrived, we played soccer in the ninety-degree sun. It was fun and all, but the heat killed off my energy. After playing some volleyball, I made a return trip to the dam before sunset. We concluded with a fireside, during which I was asked to bear my testimony. I was exhausted by the time we returned home.

DECEMBER 11ᵀᴴ. Our main investigator, Señora Grigoris, was doing great and on schedule for baptism. But a trancelike state was creeping into my life. I couldn't accept the fact that I was going home, yet I was fading from the scenery. Soon there'd be no more district meetings. No more baptisms. No more conferences or gamma globulin shots or new programs started to find new investigators. I was proud of the fact that I wasn't trunky. But what exactly was I? I wanted to work, but to what end?

FOUR DAYS LEFT. We went to the mission home to pick up some money I had coming to me. They didn't have it, but on the way home, I learned something new. President

351

Parón had pulled my comp into his office to tell him about a letter he'd received from Elder Chuparro, in which Elder C talked about the Cosquín activity: how the elders in the district had misbehaved; how some of the members were offended; worst of all, how Elder Cooper and I had done the unthinkable: we'd gone *swimming*. Scovill tried to defend me, to which Parón responded: "You can be an honest person all your life, but if you steal something just before dying, you are now a thief." What the hell was Parón saying?

The president told Scovill that he planned to interview me on Friday and discuss how I'd broken mission rules. This bit of news made me sick. Then I got pissed. Several things were obvious: I had not gone swimming; Parón was wrong; and my district leader was a grade A, top-of-the-line, world class ass-kisser. I was beside myself with frustration and helpless outrage the rest of the ride home. Scovill's only suggestion was that after I return home, I write a letter to Chuparro telling him what a sphincter he'd been.

And from there things just got better. The following evening, we stopped by the apartment for a minute. Tania was there, talking to our landlady.

"Elders," she said. "Guess what happened?"

"What?"

"I was finally baptized in the Adventist church!"

She was smiling, as if we were supposed to jump for joy at the announcement. Instead, I felt sick, saddened beyond words. What was wrong with her? Didn't she realize how much this hurt us? In order to not start weeping, I bore my testimony. Then—

"Sister Canto, I hate to say this, but it would have been better for you to not have been baptized into our Church." As I spoke, my heart felt like it would leap from my chest. "Someday you'll have to answer to the Lord for your decision. You felt the Spirit testify to you of the truth of our message. I know it and you know it."

Tania was listening, but there was a wall there now— as if she could no longer comprehend what I was saying.

"Out of all the people I helped baptize over the last two years, you are the first to turn against the Church and its teachings. I just don't understand."

I didn't hate Tania. I knew the Lord would be merciful. She was new to all of this, and maybe she would figure things out someday. But for now, the disappointment hurt. It hurt a lot.

"Goodbye, Tania," I said as I shook her hand for the last time. All that work. All that teaching. All those words. And what had it amounted to?

IN THE END, it became just another piece in the emotional jigsaw puzzle that was to mark those last few days and hours and minutes. A nice home evening with Señora Gregoris at the Flores home that evening. Waking at 4 a.m. the next morning to swat at the mosquitoes and the heat. Making the rounds that afternoon to visit Nakayama, selling him my tape recorder and a few cassettes for 33,000 pesos. Saying goodbye to Zobell and the Versaci family, the latter being the most faithful, friendly members we'd encountered in La Guerra. Buying one last souvenir—a llama-hair shawl. Then packing and taking the bags to get weighed. Wishing I'd never baptized Tania, or argued with her minister, or stood under that waterfall, or not taken Fallon to the mission home and just left him there.

And what did I have to look forward to now? Instead of a "Congratulations-on-serving-a-faithful-mission-Elder-Hiland" interview, I'd be getting a new orifice carved into me by President Parón. And for something I didn't do. The fact that the President took Elder C's word for the event without even asking me only added to the sting. I wondered for a moment how Elder Southern had fared during his final interview. That I slept at all that final night was a miracle.

LEAVING

THURSDAY, DECEMBER 17. We tried to be extra quiet while going down the stairs and out the front door. I didn't want to run into the Señora or her son and risk yet one more confrontation. Maybe I was being over-cautious. Given the surreal nature of my mental state, anything was possible. We left La Guerra by bus at 7:45 a.m. After arriving in Palacio, we took care of some business, then went to Elder Clark's place. I thanked Elder Scovill for all he'd done. He'd not only been a good comp, he'd helped salvage the last part of my mission.

As Scovill walked away, I shifted my focus to the task at hand: getting ready to reunite with the old Santa Fe district from the LTM. Elder Gabi was the first to arrive. We talked for a while, expecting the others to show up any time—but they didn't. As tired as I was, I felt a restlessness that wouldn't go away. After resting for a bit, Gabi and I went downtown to look around, then returned. No one there, we left yet again, and around 8 p.m. people started showing up. Then the reunion began. I passed out the previously requested boxes of Havana Alfajores, though

I doubt that many of the containers made it through the night, let alone back to the States.

Friday morning, we loaded up our stuff and traveled by taxi across the city to the mission home. Ignoring Church policy, which required that the mission president hold a final personal interview with all departing missionaries, Parón instead gathered all of us in the living room for a going-home talk. Maybe there were too many issues to discuss, and too little time or emotion from which to draw. I assumed that Parón wanted to clear the air, and I was nervous about what we might say to each other. But the way things were looking, when would I be able to squeeze in the few moments needed to do so?

As I looked around the room, I felt strange. I had known all of these people for two years. But they each looked different now. It wasn't their clothing. It was the way they acted and the manner in which they spoke. And with one exception, they all seemed more mature. But had I really changed that much? Had I changed at all? The obvious answer was Yes. How could anyone go through the experiences each of us had and not have been changed in some way? But then I thought back to Fallon, and that Elder in Santa Fe who'd been sent home early, as had the sister missionary who'd suffered the nervous breakdown. And my first companion. They'd gone home worse off than when they started.

After the president shared some words of wisdom with us, he informed the group that it was time to head to the airport. Realizing that Parón didn't plan on talking to me, mixed feelings of relief and frustration welled up. No clearing of the air or my good name. I wondered how the other elders felt about this deviation from policy, but decided it was pointless to dwell on it. It wasn't going to happen, so drop it, Dan.

The short ride to the airport over, we gathered in a line to take that last walk out the door and across the tarmac. Parón was there to give each of us a handshake and a hug. When my turn came, he was all smiles as we exchanged farewells. He mumbled something. When I asked him to repeat it, he said "You just don't understand, do you?" And with that I was rushed out the door to join the others on our small plane, the sour taste of an unresolved situation trailing behind.

NORTH, NORTHWEST, AND HOME

THE PLANE HEADED EAST, and then we were in Buenos Aires airspace, the landing rough, scaring the hell out of me. That was where the first split in the group occurred. Bertram, myself, and three other missionaries boarded a plane destined for Florida, the rest bound for New York.

At 10:30 that evening we were in Río de Janeiro. During the forty-five-minute layover, I went for a walk by myself. Without an assigned companion for the first time since that solitary week in Coronel Diaz. I was carrying a lot of pesos, as well as some dollars, but couldn't find anything to buy, finally deciding on postcards.

"How much are they?" I asked the woman behind the counter.

She responded, looking at me funny. I asked again, for I'd not quite understood what she was saying. She repeated herself, a cross look on her face. I couldn't quite understand her. Then I remembered we were in Brazil. The largest non-Spanish speaking country in South America. And she was speaking Portuguese. Feeling foolish, I handed her some money and she gave me back more change than I expected. Back on the plane I went, and we were in the air.

We stopped at another airport somewhere near Central America. More wandering around, more stewing over how to unload pesos and dollars, yet finding nothing of interest. Then I was back on the plane. Exhausted after many hours of flying, I fell into a deep sleep.

APPROACHING FLORIDA, I tried on some earphones. The music sounded strange. Was this that "disco" music I'd heard rumors of in letters from home? I looked down and saw the outline of the southern states, up against an endless ocean. Then we were banking and soon enough on the ground. Apprehension was replaced by anticipation as I stepped off the plane and walked along a sealed walkway. That feeling of knowing I was back on American soil was all I'd come to expect. I did want to kiss the ground. No police standing guard at the entrances and exits, watching my every move. No unsafe water fountains. No fears about saying the wrong thing to someone who might turn me in to the local constabulary. No military dictatorship.

As our group of missionaries fanned out across the area past the boarding gate, the sense of freedom was exhilarating. And with that came a desire to start catching up on what I'd missed. Bertram and I and several others headed for a store that sold magazines, newspapers, books, and candy. I walked along the aisles, eyes wide open, staring at magazines, books, and everything else I realized I'd missed for two years. Lots of mag covers showing something called *Saturday Night Live*, disco news, and reviews of a new movie called *Star Wars*. Things had changed since I left. We had a new president. The Olympics had come and gone, as had the Bicentennial, both events still deemed newsworthy, judging by the amount of publications still trying to commemorate them. Then there was the candy, sought after due to a two-year deprivation.

But time marched on. Off we went to Texas, where other missionaries walked off in search of their respective flights home, leaving me, Bertram and one sister. But after so many hours together inflight, I had tired of missionary company, Bertram spending most of the flight talking to Sister Price. By the time we got to Denver and said our goodbyes, I was ready to be by myself. This wasn't what I'd imagined it to be: my district gathered for a final farewell and some reminiscing. Instead, exhaustion replaced those musings about the good times with sleep and brief conversations, followed by long periods of silence, as I contemplated the future.

The plane now on its way northwest, I was in a muddle. Expecting to feel like the knight returning home after a successful quest, I was instead a mix of happiness, sorrow, uncertainty, and confusion. A dazed feeling overcame me. It was done. Finally over. And for better or worse I needed to deal with it. But how? The way I felt, the best I could do was enjoy the ride, and hope my faculties for dealing with reality came back from vacation before I did.

I looked down at the Rocky Mountains, other geography I couldn't recognize, then remembered I was still a missionary, and began talking to a man next to me. The conversation eventually led to my mission ending, which led to a discussion about what we believed. So I still had it. I could do missionary work, even at the eleventh hour. Just as I was getting up a head of religious steam, I recognized the landscape below. Mt. Hood. The Columbia River. The Gorge. And then we were on the ground.

THEY WERE ALL THERE to greet me. Mom. Dad. My sisters and grandparents. A stepparent or two. The feeling of being back with them was overwhelming. As we walked out of the terminal, I did feel sort of like a conquering hero. I'd survived. I'd overcome. Since I was the only Mormon in my family, I believed it would be a long time before they understood my victory over self and the world. But in their own way, they already knew. They'd been hearing about that struggle, those little triumphs over environment and adversity for two years. I needed to give them credit for trying to understand, to see into the world I'd entered and lived in for two long years.

As I rode home with Mom, I finally let go and relaxed. But I was still a missionary. And there was still one thing left to do . . .

RELEASE

4:30 AM. DAD PICKS ME UP at Mom's place, and we head out through deserted city streets. I can't help but notice the icy shine of frozen puddles, frost on everything. My body is still in shock about this sudden change from summer to winter—a fifty-degree drop—though being inside a warm car shields me from the worst of its frigid effects. At least my stomach is behaving itself.

Dad finds the freeway entrance and we're finally on our way east. Now we can talk. I don't remember what we say, but I can tell he's glad to see me again. He didn't write to me too much while I was gone, but I don't hold that against him. I tell him why we're going back to La Grande: that until I'm released by the same fellow who set me apart—Stake President Lindsay—I'm technically still a missionary. It doesn't make much more sense to me than it does to Dad, but he accepts it. That's just the way he is. As we speed along the Columbia River Gorge Highway, we travel the same route I did before leaving for Utah and South America, over two years ago. It seems like a lifetime has passed. The river is shut down for the season, dark, cold, gray on the best days, until spring and summer will bring it back to life. Excepting winter wheat crops, the surrounding farmland is much the same.

We stop somewhere for breakfast, as it's close to 300 miles we have to travel. Then we're on the road again, the temperature rising as the sun comes up, then dropping, the further east and the higher we climb. Especially that last section, where we leave Pendleton behind and ascend Cabbage Hill some 3,700 feet or so to pass through the Blue Mountains.

For the next hour we climb and descend, climb and descend before exiting I-84 to drop down into the valley that protects and nourishes La Grande, population 10,000. Even at 2,784 feet, there's a lot of snow here. We work our way along the narrow two-laner as it winds down to the city's main drag. Off we go on a side street, out past the college and all those memories locked inside my head—of not only the college but the town, its people, my friends, the weather, the seasons. And now we're at the church building, out near the snow-blanketed foot-hills on the edge of town.

I wonder how my father will handle being in a church building. Organized religion is an oxymoron to Dad, his contempt for most denominations borne of a witnessed hypocrisy going back to his teenage years. Pomp and circumstance, ceremony for its own sake, kneeling to kiss someone's hand—these are anathema to him. His religion is existential, hard to pin down, nature and the outdoors his ideal church. But he follows me inside, respectful and pleasant, unless given a reason to behave otherwise. And as I've told Dad before, he will see no pomp, no adoration of the dead, no rolling in the aisles here. If there were such a thing, I remind him, I would have left this church long ago.

I give him a short tour of the chapel, the hallways laden with scenes from the Bible, likenesses of the Savior—not on a cross, but teaching people, holding little children, speaking with the Woman at the Well, beckoning workers from the fishing boats to come follow him and become fishers of men. Dad appreciates the beauty of the building and the furnishings and the art work. He likes what he's seeing. He meets some of the local Church members, shakes their hands and is impressed with their candor, their down-to-earth demeanor, their humor.

After an hour, we part ways, my father to a meeting with the priesthood, me to a small office for my talk with President Lindsay. He asks me how I've been these last two years, and welcomes me back to the United States. Then he hands me a five- by six-inch sheet of paper. It looks like an award of some sort—but no, it's my release certificate. The stake president asks me to read it to him, since it's in Spanish. After I finish, he tells me I've been officially and honorably released from my mission. With that proclamation, I feel a weight lift off of me, though not something too dramatic—or the load has been leaving me by degrees ever since I walked out of that apartment in La Guerra. Or maybe even earlier, when Tania gave me the bad news. Possibly as far back as the day I sold my bicycle to Rosales, the realization that I'd no longer be relying on all that pedaling to get around being a sure sign the end was near, and with it the burden of responsibility shifting to Elder Scovill.

"Never forget who you are, who you've become," President Lindsay tells me. After some brief counsel about being careful who I date, he shakes my hand and welcomes me home. I walk out of the room a civilian— a "regular" member of The Church of Jesus Christ of Latter-day Saints.

Dad's waiting out in the foyer. After another glance around the building, we walk to the car and leave for home.

"How did you like the meeting, Dad?"

"It was nice. It felt good, like a church meeting should."

And I have to agree.

One Last Thing

I N MID-2008, Knight Mangum Hall, was in the first stages of demolition, workers hauling out anything easily removed before the structure itself was razed to the ground.

A BYU professor walking by the site noticed that scores of white ceiling tiles were being stacked to one side. Upon closer examination, he saw something else: words and drawings inscribed on the acoustical tiles. Contacting a fellow teacher, he told him to get over to the site as soon as possible. And to bring his camera.

In the short time they had, the two educators found poems, caricatures, hand-drawn maps and missives from hundreds of former missionaries—young men and women who were now middle-aged and with grown children, their retirement years dead ahead. The two men photographed as many of the tiles as they could. Later, one of the professors included the photos in an essay about KMH and the LTM era.